THE MAKING OF THE EUROPEAN SPATIAL DEVELOPMENT PERSPECTIVE

NO MASTERPLAN

ONE WEEK LOAN

THE RTPI Library Series

**Editors: Cliff Hague, Heriot Watt University, Edinburgh, Scotland
Robin Boyle, Wayne State University, Michigan, USA
Robert Upton, RTPI, London, UK**

Published in conjunction with The Royal Town Planning Institute, this series of leading-edge texts looks at all aspects of spatial planning theory and practice from a comparative and international perspective.

The series

- explores the dimensions of spatial planning and urbanism, in relation to people, place, space and environment;

- develops the theoretical and methodological foundations of planning;

- investigates the relationship between theory and practice;

- examines the contribution of planners to resolving social, economic and environmental concerns.

By linking planning to disciplines such as economics, anthropology, sociology, geography, environmental and urban studies, the project's inherent focus on sustainable development places the theoretical and practical relationships between social, economic and environmental issues in their necessary spatial context.

Planning in Postmodern Times
Philip Allmendinger, University of Aberdeen, Scotland

Sustainability, Development and Spatial Planning in Europe
Vincent Nadin, Caroline Brown and Stefanie Dühr, UWE, Bristol, UK

Planning for Crime Prevention
Richard Schneider, University of Florida, USA, and Ted Kitchen, Sheffield Hallam University, UK

The Making of the European Spatial Development Perspective
No Masterplan
Andreas Faludi and Bas Waterhout, University of Nijmegen, The Netherlands

THE MAKING OF THE EUROPEAN SPATIAL DEVELOPMENT PERSPECTIVE

NO MASTERPLAN

ANDREAS FALUDI AND BAS WATERHOUT

London and New York

First published 2002 by Routledge, 11 New Fetter Lane, London EC4P 4PP
Simultaneously published in the USA and Canada by Routledge, 29 West 35th Street, New York, NY 10001

Routledge is an imprint of the Taylor and Francis Group

Typeset in Akzidenz Grotesk by GreenGate Publishing Services, Tonbridge, Kent
Printed and bound in Great Britain by Biddles Ltd, Guildford and King's Lynn

British Library Cataloguing in Publication Data
A catalogue record for this book is available from the British Library

Library of Congress Cataloging in Publication Data
Faludi, Andreas.
    The making of the European spatial development perspective / Andreas Faludi and Bas Waterhout.
       p.cm. – (RTPI library series)
    Includes bibliographical references and index.
    ISBN 0-415-27263-7 – ISBN 0-415-27264-5 (pbk.)
    1. Regional planning–European Union coutries. 2. Space in economics. I. Waterhout,
    Bas. II. Title. III. Series.

    HT395.E87 F35 2002
    337.1'42–dc21

2001048578

CONTENTS

The European Spatial Development Perspective, you might say, is a rather esoteric subject. Even those claiming the title of professional planner may not know too much about it. The same could probably have been said of the Treaty of Rome when it was signed by six European countries in 1957, an event which apparently went almost unreported in the British media. Ignorance can sometimes have serious consequences. In fact the ESDP is likely to have profound consequences for the lives of the 300 million people of the European Union and the many others soon to join it. Though they do not know it, it is already shaping the process of land-use planning at every level, from national to local. In the future, its influence can only grow.

So an account of its making – its *construction*, to use a favourite word of Brussels afficionadi – is of great value: not only for planners, but more widely for any serious student of the processes of policy making and governance within the European Union. To most people, even sophisticated citizens, the decision-making processes of the Union are seen as arcane, secret, and even undemocratic. That is why this book is so profoundly important. It tells the long story of the ESDP's gestation, session by session, negotiation by negotiation, draft by draft. Its particular value is to unpick the tangled skein of interests, opinions and power structures that progressively shaped the report. Europe, it emerges, is not in the least obscure or monolithic. On the contrary: policy is shaped in it as in any other democratic entity. The distinctive feature is that in such an enormous and heterogeneous unit of governance, the entire process is just that much more complex.

Andreas Faludi and Bas Waterhout have performed an enormous scholarly service, therefore, not merely for urbanists, but for all serious students of politics. American political scientists, thirty and more years ago, wrote studies of decision making in one city, which became classics in their time. This is a far more ambitious and daunting exercise in analysis, which equally deserves the status of instant classic.

SIR PETER HALL
Bartlett Professor of Planning
University College, London

PREFACE

As the title indicates, this book is about the making of a document called the *European Spatial Development Perspective*, referred to here by its English acronym as the ESDP. Although not a product of the European Community, the European Commission has been involved in preparing it, in ways which will be described. Being published in the official EU languages, the ESDP is arguably the most international planning text that exists.

Beyond this, the precise significance of the ESDP is as yet difficult to predict. Much depends on the follow-up, what the ESDP describes as its 'application', and also on how this type of policy will be embedded in the ongoing business of European integration. When relevant choices, documentation of the ESDP process will prove to be useful, and this is what this book aspires to provide.

The target group may be thought of in terms of three concentric circles. Those immediately involved form the innermost circle. It is to this group the book will, hopefully, be of most relevance. Professionals engaged in the application of the ESDP, in one way or another, form the second circle. Students entering the field of planning form the third circle.

The world is becoming more and more 'globalized'; cross-border, transnational and international planning therefore pose many more challenges. The ESDP represents the most sustained effort so far to confront these challenges, thus making it worthy of study.

The book portrays players from various parts of Europe, most of them planning officials, and their interactions. Varied though their backgrounds are (as *The EU Compendium of Spatial Planning Systems and Policies* shows, there is no common profile of planning throughout the European Union; see CEC, 1997a), these players have one thing in common. It is that they play 'simultaneous chess', not only internationally, but also on their home fronts where the line departments, commonly described as 'sectors', have a profound and often negative influence on planning. Occasionally, this book gives glimpses of these domestic struggles. In the main, though, this book is about the interactions that take place in the European arena.

The makers of the ESDP, who are all on the Committee on Spatial Development (CSD), have been through some difficult times together. Occasionally, conflicts have arisen, mainly because their administrations have constrained them in acting the way that they, as international planners, may have wished. This is important; without appreciating the pressures that the makers of the ESDP have been under, the reader may form an unduly negative view of the convoluted processes described in these pages. In fact, on the whole the makers of the ESDP have shown a co-operative spirit. As Hix (1999: 55) said in general about the experts on the many committees in Brussels, they are forming a 'European vanguard'. Maybe this is the outcome that augurs best for the future of European spatial planning.

The term 'spatial planning' warrants an explanation. Spatial planning is 'Euro-English': a non-British (and non-American) concept conveyed in English words (Williams, 1996: 57). Euro-English combines concepts drawn from various different contexts. Albeit in combination with regional planning, the concept of spatial planning has already figured in the *European Regional/Spatial Planning Charter* (Council of Europe, 1984). The Charter portrays 'regional/spatial planning' as giving geographical expression to the various policies of society; giving direction to a balanced regional development and the physical organization of space, according to an overall strategy. So conceived, spatial planning is similar to what Dijking (1996: 11) describes as 'geopolitical vision'. According to him, the cognitive discourse covered by the latter concept relates to

> any idea concerning the relations between one's own and other places, involving feelings of (in)security or (dis)advantage (and/or) invoking ideas about a collective mission or foreign policy strategy.

The definition fits spatial planning remarkably well, in particular since according to Dijking a vision must say something about identity, territorial borders, core areas and so on. The latter are of course the categories which planners use when formulating spatial strategy.

The *Compendium* mentioned above is more specific than the *European Regional/Spatial Planning Charter* with regard to the meaning of spatial planning:

> Spatial planning refers to the methods used largely by the public sector to influence the future distribution of activities in space. It is undertaken with the aims of creating a more rational territorial organisation of land uses and the linkages between them, to balance demands for development with the need to protect the environment, and to achieve social and economic objectives. Spatial planning embraces measures to co-ordinate the spatial impacts of other sector policies, to achieve a more even distribution of economic development between regions than would otherwise be created by market forces, and to regulate the conversion of land and property uses (CEC, 1997a: 24).

Here another element is added to that of spatial strategy: land-use regulation. However, although spatial strategy may be effectuated by passing regulations, amongst other means, land-use regulation sits uneasily with the idea of spatial planning being about strategy. The purpose here is not to analyze words but to highlight an issue in European spatial planning. Various state bodies have already assumed powers of land-use regulation. So if this is what European spatial planning is about, then this implies transferring powers and responsibilities to the European level. This is a sensitive matter that will be described as the 'competency issue'.

Concerning the competency issue, a position often taken on the CSD is that spatial planning is not, and should never become, a Community competency. As far as land-use regulation is concerned, this seems straightforward: the Community must stay out of it. However, what if spatial planning is about strategy? One can hardly ban players like the Community from having a strategy. On the contrary, strategy development is to be positively encouraged. Strategy gives direction to policies, makes them mutually consistent and, to use a term often applied to European policy making, it increases their transparency. The inevitable conclusion is that, if spatial planning is about strategy, then competency is a non-issue.

One of the participants has experience of both sides of the process, being representative of a member state and on the Commission, and has pointed out that unfortunately, many participants veer towards the view of spatial planning as regulating land-use (Doucet, 1998). They thus read Commission attempts to formulate strategy as interfering with sovereign state powers. This is manifested in the fear of Brussels imposing a 'masterplan', the latter being a characteristic instrument of land-use regulation. Indeed, taken literally, a European masterplan would imply a pattern of land-use imposed by the EU. This is the case if, following the *Compendium*, the purpose of a masterplan is to '... identify a general spatial framework and criteria for the regulation of land-use over an area' (CEC, 1997a: Table B.1). The rejection of a masterplan, so conceived, has been a leitmotif throughout the ESDP process, and so *No Masterplan!* has been chosen as the subtitle of this book.

Conceptual problems such as the one discussed are inherent in policy making, and even more so in an international context, where misunderstandings are common. The difficulties are more fundamental than mere communication problems. They have a great deal to do with the different contexts in which the protagonists operate. This book attempts to understand the contexts in which the chief players in the making of the ESDP operate. Naturally, in so doing, the authors are constrained by their own background, which is north-west European. Their understanding is thus far from comprehensive.

Another problem with writing a book about the ESDP is language. Whilst having made every attempt to write in proper British-English, the authors (themselves not native English speakers) have felt constrained by the nature of what this book is about; a multi-lingual discourse in which most of the exchanges are conducted in that idiom described above as Euro-English. Naturally, where available, the authors have made use of appropriate texts, and since this book attempts to allow the reader to follow the discourse without having to go back to the original documents, reference to such sources is sometimes extensive. Often these texts have been produced under pressure of time, with copy-editing by native English speakers an unlikely prospect. Linguistically, therefore, the source material may leave something to be desired, so where this book quotes or paraphrases it, native English speakers will occasionally raise an eyebrow. The authors are, of course, also open to criticism, but the reader should bear in mind that the problem is sometimes inherent in the material on which they draw.

Lastly, with the exception of commissioners and ministers, the authors have refrained from referring to the persons involved by their names. This has not been done to protect their anonymity; after all, it would take little effort to work out the identities of the handful of people per member state involved. The reason is rather that these people carry out roles, and it is these roles, circumscribed by their functions, that count. In some instances, they undoubtedly have been forced to take up positions not to their liking, for instance when the British delegation to the Committee on Spatial Development had to act cautiously on any issue that smacked of planning, let alone European planning. This is of course inherent in the position of civil servants, and is the reason why they are referred to by their positions rather than their names.

Finally, the authors admit to being biased. The grand, some would say over-ambitious, enterprise of ESDP fascinates them, and they hope that European spatial planning will prosper. If this colours their account of the ESDP process, then so be it!

ACKNOWLEDGEMENTS

When one compares the authors' research of the ESDP, which has extended over several years, with the intricacy of an international project spanning an entire decade, it is bound to appear somewhat feeble. The authors have a command of only a fraction of Community languages, and limited access to the many arenas in which the ESDP has been prepared. The places they have managed to access include, in the first instance, the archives of the National Spatial Planning Agency at The Hague and later the German archives in Bonn and Berlin. Naturally, the authors have also interacted with the small community of academic ESDP 'watchers'. Published sources are referenced in the usual way.

In late 1998, one of the authors had the privilege of meeting the full CSD at their seminar in Vienna, described in Chapter 10. On several occasions the authors have also had the welcome opportunity of speaking to many of the players involved with the ESDP. Sometimes, the discussions took the form of formal interviews, with the minutes subsequently authorized by the participants. Often, the setting was more informal, comprising the authors and participants conversing in the anterooms of the many meeting rooms in which the policy making of European integration is carried out. As mutual trust grew, international telephone calls and in particular countless exchanges by e-mail became the preferred means of interaction. Some of the authors' contacts have kindly taken the trouble of commenting on early drafts of this book.

There have also been various occasions when the authors have been able to become involved with some of the protagonists in the ESDP process, in joint reflection on its meaning. This collaboration has resulted in, or is in the process of resulting in, the production of parallel and complementary works. Thus, the Lincoln Institute of Land Policy sponsored a session on 'European Spatial Planning' at the annual National Planning Conference held by the American Planning Association at New Orleans in March 2001. This featured papers on the British, Dutch and German positions with regard to their contributions to the ESDP. Augmented by other contributions, including ones on France and the Nordic member states, these papers have appeared in a special issue of *Built Environment* under the title of *Regulative Competition and Co-operation in European Spatial Planning* (Faludi 2001b).

Having an abiding interest in stimulating strategic planning debates in the USA, the Lincoln Institute convened yet another seminar on 'European Spatial

Planning', held at its headquarters in Cambridge, MA in June 2001. The Lincoln Institute intends to document the proceedings by publishing papers from nine authors, including the co-authors of this volume, as well as papers by several key participants in the process who have also been amongst the sources on which this book draws.

Whilst writing this book, the authors have also been involved in an INTERREG IIB project called EURBANET, with the research institute OTB of Delft University of Technology being the lead partner. Our role has been to evaluate the ESDP, in particular its application. Although this is not the topic of this book, it will be clear that working on two parallel projects has produced some synergy. In particular, it has allowed us to strengthen our links with the network of players involved.

The names and affiliations of participants, who gave so freely of their time, are to be found on pages XVII–XX. Naturally, the authors are grateful for all the help they have received. Needless to say, if this book has any shortcomings, it cannot be for want of any outside help.

LIST OF FIGURES

LIST OF TABLES

AUSTRIA

Roland Arbter is Desk Officer in charge of European spatial development policy at the Federal Chancellery (unit for co-ordinating regional and spatial policies).

Wolf Huber is head of the unit responsible for co-ordinating regional and spatial policies at the Federal Chancellery.

Friedrich Schindegger is a senior consultant at the Austrian Institute for Regional Studies and Spatial Planning.

BELGIUM

Frank D'hondt is a Flemish consultant who worked from 1998 until 2001 at the Dutch Spatial Planning Agency where he was responsible for elaborating the international aspects of the 5th Planning Report.

Sofie Houvenaghel is Deputy Director at the spatial planning department of the Flemish Administration. She is involved in the ESDP process and in the NWMA Spatial Vision Project.

René van der Lecq works at the spatial planning department of the Flemish Administration and was involved in the preparations for the informal meeting of ministers responsible for spatial planning on 14 July 2001.

DENMARK

Peter Baltzer Nielsen works for the Ministry of Environment and Energy.

Niels Østergaard is Director-General for Planning at the Ministry of Environment and Energy.

EUROPEAN COMMISSION

Pierre-Antoine Barthelemy is a French official at DG REGIO involved in the ESDP process and its application.

Philippe Doucet is Programme Manager of the INTERREG IIIB NWE programme in Lille. He has been involved in the ESDP process, first as a Walloon civil servant, later on as an *expert national détaché* at DG XVI.

Jean-François Drevet is a French senior official at DG Regio and deals with EU enlargement. Until 1995 he was involved in the ESDP process, first as an official of the French planning agency DATAR, then as a member of the Chérèque cabinet and finally as senior official at DG XVI.

Eric Dufeil is French and a deputy head of unit at DG Regio. He was closely involved in the ESDP process from 1995 to 2000. Also he was one of the architects of the Community Initiative INTERREG IIC and helped to launch the programme.

Reinhard Klein is a former German head of regional planning and is now Head of the Tourism Unit at the Enterprise Directorate-General, after having been co-ordinator of the INTERREG IIA cross-border cooperation Community Initiative for several years. He was involved in the working group of the Commission's Services and closely followed the Commission's work on the ESDP from 1995 to 1999.

Peter Mehlbye is a former Danish official involved in the ESDP process; he served subsequently as an *expert national détaché* at DG XVI. He is now a consultant.

Rudolf Niessler is Austrian and was head of a unit in DG Regio. In that capacity he was involved in the ESDP process from 1997 to 2000.

Mario Rodrigues is Portuguese and within DG XVI was responsible for the co-ordination of all INTERREG IIC programmes and Article 10 Pilot Actions.

Charles White is British and Principal Administrator at DG Regio, responsible for communication.

Monika Wulf-Mathies comes from Germany and was Commissioner of the European Commission responsible for Regional Policy and Cohesion under the Santer Presidency.

FINLAND

Ulla Blomberg is Senior Advisor at the Department for Regional Development of the Ministry of the Interior and in that capacity has been involved in the ESDP process since 1994.

FRANCE

Claude Marcori works at DATAR and has been involved in the ESDP process from the very start.

Jean Peyrony has worked at DATAR since mid-1999 and was previously responsible for the organization of the French EU Presidency.

Jacques Robert is a consultant and carried out a number of studies commissioned by various CSD delegations.

Jérôme Vignon was Director for Long-term Strategy at DATAR. Before that, he was a member of the Delors cabinet. Since late 2000 he has once again been working for the European Commission.

GERMANY

Lothar Blatt became involved in the ESDP process when the first ideas began to emerge with regard to the application of the ESDP. He advised the German federal ministry responsible for spatial planning on how to deal with the European Structural Funds.

Joachim Gazecki is with the German Federal Ministry of Transport, Building and

Housing. He was involved in the drafting of the Potsdam document. He commented on drafts from the perspective of his involvement with economic policy in relation to spatial planning.

Michael Krautzberger was Director-General for Spatial Planning at the German Federal Ministry of (as it was then called) Regional Planning, Building and Urban Development from 1991 until 1999.

Ute Krönert is with the German Federal Ministry of Transport, Building and Housing. She has been involved with the ESDP process since early 1997. She has attended CSD meetings and has had a central role in the drawing up of the Potsdam document.

Wolfgang Schneider was Head of Unit at the Ministry for Environment, Spatial Planning and Agriculture of the German *Land* North Rhine-Westphalia. He was also involved in the NWMA Spatial Vision Project. Now he is on the cabinet of the Prime Minister of North Rhine-Westphalia.

Karl-Peter Schön is an expert at the Bundesamt für Bauwesen und Raumordnung and has been involved in the ESDP process since 1995.

Welf Selke is Head of the International Planning Unit at the German Federal Ministry of Transport, Building and Housing. He has been involved in the ESDP process from the start.

Manfred Sinz has been involved in the ESDP process at various stages as an expert. Since 1999 he has been Director-General for Spatial Planning at the Federal Ministry of Transport, Building and Housing.

THE NETHERLANDS
FROM THE NATIONAL SPATIAL PLANNING AGENCY:

Paul van Hemert is a cartographic expert and has been involved in the ESDP process since 1995.

Rob Kragt is a senior official concerned with cross-border, transnational and European spatial planning in the International Affairs Division.

Derek Martin is Head of the International Affairs Division and has been involved in the ESDP process since Nantes, both as an Agency representative as well as from within the European Commission.

Peter Petrus was Co-ordinator for International Spatial Planning Affairs from 1990 to 1993. Prior to the informal council in Leipzig he was seconded to the International Planning Unit of the German Federal Ministry of (as it was then called) Regional Planning, Building and Urban Development. He was involved in the ESDP process until 1996.

Gerda Roeleveld is a senior official and was involved in the cartographic and expert groups during the ESDP process. She was also project leader of the NWMA Spatial Vision.

Hans ten Velden was Co-ordinator for International Plan Development at the National Spatial Planning Agency and was part of the international writing group of 1996/1997 that produced the *First Offical Draft* of the ESDP, carried out under the Dutch Presidency; he also co-ordinated the Dutch contribution to the SPESP.

OTHERS:

Jenno Witsen was Director-General of the National Spatial Planning Agency until 1990. In other functions he stayed involved in the Dutch debate on European spatial planning. He is Emeritus Professor at the University of Nijmegen.

Wil Zonneveld is a senior researcher at the research institute OTB of the Delft University of Technology and co-operates in various research projects, together with the authors of this book.

SWEDEN

Sverke Lindeblad works for NUTEK, a Swedish government agency, and is a member of the CSD.

UNITED KINGDOM

Jim Mackinnon is Chief Planner at the Scottish Executive and has been involved in the ESDP process since the UK Presidency.

Christabel Myers is Head of the International Planning Unit at the planning department of the Department of (as it was called during the period covered in this book) the Environment, Transport and the Regions and has been involved in the ESDP process since 1997.

Vincent Nadin is Director of the Research Centre for Environment and Planning at the University of the West of England (UWE). He was project leader of the EU Compendium of Spatial Planning Systems and Policies, led the consultant team preparing the Spatial Vision for North-West Europe, and has undertaken research for the UK government on issues relating to European spatial planning.

Sean Ryan worked for the international planning division of the DETR during the initial INTERREG IIC period. In this capacity he was a member of the INTERREG IIC steering committee for the NWMA.

Chris Williams is Director of Environmental Services at Buckinghamshire County Council and has been involved in CRONWE. Now he is involved in transposing the ESDP into the British planning system and in an INTERREG IIC project.

John Zetter was head of the DETR division responsible, *inter alia*, for international planning. He led the UK team working on the ESDP from 1993 to 2000. He is now a Visiting Professor at University College London, directing a course on European Spatial Planning.

CHAPTER 1

ROOTS AND CONTEXT

On 10/11 May 1999 a meeting took place in Potsdam, capital of Brandenburg. Ministers of the member states of the European Union responsible for Spatial Planning and the Member of the European Commission responsible for Regional Policy and Cohesion, Dr Monika Wulf-Mathies, were present. With the German EU Presidency in the chair, they deliberated about the European Spatial Development Perspective (ESDP). Advisers on the Committee on Spatial Development (CSD) had had drafts since before Christmas 1998. The CSD had ironed out any remaining differences, so the proceedings at Potsdam passed smoothly. Seated according to European protocol, heads of various delegations read out prepared statements giving the ESDP their blessing. In its Conclusions, the Presidency duly recorded the positive outcome of the meeting.

Had this been a Council of Ministers meeting on official Community business, the venue would have been either Brussels or Luxembourg. However, the ESDP is an informal document and thus the meeting was informal too. This does not mean that making the ESDP was straightforward. This book takes the reader along the route of policymaking to Potsdam, documenting the events and describing the difficulties that have occurred. It does not attempt to theorize European planning. Rather, it relates how the ESDP has come about, introduces the chief protagonists and explores their motives. It does so in the conviction that practices developing out of the 'flow of policy' (Wallace, 2000: 525) have a dynamic of their own, which is worth exploring.

As indicated in the Preface, a masterplan is the one thing that its makers did not want the ESDP to be. Rather, as they said all along, it was to be a framework and a source of inspiration. To come to fruition, frameworks need to be applied (Faludi, 2001). The application of the ESDP is on its way, and in time this may lead to a revision of the document. With the enlargement of the EU, revision will eventually become an issue anyhow.

Even though it was informal, the meeting at Potsdam was not a minor affair. Apart from ministers and the Commissioner, those present included representatives of European institutions. Including the retinues of heads of delegations, the participants numbered close to one hundred. Until the previous autumn it had seemed as if the venue would be Munich, capital of the Free State of Bavaria, which was ruled by one of the coalition partners of the then federal government. In the meantime, though, the government had changed. An additional consideration in favour of changing the venue to Potsdam was that as a beneficiary of the so-called 'Structural Funds', Brandenburg was likely to give Commissioner Wulf-Mathies (a German Social Democrat and former trade union leader) a warmer welcome than the Bavarians. One of the lessons from the ESDP process is that the 'opportunity structure' of the players, shaped as it is by the contexts in which they operate, is important.

THE ROOTS

Those who have been involved in the ESDP process for a long time may have reminisced at Potsdam about where and when it all started: ten years previously in Nantes, France. This is the subject of Chapter 3; this chapter sketches the roots and contextual framework of the ESDP process.

Planners are notorious internationalists. After the First World War, the reconstruction of war-torn Belgium drew the attention of no less an authority than Patrick Geddes (Boardman, 1978). There were international organizations, like CIAM and the International Garden Cities and Town Planning Association. In 1930, Amsterdam played host to a World Social Economic Planning Conference (International Industrial Relations Institute, 1931).

Jean Gottman's identification of a megalopolis on the East Coast of the USA (Gottman, 1961) after the Second World War inspired the permanent Conference on Regional Planning in North-west Europe to look for similar developments in Europe. The conference also deliberated about a Channel Tunnel, then still on the drawing board, and a Structure Sketch for North-west Europe (Figure 1.1). Participants were hoping that the European Coal and Steel Community (ECSC), the first step towards a European Union, would take planning on board. The Dutch were particularly keen on this. When the European Economic Community (EEC) was subsequently formed, they thought it, too, should assume a planning role. German planners saw the Council of Europe as being a forum for international planning. The Council of Europe set up CEMAT, the acronym for *Conférence Européenne des Ministres de l'Aménagement du Territoire* (known as the 'European Conference of Ministers responsible for Regional Planning' in English, although the French acronym is more commonly used). CEMAT reached its peak in the early 1980s when it adopted the *European Regional/Spatial Planning Charter* at Torremolinos (Council of Europe, 1984; see also Williams, 1996: 80), mentioned in the Preface for toying with the concept of spatial planning. The Charter identified common planning principles, some of which were to appear on the agenda of the ESDP.

Subsequently, CEMAT went somewhat into limbo, but a CEMAT meeting at Lausanne in 1988 was the occasion for preliminary discussions about Nantes. With the development of the ESDP, CEMAT is once again in the picture. For all the

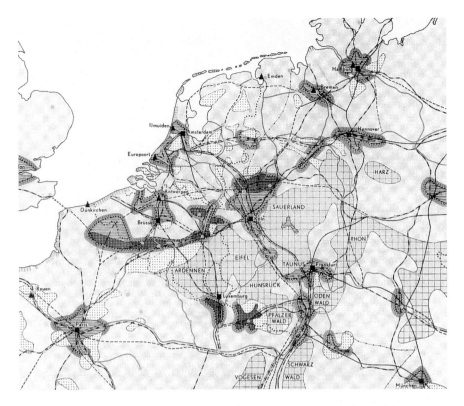

Figure 1.1 Structure Sketch by the Conference on Regional Planning in North-west Europe (1967) (Source: National Spatial Planning Agency 2000)

so-called accession states hoping to join the EU, CEMAT is a vehicle for something that they have clamoured for, unsuccessfully it must be said, which is a voice in European spatial planning (Richardson and Jensen, 2000: 508; Finka, 2000: 437–8). Indeed, at Hanover, Germany, in September 2000, CEMAT drew on the ESDP as a source of inspiration and adopted what are known as the *Guiding Principles for the Sustainable Development of the European Continent* (European Conference of Ministers responsible for Regional Planning, 2000).

The European Regional/Spatial Planning Charter of 1984 was the occasion on which the fledgling European Parliament argued for a form of European planning. It was not to be for the last time (Noetzel, 2000: 10; Husson, 2000). However, the European Parliament has no say in the matter. To explain why, a brief exposition of the nature of European integration is needed, which is given in Chapter 2. First, the discussion explores one of the chief reasons why there needs to be some form of European spatial planning, that is, that there are already European spatial policies in place that require co-ordinating.

EUROPEAN SPATIAL POLICIES

The European Community, as it is now called, engages in various policies that are 'spatial'. The term 'spatial policy' is understood to refer to:

> [A]ny policy which is spatially specific or is in effect spatial in practice, whether or not it is deliberately designed to be, and any policy which is designed to influence land-use decisions, to be integrated with local planning strategies or to be implemented by local and regional authorities as part of their spatial planning responsibilities (Williams, 1996: 7).

With the exception of transport policy, spatial policies were not the object of the original Treaty of Rome, which established the EEC in 1958. Creating an integrated 'Common Market', as it was then known, amounted to spatial policy anyway (Swyngedouw, 1994). In the words of Article 13 of the Single European Act (the first amendment more than thirty years after the Treaty of Rome; see Chapter 2), 'single market' stands for the creation of '... an area without internal frontiers in which the free movement of goods, persons, services and capital are ensured' (Rosamond, 2000: 99). These 'four freedoms' assume a barrier-free space where there is 'frictionless mobility' (Richardson and Jensen, 2000: 512); a 'Europe of Flows' (Hajer, 2000). Of course, the idea is that a single market will discipline producers, thus increasing efficiency and progressively eliminating development differentials between states and regions (Taulelle, 2000: 58).

This abstract notion of a single market is being imposed on a situation characterized by long distances and physical barriers. These serve to exacerbate social, economic, cultural and linguistic diversity in which gains tend to be unevenly distributed (Héritier, 1999: 31). The preamble of the Treaty of Rome faintly recognizes this, referring to the need to '... reduce the differences between the various regions and the backwardness of the less favoured regions. In addition, some of the sector policies ... assumed a regional character in their early phases' (Calussi, 1998: 225–6).

Chapter 2 of the ESDP lists Community spatial policies, identifying the Structural Funds, the trans-European networks and environmental policies as being of particular significance (CEC, 1999a: 13). What follows are brief descriptions of these spatial policies.

STRUCTURAL FUNDS

Regional disparities have always been seen as barriers to what the Treaty of Rome has termed 'harmonious development' (Allen, 2000: 245). The formulation of appropriate policies has taken time. When the European Regional Development Fund (ERDF) was eventually established in the early 1970s, it gave member states fixed sums to be disbursed among their regions. Their distribution and use was at the discretion of the member states. Some of them formed special agencies for modernizing less developed regions, like the Italian *Mezzogiorno* (CEC, 2000a: 23).

With the passing of the Single European Act in 1988, regional policy acquired a treaty base. By that time, Directorate-General XVI already existed. Since the current Commission President at the time of publication, Romano Prodi, has done away with arcane Roman numerals, it is referred to as the Directorate-General Regio, but for most of the period covered in this book it was known as DG XVI. DG XVI became important when a 'non-quota' title was created (Héritier, 1999: 63). Governed by detailed Council regulations, which are subject to the unanimity rule, the discretion that this title gave to the Commission, and with it to DG XVI, was, however, limited. Eventually though, the doubling of the Structural Funds in the late 1980s was to enhance the position of DG XVI.

The passing of the Single European Act also marked a period in which the term 'economic and social cohesion' entered Community discourse, providing a broader justification for regional policies. Since then, the reduction of economic and social disparities has been a fundamental objective of the EU (Dinan, 1999: 430). A standard text by Hooghe (1996a) refers to regional policy as 'cohesion policy'. (As will become evident in Chapter 10, as the popularity of the term 'cohesion' increases, the Commission now seems to regard 'territorial cohesion' as a functional equivalent of spatial planning.)

Regional policy is the second largest spender (after the Common Agricultural Policy, or CAP) amongst Community policies. There are altogether four so-called Structural Funds – the European Regional Development Fund (ERDF), the European Social Fund (ESF), the European Agricultural Fund for Guidance (EAFG) and the Financial Instrument for Fishery Guidance (FIFG). There is also a 'Cohesion Fund', established under the Treaty of Maastricht; this has made the 'cohesion countries' of Greece, Ireland, Portugal and Spain the beneficiaries of grants, which are to be used mainly for infrastructure investments and environmental improvements.

For the current Programming Period, 2000–2006, EU spending amounts to 213 billion euro. Funding is mainly for three objectives. Objective 1, which absorbs 70 per cent of the funds, is to help regions that are lagging behind economically (Figure 1.2). Objective 2 is to provide for the social and economic renewal of zones experiencing difficulties. Objective 3 is non-spatial in that it is for training and employment throughout the Community. In addition, there are four so-called Community Initiatives. They are financed by the budget for the Structural Funds. The one promoting co-operation between regions (called INTERREG IIIB) is particularly important for the application of the ESDP. There is also the Cohesion Fund, mentioned above, and there are the so-called Innovative Actions and Structural Instruments for Pre-Accession. During the period when the ESDP was being prepared, there were six objectives and fourteen Community Initiatives, with INTERREG IIC (transnational planning) easily being the most important one in relation to the ESDP. A recent publication (CEC, 2000b) describes the precise differences between the current Programming Period and the previous one.

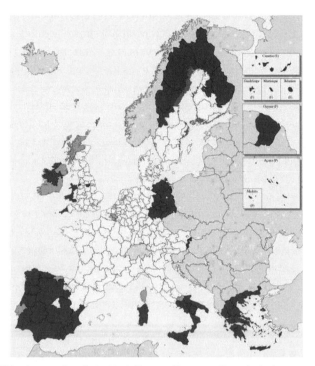

Figure 1.2 Objective 1 regions in 2000–6 (Source: European Commission)

The policy regarding the Structural Funds will have to be adjusted to cope with the accession of central and eastern European countries (Hix, 1999: 260). The reasons for this are the disparities between existing and potential new member states (Drevet, 2000: 28). The recent *Second Report on Economic and Social Cohesion* (CEC, 2001a) analyzes the prospects of the Structural Funds in a European Union of twenty-seven members. This is a relevant issue for the future. What is important here is the fact that Community regional policy has been the cradle of European spatial planning, as will become evident in Chapter 3.

ENVIRONMENT

As with regional policy, the Treaty of Rome made no reference to the environment, so when the need to formulate environmental policy became urgent, as with regional policy, provisions addressing new concerns were invoked. One was Article 100 of the Treaty of Rome, dealing with the harmonization of laws with respect to the establishment and functioning of the internal market. Another one was Article 235, allowing measures necessary to achieve the goals of the Community to be taken, even in the absence of explicit treaty provisions (Allen, 2000: 247; Bursens *et al.*, 1998: 28). (Note that the Treaty of Amsterdam has consolidated the numbering system so that the once infamous Article 235, for instance, is now Article 308.)

In the case of environmental policy, these articles were invoked to respond to the growing concerns of 'green-minded' governments like the Danish, the Dutch and, in particular, the German, and of certain advocacy groups (Sbragia, 2000: 296). The occasion was one of the so-called summits; the six-monthly meetings of the heads of state and government of the member states, now styled European Councils. This summit was held in Paris in the aftermath of the 1972 United Nations Conference on the Human Environment in Stockholm. It provided the impetus for the European Commission's formulation of 'Environmental Action Programmes' (EAPs). Three such programmes operated until, once again, the Single European Act of 1988 gave this policy a treaty base. The Treaty of Maastricht and the Treaty of Amsterdam give even more prominence to environmental concerns. Lenshow (1999: 44) says approvingly that on the EC level '... the wider and more systemic environmental problem perceptions formulated in global environmental fora are taking root', a factor that has also become evident at world climate conferences held in both The Hague and Bonn in 2001.

European environmental policy impacts upon spatial development in various ways. The two most obvious effects are, first, the requirement of Environmental Impact Assessments (EIAs) under EC Directive 85/337, currently in the process of being supplemented by one on Strategic Environmental Assessment, and second, the setting aside of Special Protection Areas and Special Areas for Conservation, under the Birds and Habitat Directives. Such areas are the building blocks of the European ecological network, 'Natura 2000'. (Note that these directives are sometimes considered intrusive, particularly in countries that believe they have already integrated environmental concerns into their routine planning operations.)

The European Commission itself seeks to inject environmental awareness into all its policies. The ESDP, too, embraces the sustainability agenda.

TRANS-EUROPEAN NETWORKS

As against regional and environmental policy, the Treaty of Rome did make provisions for a transport policy, but this was not followed through (Aspinwall, 1999: 119). Eventually, the European Court of Justice forced a reluctant Council of Ministers to act (Héritier, 1999: 33). Lobbying by the European Round Table of leading industrialists helped to jolt the Community into action (Richardson, 1997). As part of the so-called 'Delors II Package' (after Jacques Delors, President of the European Commission for a crucial period during the 1980s and 1990s) the 1993 Edinburgh Summit received Commission proposals with regard to the trans-European networks (TENs). The TENs cover transport, telecommunications and energy supply infrastructure, with transport networks receiving a full 80 per cent of available Community funding.

Infrastructure is not the only concern of Community transport policy, which is also about liberalizing market access and so on. Since 1995, there has been more emphasis on the development of sustainable forms of transport, to limit the impact of transport activity on climate change (Banister, 2000: 177). However, the main rationale is still that of creating the preconditions, in terms of infrastructure, for a smoother operation of the single market. Following the logic of what has been described as the 'Europe of Flows' (see page 4), national networks need to be integrated and access to them improved.

Based on a report prepared in co-operation with the transport industry, the Commission prepared a Community Guideline for the most visible TEN, the Transport TEN (T-TEN). In Essen in 1994, the European Council amended it to take account of the pending accession of Austria, Sweden and Finland. As it stands, the policy is to promote the creation of fourteen so-called 'missing links', needed to bridge gaps between national networks (Figure 1.3). This is obviously spatial policy in that it addresses perceived shortfalls in the provision of infrastructure. Involving the creation of high-speed rail connections, among other policies, the T-TEN is of great interest to many people. It should be noted that, as with the other policies discussed, T-TEN policy has been developed by a dedicated network of players. There has been no sustained effort to co-ordinate it with other spatially relevant policies. However, as the ESDP points out, the effectiveness of transport policies in achieving the desired shift towards more environmentally friendly modes of transport can be improved by co-ordination with spatial development policy and urban development measures (CEC, 1999a: 14). It is therefore the ESDP's ambition to contribute to the ongoing debate about the revision of the TENs. Common sense would dictate nothing less.

Indeed, common sense would suggest that all Community spatial policies should be co-ordinated to prevent such cross-impacts, as when TENs interfere with policies designed to protect nature and the environment. Co-ordination would also make Community policy more accessible to local, regional and national authorities. This is what spatial planning could and should achieve. However, there are institutional issues involved, which will be discussed in Chapter 2.

THE ROLE OF DG XVI

The quest for European spatial planning was a response to opportunities created by the rising fortunes of the European Commission in the late 1980s. Seen as the formulation of strategy rather than as land-use regulation (the distinction having been explained in the Preface), spatial planning fitted into the greater picture. It was also an area that Delors was personally interested in, having had previous exposure to urban issues (Milesi, 1995).

Spatial planning was not, however, a high-profile issue on the European Commissioners' agenda. Rather, it was a matter discussed within the bureaucratic

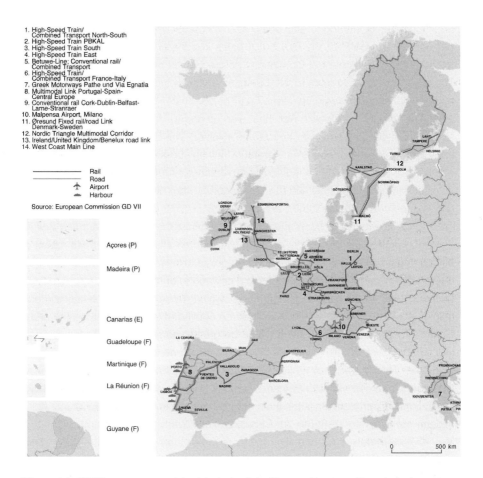

1. High-Speed Train/
   Combined Transport North-South
2. High-Speed Train PBKAL
3. High-Speed Train South
4. High-Speed Train East
5. Betuwe-Line: Conventional rail/
   Combined Transport
6. High-Speed Train/
   Combined Transport France-Italy
7. Greek Motorways Pathe und Via Egnatia
8. Multimodal Link Portugal-Spain-
   Central Europe
9. Conventional rail Cork-Dublin-Belfast-
   Larne-Stranraer
10. Malpensa Airport, Milano
11. Øresund Fixed rail/road Link
    Denmark-Sweden
12. Nordic Triangle Multimodal Corridor
13. Ireland/United Kingdom/Benelux road link
14. West Coast Main Line

———————— Rail
— — — — Road
✈ Airport
⚓ Harbour

Source: European Commission GD VII

Açores (P)

Madeira (P)

Canarias (E)

Guadeloupe (F)

Martinique (F)

La Réunion (F)

Guyane (F)

Figure 1.3 T-TEN programme and the 14 missing links (Source: European Commission)

system. In questions of European integration, the prominent role of the administrative élite is often commented upon (Bach, 1994; Benz, 1998). More specifically, the key mover was a small section within DG XVI.

As indicated, DG XVI administers the Structural Funds, in particular the European Regional Development Fund (ERDF) established in 1975 (Damette, 2000: 67). Initially, it provided financial support with few conditions attached. As indicated, however, the Single European Act of 1988 changed this. It was believed that the single market would mean more growth, but mainly in the inner core of Europe (John, 2000: 880). In 1988, Spain therefore vetoed the EC budget, thus forcing a doubling of the regional funds (Morata and Muñoz, 1996: 195). The literature describes this as a 'side-payment' which, much as 'package deals', are an important mode of operation in European integration (Scharpf, 1999: 168–9).

Community funding for this policy seems impressive (the maximum being 0.46 per cent of the GDP of the EU) but it pales in comparison with the spending of nation states. The impact of Community policies lies in their agenda-setting nature. The majority of funding goes to 'NUTS-areas' (these being European statistical units such as provinces or regions) with a GDP of less than 75 per cent of the EU average. The Single European Act has also changed the ground rules, in that sub-national governments now need to be involved. The European Community, originally a club of member states, is therefore drawing sub-national players into its span of influence. There is talk of 'multi-level governance' (Hooghe, 1996b). Some centralized member states may find this disconcerting (but not France, a country that is taking decentralization seriously; see Chapter 3).

Once again, this all bears the stamp of Commission President Jacques Delors. Cohesion policy was part of his defence of what he called the 'European model of society' against radical free-market protagonists (Ross, 1995; Hooghe, 1996b). Seizing the opportunity Delors proposed a new mode of operation, using experimental 'Integrated Mediterranean Programmes' which Italian Commission officials had helped to create. European funds were to be applied in an integrated way to attain Community objectives. Also, there would be greater partnerships between regional and local players. In this way, what Delors described as the *forces vivres* would be mobilized. This is a French philosophy, which will be described in more detail in Chapter 3. It agrees well with Putnam's findings (1993) on Italy, suggesting that political and social participation is the main determinant of institutional performance (for a critique see Ritaine, 1998: 69–70; Bagnasco and Oberti, 1998: 150–2).

Delors preferred ad hoc arrangements rather than working via existing channels (Cini, 1996: 180). He set up a small Directorate-General XXII for this new type of cohesion policy. However, DG XVI had responsibility for the Structural Funds and had acquired the capacity for conceptualizing policy by making profuse use of so-called *experts nationaux détachés* (delightfully rendered in Euro-English as 'Detached National Experts') on short-term contracts. The hand of DG XVI was strengthened further by the appointment of the member of the Delors cabinet responsible for cohesion policy who, as a director, was to play an important role in formulating the policy of DG XVI regarding planning in general and the ESDP in particular. Eventually, DG XXII was superseded by DG XVI (Hooghe, 1996b).

CONCEPTUALIZING EUROPEAN SPACE

European planning implies the conceptualization of European space. When the ESDP process first started, the dominant view of Europe was shaped by the notion of the 'Blue Banana'. This came out of a study (Brunet, 1989) of the position of

French cities. The study had been commissioned by the French planning agency DATAR (*Délegation à l'aménagement du territoire et à l'action régionale*; 'Delegation for Spatial Management and Regional Action' in English, according to Lagrange, 1997: 333, although recent publications talk about 'Regional Development and Action Delegation'). Based on an analysis of all 165 major cities in twelve countries of the European Community plus Austria and Switzerland, the Brunet study pointed out that almost half of them were situated in a megalopolis. The study called this the *dorsale*, reaching from England to Lombardy and bypassing the French heartland, including Paris.

It was quite accidentally that the *dorsale* got the name 'Blue Banana'. On a visit to DATAR, the French Planning Minister, Jacques Chéréque, saw a map of Europe with the *dorsale* painted in blue and asked: 'What is this blue banana for?'. A reporter from the weekly *Le Nouvel Observateur*, after overhearing this comment, published an article under the title *La banane bleue*, and the name stuck.

Covering barely 18 per cent of the territory of the fourteen countries studied, the Blue Banana comprised no less than 47 per cent of urban agglomerations with more than 200,000 inhabitants. The Channel Tunnel would further consolidate the situation. Another development was the prosperous 'North of the South' stretching from northern Italy to north-east Spain, where the third industrial revolution had resulted in much economic growth.

What is noteworthy is the attention that the Blue Banana received, for instance in the work of Kunzmann and Wegener (1991: 63), commissioned by DG XVI. They rejected the underlying view of Europe as 'competitive' and substituted it with the 'European Bunch of Grapes', in their eyes a more co-operative view, 'more suited to represent the polycentric structure of the urban system in Europe and the fundamental *similarity in diversity* of the interests and concerns of its member cities' (Figures 1.4 and 1.5). Like the Banana, this was also a powerful metaphor (Williams 1996: 96) that would resonate in discussions on the CSD. In the end, the polycentric image of Europe would prove to be the more enduring.

Perhaps, though, the critique of the Blue Banana was exaggerated. To reiterate, the underlying Brunet study was about the European urban network. Its main point was that in the *dorsale* the network was more compact than in other areas. The fact that the Blue Banana has received enormous attention since then merely demonstrates the need for concepts that are easy to grasp. In policy making, the need for such concepts is evident. Policy would be impossible to formulate without the order that they impose on one's perception of reality.

This does not mean to say that the Blue Banana represents the only way of conceptualizing European space. Rather, the images of a 'Banana' and a 'Bunch of Grapes' stand for alternative conceptualizations: the former a 'one-dimensional Europe', based on the single principle of density, and the latter a 'diversified Europe',

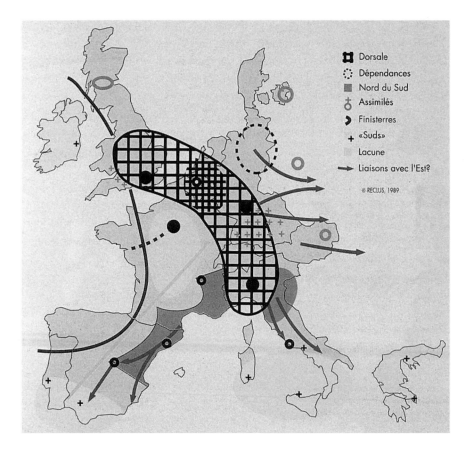

Figure 1.4 The dorsale or the 'Blue Banana' (Source: National Spatial Planning Agency, 2000)

which is based on a more multifaceted model of reality. Throughout the book, these two views of Europe will be shown to be in a dialectic relation to each other.

PLAN OF THE BOOK

The next chapter gives a brief account of the institutions of the EU. Subsequent chapters follow the 'flow of policy', with emphasis on the ministerial meetings that steer the process. For reference purposes, Table 1.1 summarizes the venues and topics of these meetings.

Chapter 3 deals with Nantes and also its follow-up, Turin. These two meetings articulated one important theme in the ESDP process – regional policy, serving economic and social cohesion, allowing itself to be influenced (and this is where the innovative element came in) by an appreciation of space and spatial relations. Still, the view of Europe was fairly one-dimensional.

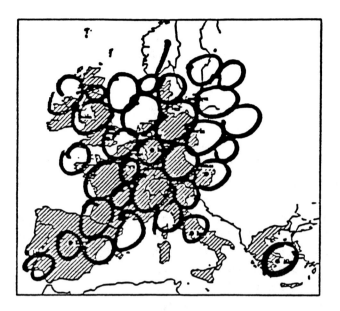

Figure 1.5 The European 'Bunch of Grapes' (Source: Kunzmann and Wegener, 1991)

In the run-up to Nantes, The Netherlands had co-operated with France 'behind the scenes'. Italian enthusiasm in organizing Turin enabled the Dutch to organize the third meeting at The Hague in 1991. The Dutch produced a document on *Urban Networks in Europe*, and there was agreement on setting up the Committee on Spatial Development (CSD). The CSD met for the first time under the Portuguese

Table 1.1 Venues, dates and topics discussed at gatherings 1989–99

Venue & date	Topic
Nantes '89	Start-up
Turin '90	Uneven development
The Hague '91	Urban networks, set-up CSD
Lisbon '92	TENs, spatial vision
Liège '93	Go-ahead for ESDP; member states propose INTERREG IIC
Corfu '94	Working methods
Leipzig '94	Leipzig Principles
Strasbourg '95	Scenarios; Commission set to launch INTERREG IIC
Madrid '95	Indicators; start of INTERREG IIC
Venice '96	Commitment to finish ESDP
Noordwijk '97	'First Official Draft'
Glasgow '98	'First Complete Draft'
Potsdam '99	The ESDP
Tampere'99	Action Programme

Presidency. The latter also organized the Lisbon meeting, which focused on trans-European networks. An outcome of this meeting was the call for a 'spatial vision' of Europe. The Hague and Lisbon provide the subject matter for Chapter 4.

Chapter 5 describes the turning point reached at Liège, where ministers heeded the call for a spatial vision and laid the foundations for the successful Community Initiative INTERREG IIC. By that time, with their 1994 Presidency in mind, the Germans had already decided to get involved, even entertaining hopes of seeing the ESDP through. However, the question remained: was the ESDP to be a document of the European Community or of the member states? This is the 'competency issue' mentioned in the Preface. There were other problems as well: where should the emphasis lie? On cohesion or on sustainability, pushed increasingly by north-west Europe? Was the focus to be exclusively on problems in the periphery or also on problems in the core of Europe? As a result of these issues, the Germans made no further progress than setting up the so-called Leipzig Principles, named after the venue of the ministerial meeting at which they were accepted. Meanwhile, there had also been a meeting at Corfu where the CSD had settled on a mode of operation which reflected the inter-governmental setting of the ESDP process and the concomitant need for unanimity.

Chapter 6 takes the reader through three Presidencies. First of all, there was the second French Presidency of 1995, begun ambitiously but handicapped by the general elections, which were bringing down the French government. The next Spanish Presidency was sceptical about the ESDP and used stalling tactics. Under the Italian Presidency, the ministers entrusted the Dutch with concluding the ESDP process.

Then the emphasis changed. This was because, with key players more or less in position, a period of practical work rather than of political manoeuvring started. The three chapters that follow give fairly detailed accounts of how the players co-operated in producing the ESDP.

Chapter 7 is about the collective effort that the *First Official Draft* of the ESDP represented and about Noordwijk, where it was approved in 1997. During this part of the process, working methods were refined and the Leipzig Principles were amplified. However, the implications of the ESDP were left for other Presidencies to explore.

Chapter 8 is about the role of the UK. The new Labour government was enthusiastic about the ESDP. However, the results of consultations and a series of transnational seminars took time to digest, thus preventing the UK Presidency from finishing the job. The UK achievement was the *Complete Draft*, presented at Glasgow in 1998.

By that time it had become clear that the task of completing the ESDP would fall to the German Presidency, one year further down the line, and this is how ministers came to give their blessing to the ESDP at Potsdam. This home run is the topic of Chapter 9.

Chapter 10 looks at what is nowadays being described as the 'application' of the ESDP. This includes an explanation of how the Finnish Presidency finished the business begun at Potsdam, by getting another ministerial meeting to accede to a 12-point Action Programme. There is also an overview of how the Commission takes the ESDP on board. The chapter touches upon the prospect of revision and the unfinished business of deciding what spatial planning actually means in terms of European integration. The urgency of this issue was made evident by the financing of the European Spatial Planning Observatory Network (ESPON). In late 1997, the Luxembourg Presidency made valiant efforts to get this much-coveted research network off the ground. They encountered unresolved problems relating to the status of the ESDP, which were discussed at a CSD seminar in Vienna in 1998. At the time of writing, decisive steps are being taken with regard to the future position of the CSD.

Still, the future remains uncertain. The Epilogue focuses on the skills of international planners, skills that will be indispensable, whatever the future arrangements are likely to be.

CHAPTER 2

A EUROPEAN PRIMER

Attitudes towards European spatial planning are shaped by people's attitudes towards European integration. The purpose of this book cannot be to address all the issues involved. Rather, its purpose is to provide information that is essential in order for one to be able to follow the making of the ESDP. Chapter 1 has shown that this requires a grasp of the nature of European institutions and the ways in which they interact in pursuing the elusive goal of European integration, what is known as the 'Community method'. In brief, the European Commission makes legislative and policy proposals and legislative and budgetary acts are then adopted by the Council of Ministers (representing the member states), the European Parliament (representing the citizens) and the European Court of Justice, guaranteeing the rule of law (CEC, 2001b: 8).

No state

The Community method diverges from decision-making routines in member states. This is related to certain distinguishing features of European integration. What are these features?

Unfortunately, on this issue there is no consensus, either in the literature or in political discourse. European idealists (of whom there seem to be few left) and Euro-sceptics alike, tend to interpret European integration as the eventual formation of a European state. This state, so it is believed, will superimpose itself on existing member states. After all, the latter have plunged Europe into a series of devastating wars. It is doubtful, however, that European integration can be seen in terms of state formation. As indicated, the modalities of European policy making are in many respects different from those of nation states. This is related to the history of integration.

Leaving aside the Council of Europe, an assembly of parliamentarians established at Strasbourg in 1949, European integration started in earnest under Jean Monnet with the establishment of the European Coal and Steel Community (ECSC). It comprised six member states: Germany, France, Italy and the Benelux countries, who agreed to pool their war-making capabilities, believed to be based mainly on coal and steel production. The ECSC was soon augmented by the European Economic Community (EEC), established under the Treaty of Rome in

1958. The members were the same as those in the ECSC. In fact, the two organizations co-existed, alongside a third one, established concurrently, called Euratom.

The EEC became by far the most important of the three. As indicated in Chapter 1 the synonym for EEC soon became the 'Common Market', a term that has now fallen into disuse. Since its establishment, the EEC has assumed new tasks, accepted new members and restyled itself as the European Community (EC), absorbing both the ECSC and the European Atomic Energy Agency (Euratom). Finally, on 1 November 1993, the European Union (EU) came into existence. It currently comprises fifteen member states. It is anticipated that the EU will expand, to include countries of central and eastern Europe and the Mediterranean. The Commission's recent publication, mentioned briefly in Chapter 1, *The Second Report on Social and Economic Cohesion* (CEC, 2001a), explores what the future of the Structural Funds would be if the EU comprised a total of twenty-seven member states. It is, indeed, a common assumption that this will occur, although precisely when and how and to what extent is as yet unknown.

So what is this European Union? A natural inclination is to compare it with the United States of America. Indeed, in a famous speech which he gave in Zurich in 1946, whilst receiving an honorary degree, Winston Churchill (1997: 26) argued for the formation of a 'United States of Europe'. (The UK would not be included, perhaps because of the 'special relationship' with the USA that Churchill himself had carefully nurtured during the Second World War, although Churchill used the Commonwealth as the reason why the UK would not be part of it.) For a war-torn Europe, looking to the US, not only for intellectual stimuli but also as a social and economic model, this was an attractive proposition. It soon became attractive to the USA, too, as they were concerned that a weak and divided Europe might fall prey to Communism (Lieshout, 1999). It is still attractive to France, who would like to form a counterweight to US hegemony. The fact is, the EU bears little resemblance to the USA.

To start with, the EU is just the roof over three pillars. Of these pillars, the European Community is the only one with real supra-national powers and a budget (pegged at 1.27 per cent of the GDP of the EU, way below the percentage that national governments are used to spending). The other two, much weaker pillars deal with common foreign and security policy and with home affairs and are not supra-national; rather, they provide the arenas for inter-governmental co-ordination. The European Community wields all the power, certainly with regard to spatial development. So although it is commonplace to equate the two, the subject of this book will mostly be the EC, also called the Community, and not the EU.

Whether EC or EU, both are based on treaties between the member states, which govern all matters relating to European integration. So-called Inter-governmental Conferences are the occasions for making and revising these treaties. They are long, drawn-out negotiations, conducted by experts and diplomats. They culminate in meetings of the European Council of heads of state and government, one of the prominent European institutions. The European Council meets on other occasions as well. In fact, six-monthly meetings take place, popularly called 'summits'. They receive a lot of attention and are the high points of the Presidency, which each and every member state holds for a term of six months. (At present, alongside the meetings of the World Trade Organization (WTO) and other such fora, they are also the occasions of vociferous protests against the forces of globalization.)

Returning to Inter-governmental Conferences, it is here that in the end the heads of state and government reach history-making agreements, often under conditions that make one doubt whether they are in a fit state to do so. Thus, Ash (2001: 62) describes the recent Treaty of Nice, 'like all previous treaties in the history of the EU ... [as] a snapshot of the balance between the contending parties on the night of the final agreement'.

What this signifies better than anything else, and what the message of this section is, is that the EU is not a state in its own right, not even a federal one. Although the assumption is that federations are based on some form of voluntary agreement between their constituent parts, once they exist, federal states devise various mechanisms for modifying the ground rules (in the USA they are called the First Amendment, and so forth). Federal states have what constitutional scholars describe as the 'competency-competency'. This refers to some form of constitutional assembly, or a rule that sets out the procedure for inserting new provisions in the constitution or changing one or more of the existing ones. This is not so with the EU, where the supreme power is strictly a reserve of the member states. Rather than being an emergent state, the EU may thus be described as a club of member states.

This is why Inter-governmental Conferences, a sort of General Assembly of the club, are important occasions, not only due to the decisions that they make, but also because they show who is in charge. In the past, revisions of the treaties (since the Treaty of Maastricht there have been two parallel treaties, one relating to the European Community and one to the European Union) have often consolidated evolving practices. For almost three decades, the provisions of the original Treaty of Rome have actually been flexible enough to allow the business of European integration to flourish. (Naturally, there were crises, like French President De Gaulle's boycott of all Community business in the 1960s, but they had little to do with the inadequacy of treaty provisions.) In particular, there are mechanisms in place, like Article 235 (Article 308 under the Treaty of Amsterdam which consolidated the numbering system) allowing the Council of Ministers to give the European Community new powers as and when needed, to fulfil the original purposes of the Treaty of Rome. As indicated, regional and environmental policy, two of the three spatial policies discussed in the previous chapter, have been introduced in this way. Eventually, they were formalized under the provisions of the Single European Act of 1988.

Such flexibility makes eminent sense. It allows the Community to cope with new concerns, such as the growing awareness in the 1970s of environmental issues. The result, though, is now being described as 'competency creep', the unintended extension of the grip that the Community has on its member states. Before pointing an accusing finger at Eurocrats conspiring to undermine the sovereignty of member states, the reader needs to appreciate that each and every new commitment has been accepted by the same member states, the operative principle being that 'you accept my add-on and I'll accept yours' (Ash, 2001: 63).

At present, however, there is weariness about the whole process of integration, and in particular about this surreptitious expansion (albeit, as has become clear, always at the behest of member states) of the powers of the Community. So the more obvious route of formal treaty revisions is now being taken: the Single European Act (1988), the Treaty of Maastricht (1991), the Treaty of Amsterdam (1997) and the Treaty of Nice (2000). Though it may have received a bad press, the Treaty of Nice has taken steps to keep European institutions well balanced notwithstanding an increased membership. One outcome of Nice has been the undertaking to organize another Inter-governmental Conference in 2004 on German insistence, to come to a more definite allocation of powers and responsibilities between member states and European institutions (Hüttmann and Knodt, 2000). In the interim, the Commission itself is undertaking strenuous efforts to improve its image, by streamlining what it calls 'European governance' (CEC, 2001b).

The next Inter-governmental Conference is likely to take the course of a constitutional convention, to reshape the EU along federal lines. The Germans can be trusted to have already considered how this might be done. Indeed, Alfred Gomulka, the one-time President of the upper house of the German parliament, the Bundesrat (Federal Council), once commented that 'German federalism can be a very useful model for co-operation within the European Community' (Weigall and Stirk, 1992: 194), and this is a common feeling in Germany. In his famous speech at the Humboldt University in Berlin in 2000, German Foreign Minister Joschka Fischer was careful, though, to make the distinction between a federal state and a federation and to show his preference for the latter. Arcane though the distinction may seem, the message is clear: even the Germans, with their predilection for a federal Europe, recognize that the EU is not going to become a federal state.

Whatever the outcome of this debate, it demonstrates that the allocation of powers has become a major issue. The Treaty of Maastricht has tried to resolve it by introducing the subsidiarity principle. (For an exploration of the meaning of subsidiarity and the related concept of proportionality for planning, see Nadin and Shaw, 1999.) So the 'competency issue' in European spatial planning does not stand on its own but rather is embedded in a much wider debate, which makes it that much more difficult to settle!

To reiterate, the reason behind the complex nature of the debate is the preconceived view of the EU as a nascent 'state', an idea that most people at the same time reject. Experts often come to different conclusions. They say that the EU is in a category of its own, that it is *sui generis*, meaning that its trajectory does not point towards an end-state (what the French are fond of describing as a *finalité*), least of all towards the formation of a European 'superstate'. Rather, when thinking about Europe, one should try to disregard the mental model of the nation state.

NO GOVERNMENT

Although not a state (not even a nascent one), the EU/EC still has institutions that perform certain state-like functions and work towards integration. The best known of these institutions is the European Commission. This is a College of twenty Commissioners forming the EU 'core executive' (Hix, 1999: 32). It is the closest thing to a European government. However, the reader needs to avoid making facile comparisons. The Commission is not elected by the European Parliament but appointed by the member states, with the European Parliament having only a small influence. (Once appointed and approved by the European Parliament, Commissioners must swear to not take orders from anybody, especially the governments that have put their names forward!)

Whether the Commission will ever come close to resembling a European government obviously depends on the future of the EU. In a carefully leaked paper concerning strategy for the Inter-governmental Conference of 2004, the German Federal Chancellor went no further than referring to the Commission as a 'strong, executive body'. However, in the ensuing discussions this was interpreted to mean a European federal government. This is another example of the popular misconception of European integration, as pointing towards the formation of a European state with a European government.

If, however, the Commission is not a nascent European government, what, then, is its nature and its purpose? The answer is simple: to take initiatives, to administer Community policies and to represent the EU internationally. This set-up casts the Commission in the role of an institution whose explicit task is to generate what Ross (1995: 6) calls 'Europeanization'. To repeat, as part of the Community method, it has the sole prerogative of proposing new Community rules and regulations. Under Jacques Delors, now almost a legend, the Commission fulfilled this role extremely well. Delors himself conceived of the Community as a 'strategic authority', with a mission to guarantee the continuity of the European project

(Dinan, 1999: 234). And the Delors Presidencies offered unique opportunities for revitalising integration.

> The Commission had the power and institutional right to pick and choose among possible courses of action, to set agendas. The right choices, those which made the most of the political opportunity structures, could set the Community in motion again. Bad political work by the Commission would have wasted the opportunity (Ross, 1995: 12).

So there is no doubt that the Commission, although not a European government, is the powerhouse of European integration. The nature of its position means that it regularly comes under attack. Indeed, in its White Paper on European governance, the Commission complains: 'Brussels is too easily blamed by member states for difficult decisions that they themselves have agreed upon or requested' (CEC, 2001b: 7).

THE 'EUROCRATS'

The first chapter has discussed three Community policies that are spatial in the sense that they influenced spatial relations. It was also said that there were good reasons why such policies should be co-ordinated. The cross-impacts of various spatial policies may affect the territory of member states or regions in unanticipated and harmful ways. Also, co-ordinating these policies may increase their overall efficiency and effectiveness. This seems very obvious, so why is there apparently so little co-ordination? Answering this question requires taking a closer look at the organization of the European Commission beneath the level of the twenty Commissioners.

People often refer to the 'Eurocrats'. Their number is surprisingly small, 'barely matching the number of administrators of Cologne' (Pond, 2000: 9). They are organized in twenty-four Directorates-General and a number of so-called 'horizontal services', the Secretariat-General being the most important one. In addition, there are the secretariats of the other European institutions, in particular the Council of Ministers, and there is the administration of the European Parliament and the European Court of Justice. There are also special agencies and services spread around Europe.

There is no one-to-one relationship between Directorates-General and Commissioners in the sense of Commissioners directing one Directorate-General each. Rather, at the head of each there is a Director-General. After the Secretary-General, these Directors-General are the highest European civil servants. (As with Commissioners, their appointment is a matter of great concern to member states who need to ensure that they are not under-represented.) The Commissioners in turn have a small staff of political advisers who are not attached to any Directorate-General. They form what is called the political 'cabinets', more about which below. The relationship between Directorates-General on the one hand and the Commissioners (in particular their political cabinets) on the other, is often less than harmonious; Directors-General can be strong personalities with political acumen and vast experience of European politics.

Of the twenty-four Directorates-General, a few are significant in the field of spatial planning in that they pursue spatial policies. Williams (1996) gives an overview of these policies, as does the ESDP. In fact, Chapter 1 has already touched upon them.

The most important Directorate-General is the one dealing with regional policy. This relates to the so-called Structural Funds, which account for approximately one third of Community spending. The Directorate-General concerned is called DG XVI (Regional Policy and Cohesion) and at present Directorate-General Regio. It is responsible for the Commission input into the ESDP process. In fact, when referring to the 'Commission', literature on the ESDP (including this book) refers principally to a small section within DG Regio, which deals with spatial planning.

Importantly, and this is where the nature of the Brussels 'machine' becomes apparent, DG Regio cannot co-ordinate other Directorates-General. It only deals with the Structural Funds. Co-ordination between Directorates-General is the task of the Secretariat-General (Cini, 1996: 102). If it were to be entrusted with spatial co-ordination, the Secretariat-General would have to build up some kind of planning capacity. Co-ordination is also done through the political cabinets of the Commissioners, mentioned above. They are an institution imported from France (Cini, 1996: 111–2; Hix 1999: 34) where ministers routinely appoint large numbers of political advisers (Cole, 1998: 110). Cabinets are think tanks and trouble-shooters, but they do not have the capability for sustained co-ordination such as planning would require. This reinforces the point that, in discussing planning co-ordination, it is important to take the composition of the Commission into account.

Nugent believes that there is no centre of power in Brussels,

> with the authority and the internal coherence to take an overall view of EU requirements and impose an ordered pattern ... [Rather] policies have tended to be the outcome of complex and laboured interactions, where different, and often contrasting, requirements, preferences, reservations, and fears have played a part. As a result, the EU's overall policy picture is inevitably patchy and rather ragged (Nugent 1999: 349).

This, perhaps, may be why former US Secretary of State Henry Kissinger is said to have quipped: 'you say Europe, but can you tell me which number I should call?'. The recent White Paper on European governance shows that the

Commission agrees with this verdict, holding the Council of Ministers (to be dis-cussed), and in particular the General Affairs Council of Foreign Ministers, co-responsible for the situation. The General Affairs Council, according to the Commission, 'has lost its capacity to give political guidance and arbitrate between sectoral interests' (CEC, 2001b: 29).

Because of the divisions within the Commission and the Council, those involved may well smile when confronted by the talk about a masterplan, imposed by Brussels. A masterplan would presuppose that the Community has more clout and more internal coherence than it actually does.

There is yet another reason why a European masterplan is such a distant prospect. Even if it were to aspire to one (which it does not), the Commission does not have the institutional resources for formulating a masterplan. Even if a Community planning policy existed, the Commission would depend on the member states for its implementation. There is simply no implementation capacity at Brussels, and therefore everything has to be agreed with the member state or states concerned. For conceptualizing policy, the Commission also depends on expertise drafted in from the member states. This is done through a system called 'comitology' (Faludi et al., 2000). This is the term for many committees discussing, preparing and overseeing the implementation of Community policies. The attraction of this system is the fact that the members of such 'comitology' committees frequently become quasi-Eurocrats. The Committee on Spatial Development (CSD), whose work is central to this book, came close to being such a 'comitology' committee, although the competency issue prevented it from functioning as others do, as will become evident. This eventually led to a situation, in early 2001, of great uncertainty about its future, more about which on pages 173–176.

THE SEMINAL CONFLICT

The Commission may be important, but it is not responsible for passing Community law. That is the prerogative of the Council of Ministers, who represent the govern-ments of the member states, although, as with the appointment of the European Commission, under the co-decision procedure, the European Parliament now plays a role. However, the European Commission still has the important and exclusive right of initiative.

Needless to say there is conflict, not only over the extent and direction of European integration, but also with regard to the positions of various European insti-tutions. This also forms the backdrop to the struggle over European spatial planning. There is strong division between European institutions articulating the autonomy of member states on the one hand, and those institutions who represent other forces of integration on the other. The first group would like member states to retain more control over the course of European integration.

Which are the European institutions articulating the positions of the member states? First of all, member states play a leading role at the European Council of heads of state and government, as described on page 19. Significantly, the European Commission has no important role to play at the European Council.

As indicated, Community law is adopted by the Council of Ministers, which also represents the member states. The Council takes many different forms, depending on the topic of discussion. Thus, as the reader is aware, the General Affairs Council is expected to co-ordinate the work; ECOFIN, with the Ministers of Finance and Economic Affairs on it, approves the budget and economic policy and the Agricultural Council discusses important matters, such as the 'mad cow' disease. The Council of Ministers is almost continuously in session in one permutation or other. When convening on official business, they meet mostly in Brussels and for three months each year in Luxembourg, but there are also informal councils. These are held in the member state that is currently holding the Presidency of the EU. (Confusingly, there are also meetings that are informal, like the ones of the ministers of the member states responsible for spatial planning, and they are classed as such because there is no formal Community business to discuss.)

Voting on the Council of Ministers is a matter that is discussed greatly. This takes two forms: unanimous voting, which gives each and every member state the same weight, however large or small its population (the range being from 82 million to somewhat more than 400,000 million, roughly a ratio of 200:1); and Qualified Majority Voting, a complicated system of votes allocated to member states. If the Community had a spatial planning competency, then, on the recommendation of the Commission, the Council (perhaps taking the form of a Spatial Planning Council) would adopt relevant guidelines or directives, these being two types of Community law. Of course, this Council would also provide an arena for discussing European spatial planning.

Therefore, the European Council and the Council of Ministers, on a day-to-day basis, are the institutions representing member states. They are said to represent the 'inter-governmental' element in Community decision making. This is confusing because, as will become evident, in the ESDP process 'inter-governmental' has always meant something altogether different: keeping spatial planning outside the process of Community decision making and leaving it to the member states to make voluntary arrangements. The suggestion has often been that anything else, like giving the Community a spatial planning competency, would remove planning from the control of member states. It should now be clear to the reader that this would not be the case. Even if spatial planning became a Community competency, the member states could not be overruled. Rather, the Council of Ministers (thus the member states) would always have the last say in planning matters.

Other European institutions, such as the European Commission, the European Parliament and the European Court of Justice (not discussed here) represent the forces of integration. The European Commission, in particular, has the right of initiative, mentioned on page 21, meaning that the Council of Ministers (in conjunction with the European Parliament) can only pass such legislation as the Commission puts before it. This is a cherished prerogative of the European Commission. Proactive Commissions interpret the right of initiative as the institutional brief to propel the process of European integration along (Ross, 1995). On the shop-floor level of European policy making, it is often Commission officials who take the lead, cajoling member state representatives into developing a joint perspective.

THE 'DEMOCRATIC DEFICIT'

The reflex of many is to favour strengthening the institutions representing forces of integration, in particular the European Parliament. This is also seen as one way of mitigating what is often called the 'democratic deficit'. However, a huge assumption is being made. It is that the EU is a polity, or at least in the process of becoming one, along the lines of democratic nation states. There is a powerful argument for saying that this is not the case: there are no European political parties, no European newspapers and no European public.

Above all, there is no common language. Rather, there are eleven official languages, good for 110 combinations, a tally that could increase tenfold (to over one thousand!) once enlargement has run its full course and there are thirty-five languages spoken (Ash, 2001: 62). With Herculean effort, the legendary Brussels interpreters cope with present challenges, but whether this will continue to be the case is not known.

More importantly, assuming that the everyday problems involved are amenable to pragmatic solutions, it is doubtful that a polity could function under such circumstances. However, circumstances will change with the introduction of the euro as the currency of the twelve member states.

Indeed, maybe the legitimacy derived from an efficient internal market generating wealth spread equitably throughout the EU is all that Europeans expect of its institutions? Maybe the 'democratic deficit' of Europe is one that only those involved in politics are concerned about, leaving the population at large unaffected?

The German scholar Scharpf (1999: 188) argues in this vein, that the European polity will continue to 'lack the quality of *government by the people*, and that all discourses that attempt to draw on input-oriented legitimizing arguments can only exacerbate the perception of an irremediable European democratic deficit.' However, he continues saying that in many policy areas there is another, output-oriented rationale at work, and there can be 'specific institutional arrangements ... conducive to *government for the people* – meaning that they will favour policy choices that can be justified in terms of consensual notions of the public interest.'

Be that as it may, applying democratic principles as we know them to the EU would mean that the less populous member states would carry less weight than is presently the case. After all, presently the number of seats in the European Parliament is heavily loaded in their favour. Bi- and tricameral solutions to this problem have been proposed, common in federal set-ups. As always, the issue is how the rights of territorially defined minorities can be protected in the light of the one-man-one-vote system that seems to be the embodiment of democratic rule. Obviously, there is still uncertainty as to how, if ever, this issue will work itself out.

CONCLUSIONS

The greatest uncertainty, of course, is the issue this chapter started with: that of whether the EU will, or indeed should, take the path towards statehood. Perhaps it represents something altogether different, something that is unprecedented, the understanding of which still eludes us.

Against this backdrop, what does European spatial planning mean? As indicated, it could mean a form of planning initiated by the European Commission, with proposals subject to approval by the Council of Ministers. Once again, the reader should note that (as in all Community matters) member states would have much influence via their ministers representing them on the Council.

In fact, this is not the path that European spatial planning has taken. Rather, European spatial planning has taken the form of *voluntary* co-operation between member states. This has been dubbed 'inter-governmental', a somewhat confusing term as the Council of Ministers (operating in the core of the Community decision-making machine) has also been described as 'inter-governmental'. The difference is that the Council operates under European treaties, whereas 'inter-governmental' planning, when referring to the ESDP, takes place outside these treaties.

In this discussion, the distinction in Chapter 1 between spatial planning as strategic planning and spatial planning as land-use regulation is also important. If land-use regulation was the chief purpose of European spatial planning, this would place spatial planning in the middle of the contest between member states and European institutions. To resolve the issue, at a future Inter-governmental Conference, member states would need to formally transfer their powers to regulate land-use to the European Community. There is little likelihood that this would happen.

However, as the reader will learn, land-use regulation is not how the early proponents of European spatial planning have conceptualized it. Rather, they have seen it as a matter of formulating strategy. Under this conceptualization, the competency issue does not arise, nor does it under *aménagement du territoire*, the source of inspiration of the French proponents of European spatial planning at the Commission. Strategy can give coherence to policies, thereby making them transparent and easier to explain.

Others coming from member states which are steeped in spatial planning traditions focusing on land-use regulation, such as Germany, have a different view. It is for this reason that the competency issue has come to the fore. This issue will be described, along with the ESDP process. For the purposes of this chapter, it suffices to say that, in terms of the short exposition of European institutions above, the ESDP is not a 'communautarian' document but rather is based on the voluntary co-operation of member states outside the Community competencies, as defined in the European treaties. Nevertheless, the European Commission has been involved in preparing it, in the expectation that spatial planning would ultimately become a function of the European Community. As the reader will learn in Chapter 10, in its White Paper on European governance, the Commission has now reaffirmed its view that (albeit under a different name) spatial planning should become a Community concern.

CHAPTER 3

NANTES AND TURIN – THE SINGLE MARKET CASTING ITS SHADOW

The member states involved in the initial phase of the making of the ESDP were France and The Netherlands. More precisely, it was DATAR and the Dutch *Rijksplanologische Dienst* (National Spatial Planning Agency) that took the lead. If the truth be told, it was individuals who seized opportunities for transnational net-working with like-minded foreign colleagues. When 'Germany', 'France', or 'the Commission' are referred to, this actually alludes to certain individuals who are mak-ing the most of the 'opportunity structure' of their organization. Likewise, when the text talks about 'the Portuguese', 'the French' and so forth, it refers to the planners from these countries, who are playing the roles into which their spatial planning sys-tems and their positions in the wider European context have cast them.

First, the French and Dutch opportunity structures are discussed. This is fol-lowed by an account of the Nantes kick-off meeting. Confusing though it was for many, with Jacques Delors and Bruce Millan (the Commissioner for Regional Policy) participating, it was a remarkable affair. This chapter then describes the follow-up meeting at Turin. If the Italians had not initiated that meeting, Nantes might possibly have been nothing more than a dead end.

FRENCH OPPORTUNITY STRUCTURE

The French accept their loss of autonomy resulting from European integration, in exchange for greater dominance in Europe (Eising and Kohler-Koch, 1999: 281). They see integration as a 'means of enhancing French national prestige' (Cole, 1998: 237). The Brussels bureaucracy, and to a greater extent DG XVI, is French in its make-up. This is not new. 'Traditionally expansive French views of Europe depended upon a version of Europe as an extension of France, hence the emphasis placed on exporting features of the French model for the benefit of others' (Cole, 1998: 251).

Against this backdrop, DATAR saw itself as the linchpin between Brussels and Paris. How did it form this view? France was the archetype of a centralized state. Indeed, it had been a 'technocratic state elite' (Ross, 1995: 242) that had propelled a fragmented and unstable post-war France along the path of modernization, with the *Commissariat Général du Plan* in the lead, under Jean Monnet (one of the archi-tects of European integration; see Fontaine, 2000). The *Commissariat* received international acclaim for its indicative planning, which defined medium-range targets jointly with industry. It is worth noting that in the 1960s Delors worked there (Milesi, 1995).

DATAR itself had been set up under De Gaulle to 'co-ordinate the actions of the different ministries in the domain of central territorial development' (Balme and Jouve, 1996: 225). Generally, a *délégation interministérielle* is a 'means of ensuring permanent co-ordination in a policy sphere which falls [as planning does] between several ministries but which has a high government priority' (Cole, 1998: 111). Obviously, such delegations have to overcome resistance from line departments.

DATAR reports to the Prime Minister. Its area of concern, *aménagement du territoire*, has no direct equivalent in English, at least not in British-English. 'The expressions most commonly used are spatial planning and regional policy, but these do not reflect the global ambition to reach a harmonious allocation of economic activities' (Chicoye, 1992: 411). According to Dupuy (2000: 11), the least controversial definition of *aménagement du territoire* is that of 'public action envisioning the spatial disposition of people, activities and physical structures based on a balanced notion reflecting the geographical and human situation within the space under consideration'. This seems close enough to the meaning of spatial planning, but without explicit mention of land-use regulation. The *Compendium* (CEC, 1997a: 35) identifies *aménagement du territoire* as one of four European approaches to spatial planning. Because of its economic emphasis (see also Marcou *et al.*, 1994), it is dubbed as the 'regional economic planning approach'. Accordingly, 'spatial planning has a very broad meaning relating to the pursuit of wide social and economic objectives, especially in relation to disparities between different regions ... Where this approach ... is dominant, central government inevitably plays an important role' (CEC, 1997a: 36).

What DATAR did was to co-ordinate public investments in the French regions. This required no extra powers, let alone a statutory plan. In fact *aménagement du territoire* functioned without a plan, and with the exception of two short periods in the 1980s, when the work of DATAR fed into the national economic and social development plan, there was, and in fact still is, no national plan. However, as the French *Compendium* volume notes, the

> abandonment of a national economic and social development plan does not mean that there is no longer national planning. The central government determines the scope, the goals, the amount of money involved, and the matters (in broad terms) for the plan conventions to be passed within the regions for five-year periods as provided by the Planning Reform Act 1982 (CEC, 2000c: 19).

In so doing, plans, schemes or scenarios showing the location and dynamics of economic activity can naturally be of assistance. The French have a penchant for scenarios that use imaginative graphics. Witness the famous, some would say infamous, 'Blue Banana', discussed in Chapter 1. Even geography texts for secondary schools teaching spatial analysis use cartographic representations of strategic situations. As will become evident in Chapter 10, one of the French proposals for a follow-up to the ESDP is to make such geography texts available throughout Europe.

Scenarios or images are mere instruments, though, and are not the essence of *aménagement du territoire*. That essence lies in the will to manage the overall territory. If, in doing so, the government uses good minds to create imaginative schemes, the French do not ask whether it is within its rights. Competency is thus a non-issue.

The backdrop to the development of *aménagement du territoire* was the over-centralization of France. Paris was attracting too much development. In addition, French agriculture was in the process of restructuring, with the European Economic Community footing much of the bill. To reduce the attraction of Paris, investments were designed to stimulate regional development, for instance the aerospace industry around Toulouse. This was a top-down approach, taken in the interests of national unity, a sacred French goal. After the unrest in Paris in May 1968, President De Gaulle staked his political future on a referendum on decentralization. He lost and thus retired from politics; it took until 1982 for decentralization to begin in earnest.

DATAR was involved in decentralization, experimenting with plan conventions, the so-called *Contrats de Plan État-Région* (CPERs), later to become models for Community policy. In fact, the 'procedure for allocating structural funds following the structural funds reform of 1988 reflects, in many respects, the structure and the action principles of the French CPERs that were conceived while Jacques Delors was a member of the French government' (Balme and Jouve, 1996: 231). Indeed, the Community Support Frameworks presently being negotiated between the member states, the Commission and the regions concerned, mirror the CPERs. A person experienced in policy of this kind was a former regional politician from Lorraine, Jacques Chérèque (a friend of Delors), the Minister for *aménagement du territoire* who chaired Nantes. Like Delors, he was also a champion of the regions.

In the eighties, François Mitterand became president, and this shaped the broader context of the evolution of French planning. After initial attempts to forge ahead without Europe, Mitterand eventually reached the view

> that the French could profit from renewing European integration. The British were ambivalent about Europe altogether. The Germans, despite their economic power, could not lead because of their history. The French administration, good at producing quick results and overcoming opposition, was another asset, particularly in Brussels (Ross, 1998: 2).

Not all Parisian bureaucrats were amused though. Decentralization was already a threat, and they discovered that European regulations also applied to France, a message they generally took badly (Drevet, 1995). DATAR, too, was under threat (Guyomarch *et al.*, 1998; Cole, 1998: 112) but opted for a proactive approach, which the French President and the Prime Minister accepted. DATAR deemed it essential for French national policy to take account of European integration. This was to be done jointly with the regions and would result in new *contrats de plan* for 1989–93 and a programme for large-scale infrastructure investments. Pierre Méhaignerie, Minister of *aménagement du territoire* from 1986 to 1988, was also Minister of Public Works and Transport, so the combination held obvious appeal. DATAR also took the changing position of France into account. With the accession of Spain and Portugal (of which agriculture in south-west France expected nothing but trouble, see Drevet, 1997: 104) for France the Mediterranean had become more salient. Later, of course, it would be perceived as the 'Rio Grande of Europe' (King, 1997): a flimsy screen against the incoming waves of African immigrants.

DATAR was merging spatial planning and regional policy into a single concept (Bastrup-Birk and Doucet 1997: 307). At its request, the Commission was empowered under Article 10 of the European Regional Development Fund (ERDF) regulations to produce a spatial scheme or *schéma de développement de l'espace communautaire*, which later became *Europe 2000*. (Note that the French name for the ESDP is the same: *Schéma de développement de l'espace communautaire*, or SDEC. This has distinctly different overtones from the English name, European Spatial Development Perspective or for that matter the German rendering, *Europäisches Raumentwickungskonzept*.) However, the French cannot be accused of having had a European masterplan in mind. As Drevet (1995: 199) comments, the French lack a tradition of 'town and country planning' comparable with that of their counterparts in north-west Europe. 'Town and country planning' is the British expression for the more generic term, land-use regulation. It sometimes involves working with masterplans, whereas *aménagement du territoire* does not. Rather, DATAR had devised a spatial strategy to underpin policies that were undertaken already. It never occurred to anybody that this might require a new Community competency. Article 10 was considered sufficient. Only history would prove DATAR and the Commission officials concerned wrong.

It should be added that the Council of Ministers had only accepted Article 10 with difficulty. Reflecting the scepticism of the *Länder* (see Chapter 4) the German government had been suspicious. Others had been uncertain, but in the end the Commission proposal, based on the recommendations of DATAR, received the benefit of the doubt.

Discussions on such matters were limited to a handful of people, including a Dutch polyglot planner. He had been involved in previous Dutch–French exchanges on the impact of communication technology. Meanwhile, he was an *expert national détache* at the environmental DG. It is apposite to pay attention now to Dutch dispositions towards European integration.

DUTCH OPPORTUNITY STRUCTURE

The organization concerned is the National Spatial Planning Agency, a small Directorate-General within the Ministry of Housing, Spatial Planning and the Environment. Compared with other national planning outfits, the agency seems like a giant. Its track record is good. Indeed, the *Compendium* (CEC, 1997a; see also CEC ,1999b) identifies The Netherlands, alongside Denmark, as the most outspoken example of the 'comprehensive integrated approach' to planning. It is:

> conducted through a very systematic and formal hierarchy of plans from national
> to local level, which co-ordinate public sector activity across different sectors but
> focus more specifically on spatial co-ordination than economic development.
> (…) This tradition is necessarily associated with mature systems. It requires
> responsive and sophisticated planning institutions and mechanisms and consid-
> erable political commitment. (…) Public sector investments in bringing about the
> realization of the planning framework is also the norm (CEC, 1997a: 36–7).

Dutch planning may be a good representation of this system, but it works in the main with indicative rather than binding plans. In fact, local zoning schemes are the only ones that are binding. Strategic plans never are. At national level, Dutch planners have produced a succession of National Spatial Planning Reports. They are issued roughly once every ten years (at the time of writing the fifth one is in production) and are emphatically not masterplans.

Chapter 1 has already taken note of Dutch involvement in the planning con-ference for north-west Europe and the fact that the Dutch had argued for the ECSC and then the EEC to take planning on board. In 1978, the Dutch chief plan-ner once again lobbied for the EC to do so, to no avail. In the mid-1980s, as elsewhere, 'Europe 1992' began to cast its shadow. In the *Fourth National Spatial Planning Report*, Dutch planners started to focus on the competitive posi-tion of their country. Promoting EC planning became official government policy. This promised to give the Dutch a handle on developments in their surroundings. They even floated the idea of a Brussels Directorate-General for planning. However, the Dutch idea of planning differed from *aménagement du territoire*. Dutch planning was about cross-sectoral co-ordination, or 'facet planning'. All sector claims on land needed to be balanced against each other, based on a notion of what Dutch planners call 'spatial quality'. In these terms, regional policy (at the time the exclusive focus of French spatial planning) was but one of the 'sectors'.

Predictably, the context of Dutch planning, congenial though it may appear to outsiders, is marred by conflict with the 'sectors'. In the past, the ability of planners to conceptualize space and spatial development has been an asset in their struggle with the sectors (Faludi, 1996). Images have been used to paint the spectre of rampant urban sprawl. To keep intact the horseshoe-shaped pattern of towns and cities called the Randstad which envelopes the Green Heart, the Dutch need to contain urban sprawl. Unquestioned for a long time, this doctrine has formed the basis of a determined national growth management strategy (Faludi and Van der Valk, 1994; Needham and Faludi, 1999; Dieleman et al., 1999; Evers et al., 2000). At present, sectors like agriculture, nature preservation, regional economic policy and transport are formulating their own 'spatial visions' (Priemus, 1999), which only goes to show that the power of images is broadly recognized.

Anyhow, based on their understanding of The Netherlands as a European gateway, and maybe in the hope that European planning would strengthen their position *vis-à-vis* the sectors, like their French colleagues, Dutch planners were in favour of European planning. When the French minister Pierre Méhaignaire was disinclined to attend a CEMAT meeting in Lausanne scheduled for 1988, perceiving it as a talking shop, a staff member of DATAR phoned the Dutch polyglot planner mentioned on page 32 and arranged a meeting with the Dutch minister to take place in the margins. This gave Méhaignaire a reason to attend. By 1988, though, his successor Jacques Chérèque, due to assume an important role in the ESDP process, had taken his place. At any rate, in the corridors of Lausanne the idea of gathering EC planning ministers to discuss the Community's role in planning was launched.

Finishing touches were put to these plans at a further meeting between the Dutch and the new French ministers in May 1989. By that time, the staff member of DATAR who had arranged the meeting in Lausanne had become a member of the Chérèque cabinet, and was laying the groundwork for Nantes. As a Commission official responsible for spatial planning he was later to play an important role.

NANTES: ONLY SIX MINISTERS, BUT ... LE PRÉSIDENT!

As indicated, Article 10 of the ERDF regulations provided a basis for the Commission to enter the field of planning. However, there was no Council of Ministers for spatial planning.

It is often said that there cannot be a Council of Ministers for spatial planning because the Community has no competency in the matter. Undeniably though, there is a Community competency for regional policy, and yet there is no Council of

Ministers for regional policy! The reason for this is that the General Affairs Council of Foreign Ministers, charged with overall co-ordination, and the Council of Economic and Finance Ministers (ECOFIN), who hold the purse strings, want to maintain their control over the allocation of Structural Funds. Competency is not a relevant issue.

Instead of a Council of Ministers, a Regional Policy Committee of national experts, chaired by a representative of a member state, was set up in 1975, the time when Community regional policy got off the ground. After the doubling of the Structural Funds in 1988, DG XVI wanted to see the Committee replaced by a Council of Ministers, to give political legitimacy to prospective schemes related to the European territory and to facilitate co-ordination with national planning policies. Had this come to fruition, a form of EC planning related to regional policy, like aménagement du territoire, would now be established.

It is possible that Jacques Chérèque wanted to convene a Council of Ministers. However, he was not at liberty to do as he wished. The gatekeepers at the Ministry of Foreign Affairs co-ordinated all meetings to be held under the French Presidency, and they ruled out the possibility. Evidently, the reason was not that there was no Community competency, because at least for regional policy there was one. No, the purported reason was that there were already too many Council meetings. An informal meeting was all that Chérèque was allowed to organize. Also, the Ministry of Foreign Affairs laid down precise rules. There was to be no formal resolution. Instead, the Presidency would summarize the sense of the meeting. This rule is still operative, which is why in Potsdam the Germans merely noted that the deliberations had come to an end, without adding that the ministers had adopted the ESDP.

Even though the meeting was informal, Delors accepted the invitation of his friend Chérèque to attend what must have seemed a lowly affair in European terms. Commissioner Bruce Millan was also present on 24 November 1989 when ministers of the member states responsible for spatial planning and regional policy assembled at Nantes. Member states were at liberty to send whomever they wished. Few had any idea of what the meeting would be about. Six ministers turned up, with senior officials representing a further five member states. The Belgian government disagreed with the regions, who had just acquired full responsibility for planning, about how to play this, so Belgium was not represented at all. Thus the delegations numbered eleven, the majority of which were headed by ministers, a fact that pleased the hosts.

In his opening speech, Chérèque stated that the focus should be on policy, other than in CEMAT. He also said that there was no immediate need for a formal Council of Ministers, which was perhaps a question of sour grapes. What was needed was a work programme focusing on changes in Europe, on the co-ordination of EC policies, the reduction of regional disparities, on infrastructure, metropolitan developments and cross-border planning. The ESDP process would indeed evolve along such lines.

The venue, equidistant from northern and southern Europe, had been chosen with care. Coming from Lorraine, Chérèque wanted to demonstrate concern for the situation of western France. The President of the Loire Regional Council was invited to speak about the *Arc Atlantique* (Poussard, 1997), a region suffering from high transport costs and limited access to information. *Arc Atlantique* is now a household word in European planning. This is an example of the French's aptitude for conceptualizing the spatial position of France (lovingly described as the 'hexagon' because of its shape) and its regions, in ways that make the policy implications seem obvious.

Ministers read out prepared statements. The Dutch picked up the theme of regional disparities and proposed European networks as antidotes. Inevitably, there was terminological confusion. According to their records, the Dutch felt that Community spatial policy was 'not the same as in our individual countries'. But what was it? The French divined that it was about formulating a holistic perception of the development of Europe. The Dutch were only slightly more specific: 'The task of spatial policy at community level is the setting out of strategic lines of development for Europe as a whole and its regions'. What was needed was an indicative framework to clarify spatial relations between centres of economic activity and axes of development. Maybe 'strategic spatial development analysis' was a better term, the Dutch said.

In his comments, Commissioner Millan rejected the idea of a European masterplan, but then nobody had proposed one. As the reader appreciates, such a plan would have opposed the beliefs of the French hosts. Although accustomed to another planning tradition, the Dutch, too, had found out that at regional, national and especially at international levels, indicative schemes were all that they could realistically aspire to. Disowning a European masterplan was designed, rather, to allay misgivings about the ever-growing influence of Brussels.

Delors spoke too, without a manuscript, but fortunately there is a transcript. Complimenting Millan and the Director-General of DG XVI on the new programmatic approach to the Structural Funds, Delors broached two themes. First, the fact that integration means more than the creation of a free market, and second the need for a holistic view of economic and social development. As regards the first theme, he stressed that competition could not work without co-operation and a minimum of rules. He discussed this in the light of the 'subsidiarity' issue. The Community was not a super-institution. It was there to help, to ensure coherence, to make proposals and promote harmonization. What was needed was a bottom-up approach, and this was what the European Council had promulgated when adopting the new policy for the Structural Funds.

Delors then discussed various Community policies, pointing out their relationship with *aménagement du territoire*. The Structural Funds, in particular, were based on two principles, concentration and partnership. As the reader knows from Chapter 1, Delors' favourite, the partnership principle, was based on his appreciation that local knowledge and the forces of auto-development are as important as investment.

As the European economy had regained its momentum a more comprehensive view was required (Delors' second point). It should pertain to the intensity, the quality (also in the sense of sustainability) and the distribution of 'activities in space'. He did not invoke that term, but what he described was a spatial strategy. All of this needed to be seen in the context of the globalization of the economy, the technological revolution and new lifestyles and aspirations. Even without European integration, these developments would require a rethinking of *aménagement du territoire*. With frontiers disappearing and the integration of markets, a new geography was emerging. The question was one of whether it would be shaped according to our preferences. Disparities would not disappear spontaneously, but at the same time Delors warned against a dichotomous view, what in this book is described as a 'one-dimensional Europe', which focuses exclusively on disparities. Wealth is not always distributed to the rich, it goes to the poor, too. The comparative advantages of different regions were highly diverse.

Delors used this opportunity to take the Council of Ministers to task, claiming that he had heard a great deal of complaint at the meeting about the need for Commission flexibility. He advised the ministers present to direct their comments to their colleagues, and not the Commission. With the eligibility criteria for those regions due to receive Structural Funds in mind, Delors said that the Council of Ministers had created a statistical straightjacket, professing at the same time to being horrified by the thought of how and by whom the necessary data would be produced. Ministers should not ask the Commission to show the kind of flexibility that their 'grand ministers' (Delors' words) had refused to grant.

Having vented his anger, Delors went on to talk about the Community's nervous system, what was later to be described as the 'trans-European networks'. He divined that in the absence of a common transport policy, member states were spending funds ill-advisedly. However, he recognized that this was outside the area of responsibility of those present, and even beyond the area of competency of transport ministers. Rather, this was a matter for the ministers of finance. A one-time finance minister himself, Delors added that he spoke from experience: finance ministers were short-sighted, focusing on their current budget rather than on taking the right decisions now to save for tomorrow.

Delors concurred with concerns aired by the ministers, such as the position of islands, especially those on the ultra-periphery, and also the question of cross-border co-operation, favoured as a policy focus by Millan. Europe would 'come to life' in the border regions. He touched upon the less favoured regions and the need for inter-regional co-operation. In conclusion, he also addressed the emergent reality of Europe. This meeting took place just days after the fall of the Berlin Wall, so he urged ministers to show solidarity with eastern Europe and also with Africa, the Caribbean and the Pacific, affected as they were by European integration. For all these reasons, he exhorted the heads of state and government on the European Council to show the same courage in the political and financial field as they had done in agreeing with the doubling of the Structural Funds.

The speech by Delors has been reported in detail because it shows his support for *aménagement du territoire* (the use of the French term is intentional) at Community level, related as it would be to the Structural Funds. Indeed, it could be seen as an integral part of what he stood for.

Interestingly, in their report on the meeting, the Dutch said that Delors had argued for a global vision of the European territory. *Urban Networks in Europe*, the Dutch Presidency's document, which was to be presented at The Hague, repeated this recollection. Delors himself did not use the term 'spatial vision', but it certainly could be read into his speech. Anyway, what was it that Nantes had achieved? It was the rejection of a European masterplan, the acceptance of the need for a kind of spatial strategy and a concrete work programme. Above all, it would lead to a follow-up; eyewitnesses relate that the senior official representing the Italian minister left the room during the meeting to phone his Excellency, coming back with an invitation to Turin in 1990. This must have pleased the Dutch who could now look ahead to 1991, the year in which they were to hold the Presidency, and plan a meeting of their own. Without the Italian initiative, this might have been much harder to do.

Shortly after Nantes, the member of the French minister's cabinet, who originally came from DATAR, joined DG XVI. On his insistence, his Dutch partner from previous exchanges was appointed (for the second time, it should be added) as an *expert national détaché*. They were to co-ordinate work on *Europe 2000* and jointly pursue the cause of European planning.

TURIN: FOCUS ON REGIONAL DISPARITIES

At Turin, themes from Nantes were explored in greater depth, in particular that of regional disparities. With the single market nearing completion, the expectation was that these disparities would increase. Most less favoured regions were in southern Europe. In fact, in the 'Europe of Six', the Italian *Mezzogiorno* had been the only such region of any significance.

The Italian Presidency did something novel; the preparation of two Presidential documents, one technical and one political (Presidenza consiglio dei Ministri,

1990a, b). (Throughout the ESDP process there would be frequent attempts, especially by southern Europeans, to separate technical and political concerns.) The Italian documents gave a verbal analysis of European spatial structure. Accordingly, the Community territory represented a single economic area bordered by three other markets: Africa, Asia and in particular the Middle East, central and eastern Europe. This gave an inkling of what would become an issue later on: the global competitiveness of Europe. With respect to the Community territory, the Italians focused on disparities between its core, defined as the area within a 500-kilometre circle around Luxembourg, and the rest of Europe. Whereas Delors had eschewed a one-dimensional view of Europe, the Italians saw Europe more or less in precisely these terms.

Simple though it would have been to illustrate 'one-dimensional Europe' on a map, Italian style, this did not happen. Ten years later, Zonneveld (2000) did it for the Italians (Figure 3.1). The reluctance to use maps, making do with verbal accounts instead, would remain a persistent aspect of the ESDP process.

Figure 3.1 Impression of a 'one-dimensional Europe' (Source: Zonneveld, 2000)

The Italians argued for a combination of classic regional policy and what they called 'territorial planning'. No definition was given, and participants showed no excessive concern about specifying the meaning of the concept. The Italians seemed to have some form of co-ordination in mind, culminating in an agreed scheme, but emphatically not a masterplan. The notion of transnational urban and infrastructure networks also intrigued them. Infrastructure, described by Delors as the 'nervous system', was now described as the 'skeleton' of the Community territory. It connected European cities like the nodes of a network. Together with the Structural Funds, which would be administrated in accordance with the 'territorial planning' approach, this would 'ensure that the benefits ... of the Single Market are maximized and equally distributed between the regions of the Community' (Presidenza consiglio dei Ministri, 1990a).

French and Dutch initiatives have been explained in the light of the opportunity structure as it presented itself to relevant organizational players. In Italy, there is no organization comparable with DATAR or the Dutch National Spatial Planning Agency. Italian planning follows the 'urbanism' tradition, as described in the *Compendium* and also in *Europe 2000+* (CEC, 1994a, 1997a, 2000a). The emphasis is placed on local planning and design rather than on regional, or even national, planning. There is, of course, regional policy, especially with regard to the *Mezzogiorno*, a region 'untouched by the Fordist economic miracle' (Bagnasco and Oberti, 1998: 153). As a result, this region is the recipient of massive European funds. To administrate these funds, a special agency, the *Cassa del Mezzogiorno*, operated until 1984 (CEC, 2000a: 24). However, Italy has no national spatial planning. Debates on this have been inconclusive 'due to inertia and rigidity of the planning system' (ibid. 17). The Italian *Compendium* volume states:

> The Italian system, therefore, appears to have a substantial separation between decision making and the implementation of sectoral policies on one hand (each one autonomous and dependent form a ministry) and urban planning instruments, particularly those at municipal level, on the other. It follows that each sectoral policy area (energy railway plan, roads planning) even if approved by central government, also has to be verified both with the regional and municipal authorities. (...) The financial programming is sectoral and is the responsibility of the central government. The territorial specification of sector policies is responsibility of the urban planning authorities both at regional and municipal level (ibid. 18).

In addition, Italy has to cope with federalism and even 'autonomism' in northern Italy (Strassoldo, 1997). This makes national planning into a contentious issue. The upshot of this is that spatial planning is not a priority, and so throughout the ESDP process the composition and attitude of the Italian CSD delegation would continue to be fluid.

At Turin, this was not yet evident. There, a new dimension of the problem of disparities was beginning to be articulated. The implications of the fall of the Iron Curtain were becoming evident and the Commission was starting to render assistance to the new democracies. (The German Democratic Republic was joining the Federal Republic, being absorbed into the Community without much ado.) The Italian documents proposed that the external border regions should transform themselves 'from peripheral regions of individual member states into buffers (…) between the whole of Europe and the other continents' (Presidenza del consiglio dei Ministri, 1990a: 3). Internal border regions were advised to make full use of their endogenous potential. At the same time the Italians proposed a geo-political counterweight to the growing concern with central and eastern Europe. After all, the Mediterranean, too, was an external border and a potential flash point. Imbalances in the European transport system, with east–west connections said to be superior to north–south routes across the Pyrenees and the Alps, further disadvantaged the south. So a more efficient transport system was needed with 'outlets' on the Community's external borders, efficient Mediterranean ports in particular. Later on the 'outlets' would be referred to as 'gateways' and 'mainports'. For the sake of cohesion a 'new economic polarity' (ibid. 3) was needed around the Mediterranean as a counter-magnet to the north-west European core. Throughout the process, southern European member states would continue to stress the importance of developing the Mediterranean. As Chapter 7 will show, this desire to improve Mediterranean gateways would embarrass the Dutch CSD delegation in 1997, compelled as they were to defend the position of the port of Rotterdam. Be that as it may, the notion of counter-magnets would return in the Potsdam document, in the guise of new global economic integration zones outside the European core. In this document, it would be combined with the philosophy of endogenous development.

The Italians also proposed exchanging information between the member states,

> to be used not only for the definition of the problem but also for the formulation of policies. To this end, contacts will be established with the institutional bodies responsible for territorial planning in the various member states, so as to obtain the data necessary for drawing-up the technical documents (ibid. 12).

This was the first inkling of the idea of a network of research institutes, presently called the European Spatial Planning Observatory Network, or ESPON. In order to continue the process that had just begun, the Italians also proposed the 'forming of committees and permanent working groups charged with developing the technical aspects of the topics and proposals, involved in the political decisions' (ibid. 13). Both proposals were barely discussed, but they would appear again on the agenda of follow-up meetings.

CONCLUSIONS

Confident that they were on the road to some form of European planning, DG XVI was working on *Europe 2000*. In the wake of the Turin meeting, the French–Dutch pair in Brussels was making up the balance sheet. In a memorandum, they acknowledged existing differences, which could lead to confusion, but they also saw a need for 'regional strategic planning', in particular at Community level. Member states had acknowledged that momentous developments, like German unification, the opening of the central and eastern European economies, the single market and European Monetary Union (EMU), required collective responses. They had also perceived the growing influence of Community policies on their own territories, and felt that a 'horizontal' approach was required. The Community, they concluded, had the means to increase cohesion. With a view to greater policy effectiveness, it should base its intervention on insights into the spatial relationships between areas that are eligible for receiving support from the Structural Funds, and those that are not. To this end, a 'Europe-wide framework of reference' or spatial vision was needed. If misunderstandings as to the nature of regional strategic planning at the Community level could be eliminated, member states were sure to grant the Community a role, even in areas that were their exclusive competency. The following chapters show that this harmonious state of affairs was not to be achieved.

CHAPTER 4

THE HAGUE AND LISBON – TOOLING UP FOR INTER-GOVERNMENTAL PLANNING

Some form of Community planning based on Article 10 of the ERDF regulations seemed to be imminent. However, there was no Council of Ministers, not even for regional policy. Dutch planners were working on proposals for the Treaty of Maastricht, which included that of creating a Community competency for planning. They were aware of parallel German ideas and briefed their minister about them. The German train of thought was new in that the Germans wished for an inter-governmental form of planning to counteract growing Commission influence. In this way, the competency issue began to take shape.

However, in the end this issue was struck off the agenda for the meeting in The Hague. The establishment of the CSD did feature, though, this being one of the recommendations of Turin mentioned in *Europe 2000* (CEC, 1991). Beneath the surface though, the competency issue simmered on. For instance, the Dutch proposal was for member states to chair the CSD rather than the Commission. This responded to German concerns, so it seems appropriate to start with the German 'opportunity structure'. After discussing Germany, the focus will be on The Hague. Items on the agenda there, other than the CSD, were a document of the Dutch Presidency, *Urban Networks in Europe* (Minister of Housing, Physical Planning and the Environment, 1991) and *Europe 2000*, prepared by the Commission on the basis of Article 10. After The Hague, there were inconclusive discussions about the terms of reference of the CSD, and the third section reports on those. The fourth ministerial meeting at Lisbon, with which the chapter ends, focused on trans-European networks; various delegations requested a 'spatial vision'. The next chapter will show how this call was eventually heeded.

GERMAN OPPORTUNITY STRUCTURE

Support for European integration is a German article of faith written into the Constitution, or Basic Law. In Germany, as elsewhere, 'Europe 1992' was beginning to cast its shadow in the mid-1980s, and there was concern about its implications for the German competitive position (Sinz and Steinle, 1989). The position of the German *Länder* is an important consideration here. *Länder* are more like states than regions; the federal government conducts most of its business through them. In fact, foreign policy and defence are the only reserves of the federal government. However, European integration shifts competencies, including those of the *Länder*, to the

Community. The federal government participates in Inter-governmental Conferences, which set ground rules, and it is also involved in approving Commission initiatives, whereas the governments of the *Länder* are not. Therefore by necessity, the *Länder* rely on the federal government for the defence of their interests. Where European integration is concerned, the *Länder* are simply the losers (Benz, 1998: 111). Although competencies in a narrower sense are not affected, certainly not in the field of spatial planning, Eser and Konstadakopulos (2000: 792–3) also signal a shift in focus towards the federal level. The reader needs to appreciate that, in terms of population, the largest of the *Länder*, Northrhine-Westphalia, would be the sixth-largest EU member state and has forty times the number of inhabitants of Luxembourg, the smallest of the existing member states.

Admittedly, the *Länder* are represented on the Committee of the Regions. Also, since Maastricht, *Länder* ministers can represent member states in Brussels. Weariness towards Europe remains though, especially with regard to regional policy, a joint task of the federal government and the *Länder* (Drerup, 1997: 337). The Commission has successfully challenged German practices, bringing them into line with its competition and structural policies (Schrumpf, 1997: 247). It is therefore understandable that the *Länder* are weary of the Commission's intervention, particularly Bavaria (Eser and Konstadakopulos, 2000: 792), an attitude shared by federal regional policy makers (Teitsch, 1999: 105).

Of the *Länder*, Bavaria, Hessen and Baden-Würtemberg have successfully challenged existing financial arrangements for the distribution of funds within the Federal Republic in the German Constitutional Court. This has led to an order for the arrangements to be revised by 2005. The *Länder* also insist on the clarification of how powers and responsibilities are to be distributed between member states and the Community. They have made another Inter-governmental Conference in 2004 a condition of their assent to the Treaty of Nice, necessary under the German constitution. Competition policy and regional policy rank amongst policy areas that Germany would like to be reconsidered.

The German view of spatial planning is another factor in this equation. It veers towards land-use regulation rather than the formulation of spatial strategy. Perhaps it would be more accurate to say, since German plans most certainly have strategic elements to them, that these are ultimately filtered through a land-use regulation system.

As regards land-use planning, Germans draw the line between local planning (zoning and site planning) and regional, national and, where relevant, international planning. Local planning is carried out by local authorities. Above the local level, planning is called *Raumordnung* (literally, spatial ordering) and is governed by federal legislation. Within broad guidelines, *Länder* make their own laws and plans, and these have indirect impact through a system of reviews and approvals of local plans and public projects.

As in The Netherlands, planning in Germany stands for co-ordinating policies with regard to their impact upon space and spatial development. Indeed, unlike *aménagement du territoire*, both German and Dutch planners see planning as a 'policy cross-section function' (Schrumpf, 1997: 246), balancing various claims on land against each other. Naturally, this results in endemic conflict with the makers of sector policies. At the same time, German planning is more regulatory and more hierarchical than Dutch planning. Private and public development is expected to conform to local plans, which is no different from The Netherlands, but in Germany local plans must also conform to regional plans, and so forth. At a federal level though, there has never been a spatial plan, which is why Germans do not consider the federal government as engaging in proper planning. Indicative land-use plans as used in the Netherlands are not an option that the Federal Spatial Planning Act entertains, and certainly not at federal level. Instead, it stipulates a number of guiding principles 'which must be taken into account in the preparation of spatial planning by the *Länder*' (CEC, 1999c: 57).

It is not the job of federal planners to monitor the extent to which this happens, nor is their role to approve the plans of the *Länder*; keeping tabs on overall spatial development and representing Germany in the European arena is. Federal planners fulfil this role in conjunction with the *Länder* (Selke, 1999: 127). Generally though, the *Länder* jealously guard their positions and often see federal initiatives as threats to their autonomy. The position of federal planners is therefore a delicate one. The majority of business is conducted by a Standing Conference of Ministers responsible for regional planning, comprising sixteen *Länder* ministers and the federal minister. The title of the conference in German is the *Ministerkonferenz für Raumordning* (MKRO).

At the beginning of the 1990s, something unexpected happened: German unification. 'For few western states did the end of the Cold War imply so drastic a revolution in the geopolitical situation as for the Federal Republic of Germany' (Dijking, 1996: 17). Upon joining the Federal Republic (and thus the European Community), the five *Länder* carved out of the former German Democratic Republic (Breuilly, 1998: 58) became the recipients of massive Community assistance. This created divisions between the old and new *Länder*, leading to the 'bifurcation' of regional policy (Andersen, 1996). Also, unification set migratory movements into motion, giving urgency to the improvement of living conditions in the east. This demanded extensive new planning, with vast infrastructure requirements to meet. (Drerup, 1997: 339). The response was twofold.

One was a 'quick and dirty' study called *Spatial Planning Concept for the Development of the New Länder* by the Federal Ministry for Regional Planning, Building and Urban Development (1992). ('Concept' is a somewhat misleading rendering of the German term '*Konzept*'. A more adequate translation would be 'outline', 'scheme' or 'perspective'.) According to Sinz (1994: 11), this *Spatial*

Planning Concept for the Development of the New Länder (Figure 4.1) was conventional in its designation of development centres. Based on their economic and employment structures, infrastructure facilities and geographic positions, these higher-order centres, together with their development regions, seemed suitable for taking on the role of 'development engines' for the entire area of the new *Länder* (Selke, 1991). The development regions were to be designated not only in the

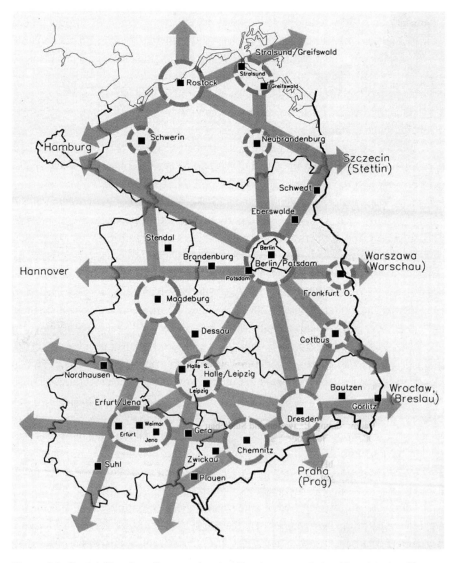

Figure 4.1 Spatial Planning Concept for the Development of the New Länder (Source: Bundesbaublatt, No. 12, December 1991, p.793)

industrial agglomerations but also in the rural areas with a less than average development potential (Irmen and Sinz, 1991).

> To improve co-operation and the integration of the individual exchanges of services, (…) transport axes and line-based infrastructure (…) will have to be developed. Priority is given (…) to the communication links between the economic centres in Western Germany and the development regions in Eastern Germany (Sinz, 1994: 15).

The federal ministry had not lost sight of the wider picture either. The new *Länder* were expected to become central European hubs. The document spelt out what this meant, not only for the *Länder*, but also for the sectors. Thus,

> the recommendations of spatial planning policy (including regional economic development policy) are formulated as a 'guiding framework' rather than as a fixed planning scheme. The sectoral ministries are asked to take this framework into account in their regionally significant plans and measures (ibid. 11).

Still in the process of building up their administrations, the new *Länder* had not been party to the formulation of this policy. Although they numbered no less than twelve, objections were raised against the concept of regional development centres, especially from rural areas, who were 'afraid of losing assistance in favour of an enforced development policy for a few central places' (ibid. 19). It seems that the sector ministries did not pay much heed to the *Spatial Planning Concept* either. However, it should be noted that in designating 'development regions', the *Spatial Planning Concept* was a forerunner of the ESDP. As Chapter 9 will show, the Potsdam document made the development of 'Global Economic Integration Zones' outside the core of Europe into one of its key policies.

The second response to unification was the joint formulation of so-called Guidelines for Regional Policy (Federal Ministry for Regional Planning, Building and Urban Development, 1993) by both the Federal Ministry and the Federal Research Institute for Regional Geography and Regional Planning, with the assistance of consultants. Eventually they were adopted by the MKRO. It was the first time that the MKRO had adopted such a non-statutory document. Guiding principles, like the ones set out in the Federal Spatial Planning Act, are called *Leitlinien* or *Leitbilder* in German, the latter term often translated as 'spatial vision'. *Leitbild*, in particular, stands for an informal instrument 'that describes, verbally and/or non-verbally, a desirable future of a region' (Knieling, 2000: 7; authors' translation). In the document, five sets of principles were put forward. They were about settlement structures (predominantly in favour of polycentric development), environment and land-use, transport planning, Europe, and one entitled 'General Principles for Planning and Development'. With regard to Europe, the Germans showed themselves to be mindful of their position, in the heartland of what was rapidly becoming a unified continent. In general, Germans are keenly aware of the fact that they are the EU member state with the largest number of neighbours, nine in total; they also feel particular responsibility towards central and eastern Europe. The Guidelines portrayed Germany as forming 'a new interface between western and eastern Europe and between northern and southern Europe' (Federal Ministry for Regional Planning, Building and Urban Development, 1993: 19).

The document went on to spell out German attitudes towards European planning. It recognized that the Maastricht Treaty contained specific objectives for spatial development (see also CEC, 1999c: 30) and that *Europe 2000* attached great importance to urban networks. The objective, though, must be to leave scope for national policies:

> Endeavours to lay down comprehensive rules and codes for regional policy at the European level must be rejected. Instead, the European regional policy concept must support the multifarious forces in the individual nations and regions, promoting and co-ordinating co-operation between them at the same time. What we need is not a new super-planning concept on a European scale but the flexible further development of the various forms of coordination (Federal Ministry for Regional Planning, Building and Urban Development, 1993: 20).

The Guidelines went on to specify issues that a European framework should address, beginning with a balanced, polycentric settlement structure. The Germans see their own polycentric settlement structure as a reflection of their federal tradition, which should thus be treasured. The list in the Guidelines included support for urban networks, and also for the trans-European networks as well as secondary regional centres. Realization of these goals depended not only on national sector policies, but also on measures taken by the European Commission. A European spatial development policy which aimed to co-ordinate these measures required an overall European spatial vision (*Leitbild*) but not a comprehensive planning policy.

It is clear why Germans were alarmed by the prospect of the Commission entering the fray. Control in the field of planning would give Community regional policy another string to its bow and it would interfere with *Länder* prerogatives. At the same time, inter-governmental European planning would give federal planners the position of linchpins between the *Länder* and Brussels, so for as long as member states rather than the Commission were in charge, the federal planners were enthusiastic about the prospect of European planning. The MKRO was sure to be involved in anything the federal planners did, so the *Länder* accepted this position. However, the reader should note that the discussions were framed in terms of the competency for regulating land use (because that was ultimately what German planning was about), which was not how the issue had been framed in the first instance. Also, as Chapter 2 has pointed out, the use of the term 'inter-governmental' in the ESDP context, for a form of planning outside the European treaties, is somewhat confusing. This is because European decision making based on the treaties carries a large inter-governmental element within it. So, even if there were a form of Community planning, the member states could not be overruled.

THE HAGUE: CREATING THE INSTITUTIONAL INFRASTRUCTURE AND MORE

At Nantes, a senior planning official, himself weary of European planning, had represented the German minister. It was his successor as chief planner who, in 1991, perceived the opportunity, described on page 48, for federal planning to become a linchpin. Upon taking office, the new chief planner invited his Dutch counterpart for discussions, explaining that it was unthinkable for Germany to grant the Community a planning competency (that is a competency for making formal plans) that the federal government itself did not have. He also floated the idea of informal co-operation with a number of like-minded north-west European neighbours. (A colleague from another ministry, seasoned in European affairs, had given him this tip.) Consequently, the Germans, the Dutch, the British and the Danish formed what has often been described as the 'Northern Group'. Later, France would join, but in the end the group dissolved.

Through such channels it became clear to the Dutch that their north-west European colleagues would not support their desire for the Community to take on a planning role. Giving up the idea must have seemed a small price to pay for achieving another Dutch goal, north-west European co-operation. Also, by that time a new Director-General, who was less enthusiastic towards the Community, had taken office. All the same, beginning with the Dutch, the Germans set European planners on a course of advocating what became known as 'inter-governmental planning'.

In preparing the meeting in The Hague, the Dutch had other concerns as well, such as the emphasis previously given to the periphery of Europe and the corresponding lack of attention for Europe's core. Planners needed to balance the interests of both, which was the argument of the Dutch document *Urban Networks in Europe*.

Turin had shown the need for a focused agenda, so the only other item on the agenda in The Hague was *Europe 2000*. In the margins of the meeting an ill-fated document entitled *Perspectives in Europe* (National Physical Planning Agency, 1991) was distributed but never discussed. Portraying Europe from a Dutch point of view, it had been perceived as presumptuous. Williams (1996: 107) gives a fuller account. In an international context, running ahead of the troops is not acceptable. At any rate, southern Europeans dislike discussion documents coming 'out of the blue'.

THE COMMITTEE ON SPATIAL DEVELOPMENT (CSD)

As indicated, from 1975 to 1988 an expert committee for regional policy existed, which was chaired by a member state official. In 1988 that committee had been superseded by a Committee of Directors-General of Regional Policy, chaired by the Commission. Subsequently, Directors-General of Planning from the member states had been invited to join. However, regional economic policy crowded out planning from the agenda, so the Dutch proposed a separate committee, following suggestions made under the Italian Presidency. (Europe 2000 was proposing the same; see pages 52–53.) However, taking account of the German position, the idea put forward by the Dutch was for the rotating Presidency, rather than the Commission, to be in the chair.

The proposals had been discussed beforehand with Commissioner Millan at a meeting hosted by the Dutch Planning Minister. The reason for this meeting was the unusual nature of the proposed arrangement. The CSD was emphatically not meant to be a 'comitology' committee, 'comitology' being the summary term for the many hundreds of committees assisting with the drafting and implementation of Community policy (Faludi et al., 2000; Hix, 1999: 30). Unlike a typical 'comitology' committee, this one would not be chaired by the Commission. The Commission was invited, nevertheless, to provide the secretariat and to foot the bill for the expenses of two officials per member state. Meetings were to be held in Brussels, with the services of interpreters provided at the Centre Borschette, a building which hosted dozens of European committees every day and was thus a nerve centre of European policy making. In agreeing to these arrangements, the Commission must have hoped that its support would ultimately pay dividends, by securing a formal role for itself.

At the time, Commissioner Millan's only concern was that the CSD might interfere with the ongoing study programme of DG XVI, pursued in the context of its Europe 2000 activities, a fear that the Dutch were successful in dispelling. They also discussed the draft conclusions of their Presidency with him. It would become common practice to circulate conclusions of ministerial meetings beforehand.

Williams (1996: 48) reports on discussions having taken place concerning the name of the committee. Apparently, the Dutch had wanted it to be known as the 'Committee on Spatial Planning', but this was unacceptable to the British. The Dutch records are silent on this. At any rate, ministers accepted the proposal to set up a 'Committee on Spatial Development'. The Dutch undertook the task of formulating terms of reference, which were to be submitted at its first meeting, scheduled for 1992.

EUROPE 2000: OUTLOOK FOR THE DEVELOPMENT OF THE COMMUNITY'S TERRITORY

As indicated, Europe 2000 had been prepared by DG XVI and its consultants under Article 10 of the ERDF regulations. The outlines had already been presented at Turin. The final document analyzed the pressures on Europe's territory arising from socio-economic developments as well as from national, regional and Community interventions. The document contextualized this by placing it against the backdrop of the completion of the single market. Although it addressed the issue of European global competitiveness, the focus was more on cohesion, reminding the reader of the conclusions reached in Turin. The single market would increase disparities, thus creating a need for a coherent overall spatial vision of the Community territory. This vision should help with the prevention of duplications or mismatches of investments and with distributing the benefits of the single market more equitably.

In the Turin document, reference was made to the situation of four peripheral member states, which at that time still included Denmark. In these states, 'relations with the centre of the Community and access to the principal markets are affected by infrastructure investment decisions in one or more neighbouring member states' (CEC, 1991: 33). However, unlike the Italian document presented in Turin, *Europe 2000* identified two European core regions as opposed to one, these being north-west Europe and an emerging region (similar to the 'North of the South' identified in the DATAR study of 1989) stretching from north-east Spain to northern Italy and southern Germany. Numbering over 200 pages, *Europe 2000* was broader in scope and went deeper into the issues than the meetings in both Nantes and Turin. It referred to other initiatives, including a resolution adopted by the European Parliament in October 1990 calling for concerted Community planning (*Official Journal of the European Communities*, 295, 26.11.1990, p. 652).

The main source of *Europe 2000* had been what the document described as horizontal studies

> on, for example, location factors for industry and services, urbanization and the functions of cities, and migration, as well as existing or developing Community programmes on specific issues such as the future development of the transport sector, energy and the environment (CEC, 1991: 35).

Not the least influential amongst them was the study by Kunzmann and Wegener (1991), mentioned above for having conceptualized the polycentric system of cities as a 'European Bunch of Grapes'. Based on such studies, *Europe 2000* discussed the demographic and economic distribution of the 1990s, and went on to identify issues such as the future of major transport and telecommunications infrastructure, energy distribution and pressures on the environment. Infrastructure apart, tourism and research and development, areas in which Europe faced competition, required co-operative efforts. Centres of excellence were needed, and less-favoured regions required assistance in establishing them. Environmental policies could also become more effective if they were implemented from a Community or international perspective, and the management of water basins belonging to different member states was carried out transnationally, the Rhine Basin being a prominent example. Clearly, sustainable development had entered the scene. In years to come both sustainability and water management would become overarching concerns.

Europe 2000 described the situation and prospects of various types of areas – urban and rural areas as well as coastal areas and islands. Cross-border planning along the 10,000 kilometre land frontiers of the European Community, as it was then known (60 per cent of which were internal borders), was a priority issue. Along borders, new links needed to be established to safeguard 'the economic unity of artificially divided entities' (CEC, 1991: 34).

It is often claimed that *Europe 2000* fell short on policy recommendations, and that this was the reason for its follow-up, what has become known as *Europe 2000+*. Retrospectively, it is apparent that *Europe 2000* set certain processes in motion. The last chapter, 'Policy implications', reiterated the need for balanced and harmonious development of the Community's territory ('harmonious' being a term already used in the Treaty of Rome). The chapter specifically referred to the consensus reached in Turin: an effective regional policy for less-favoured regions by promoting economic and social cohesion needed to be based on an overall view of the Community territory.

With regard to the competency issue, in the Foreword, Commissioner Millan stressed that the document was not, and never would be, a masterplan. Community planning could never substitute for national, regional and local planning. However, the final chapter adds 'it can provide an additional policy framework at a Community, or, to some extent, wider European level, in order to facilitate coherence between sector policies as well as inter-regional co-operation' (ibid. 197). Commissioner Millan would become more and more weary of any attempt to formulate such a framework, though. The Commission officials, keen to forge ahead, had to bide their time until he was replaced by the more enthusiastic Dr Monika Wulf-Mathies.

Europe 2000 also promised to look at adapting existing procedures of reporting on the Community's regions so that they would provide more compatible socio-economic information, thus allowing regional planners to compare different regions more easily. In addition, planners needed information on the intentions of their counterparts in the rest of the Community. The document referred to the idea of monitoring floated in Turin. It was to be a joint collaboration between member states and the future European Spatial Planning Observatory Network (ESPON). The Commission promised to assist by developing its geographic information system and a series of transnational studies that were to provide the building blocks for *Europe 2000+*.

As indicated, much space in the recommendations was taken up by a discussion of the CSD. Its purpose was described as that of holding consultations between member states and the Commission. These should cover the inter-relations between sectors such as transport, environment, telecommunications, energy and so forth, alongside their impact on territorial development. *Europe 2000* defined the agenda for the CSD as follows:

1.   Economic activity was becoming footloose. In the interest of establishing a better balance, the Community would assist by creating conditions for regions outside the development centres to be able to make better use of the opportunities this offered.

2.   The consequences of the ageing population needed to be considered with regard to both changing needs and the supply of labour. There would be a need for facilities to integrate migrants, especially in the inner cities.

3.   Economic imbalances have led to traffic congestion in urban agglomerations. Improving centre–periphery links was a partial solution to this, and at the same time a precondition for peripheral development. Regional access to the networks needed to be improved.

4.   Developments in information technology and telecommunications had created new opportunities. The Community would ensure that investments also went to areas where an economic return was only a long-term prospect.

5.   Economic development should take place in such a way as to avoid further deterioration of the environment while attempting to repair past damages. In other words, this was the sustainability agenda.

6.   The development of a single market in energy called for Community-wide transmission networks.

7.   Without prejudice to subsidiarity, there needed to be co-operation between planners, especially at the inter-regional level. 'Moreover, the Community must have a vision of its future development which makes best use of available resources' (ibid. 200).

It is clear that the authors of *Europe 2000* expected the CSD to be a sounding board for the vision proposed by the Commission. The Dutch proposal had, of course, been that of preparing ministerial meetings. By this time, the Dutch had rallied behind the German position, which held that the member states should be in charge.

URBAN NETWORKS IN EUROPE

Like the Italians, the Dutch put forward a document on *Urban Networks in Europe*. There had been prior consultation with DG XVI, and the Dutch had conducted a survey of member states. The document described urban areas as the engines of economic growth and as employment generators. The survey of member states had shown that most of them focused not only on urban areas, as such, but also on urban networks. The document made a distinction between national and cross-border networks on the one hand and the overall overall urban network on the other. In Europe, which was undergoing integration, there was an urgent need for a coherent perspective with regard to the overall urban network. Such a perspective would benefit not only Community regional policy, but also policies in the fields of transport and the environment. The Dutch position thus dovetailed with that of *Europe 2000*.

Indeed, the document referred to *Europe 2000* as conveying the same message. There was mention of Turin and Nantes and of the Delors speech, discussed in Chapter 3. What was needed was a follow-up to *Europe 2000*, focusing on the interrelationships between policies dealing with regional, environmental and transport issues. With the trans-European networks in the offing, there was particular emphasis on a framework for integrating transport and environmental concerns. This framework would become a recurring theme throughout the ESDP process. However, the reader should recall that the co-ordination effort required would be difficult for the Commission to sustain.

Dutifully, *Urban Networks* disavowed the idea of a European masterplan, stressing the need for bottom-up planning instead. The aim was to provide a basis, alongside *Europe 2000*, for a perspective to be formulated jointly by member states and the Commission. The document suggested allowing the CSD to fulfil the role of an 'observatory', as proposed in Turin, but the Conclusions of the Dutch Presidency were more ambitious. They suggested that, being representative of both the member states and the Commission, the CSD should formulate a development perspective for the European urban network. This would form a reference framework for the policies of national and regional governments, as well as for the Community's sector policies. Dutch national planning documents usually serve precisely this purpose.

There were also traces of cohesion thinking in the document. In the European context, it could hardly have been otherwise. However, in Turin the Dutch had already had their misgivings about cohesion dominating the proceedings. The recession of the late 1970s and early 1980s had taught them to perceive the competitive position of their country as depending on the health of its core, the well-known Randstad (Zonneveld, 2000). This had been translated into a policy of stimulating peripheral regions to make better use of their existing potential. By way of analogy, for the sake of the competitiveness of Europe as a whole, European planning, too, needed to address the problems of its developed core, and not just those of less-favoured regions. By putting competitiveness on a par with cohesion the Dutch reinterpreted the view of a 'one-dimensional Europe' in the sense of a more diversified Europe.

The document went into more detail with regard to urban networks. The components were 'urban regions', the flows of goods, people and information, and the 'hard' as well as the 'soft' links between them. Networks of urban regions existed on two spatial scales, the regional one and the scale of Europe as a whole. The emergent European urban network (Figure 4.2) consisted of urban agglomerations and regional networks of international significance. With the single market in mind, the document claimed that regions stood to benefit from integration, admitting at the same time that this was especially true in the core of Europe. However, secondary urban systems also needed to be linked to the primary urban regions, and so the document emphasized the need to fill in the 'missing links'. Clearly, the trans-European networks were already in the air.

The document drew a distinction between two core zones of Europe on the one hand (the same ones as identified in *Europe 2000* and previously in the Brunet study), and the peripheral regions on the other. In the core zones, congestion and environmental degradation were the major problems. In the peripheral areas, connections were inadequate. Both problems needed to be addressed. This was also true for problems within cities. Cities were essential links and as such they needed assistance in coping with environmental and social problems. (So-called 'Urban Initiatives' would eventually represent a separate strand of policy not covered in this book.) Polycentric development was the preferred method reflecting the view of a 'diversified Europe'. Because of their spatial and environmental qualities, the document envisaged a special role for medium-sized cities. It also recommended a shift in the modal split from road to rail and water transport. For intermediate distances, high-speed trains were preferred over air transport. So the threefold task was to improve the economic, social and environmental quality of cities, to improve physical links in a more environmentally friendly and sustainable way and to foster co-operation. In a similar way to their national strategy, the Dutch expected that this

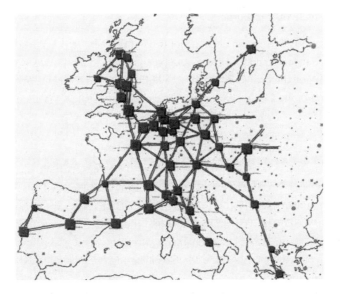

Figure 4.2 Urban Networks in Europe (Source: Minister of Housing, Physical Planning and the Environment, 1991)

would strengthen the competitive position of Europe as a whole. With regard to cross-border networks and the development of the European urban network, the document once again argued for a European planning framework.

It is obvious that, like *Europe 2000*, *Urban Networks in Europe* combined various concerns. The reader familiar with the Potsdam document will have no difficulty in tracing the influence of both documents. *Europe 2000* had, of course, been prepared with the help of a Dutch national expert, so the similarities between the two were no coincidence.

The Dutch Presidential Conclusions commended the Commission on publishing *Europe 2000*. They welcomed *Urban Networks in Europe* as fulfilling one of the recommendations of Turin and as an elaboration of *Europe 2000*, and put the acceptance of the following joint proposals of the Commission and the Presidency on record:

1. organization of a data network, (later referred to as ESPON, as the reader is aware) between existing institutes and observatories and new ones;
2. preparation of a 'Compendium' of planning systems in the member states;
3. promotion of cross-border planning, also along the external borders of the Community;
4. expansion of inter-regional and inter-urban networks of co-operation;
5. establishment of the CSD, chaired by alternating Presidencies. The secretariat was to be provided by the Commission, and it was to deal with tasks that did not specifically include the preparation of a joint document, as proposed in *Urban Networks in Europe*.

The Hague boasted two main achievements. First of all, there was agreement on the policies to be followed and a reasonable balance was found between cohesion on the one hand and the problems in the core of Europe on the other. Second, with the establishment of the CSD, a more solid basis for addressing such issues existed.

THE CSD STARTING WITHOUT TERMS OF REFERENCE

As promised, after The Hague, the Dutch produced draft terms of reference for the CSD. The preamble referred to Article 10 of the ERDF Regulations as being the legal basis for the CSD. The first article reminded the reader that the CSD had been established for the purposes of exchanging information and assisting with the joint deliberations of member states and the Commission concerning the development of the Community territory. The second article was about the tasks of the CSD. The list included not only research, but also the adoption of a perspective (as if the CSD was the decision maker) on the future development of the Community territory, the aim being to make optimal use of Community instruments. These tasks were elaborated in greater detail, including practically everything that had so far been considered. The third article summed up the provisions, as discussed above, for a rotating chairperson and the secretariat, adding that the so-called 'troika', comprising the past, present and future Presidency, should form a management board. The regulations stipulated also that this troika could allow one of its members to hold the chair for up to eighteen months. During the consultations, France had proposed that the chair be elected independently from the Presidency. Apparently, the French were too impatient to wait for their next turn after Nantes, but this was all that the Dutch would do for them. Subsequently this idea was put to rest. The Dutch also suggested an agenda for the CSD. This took place after Maastricht, so the first point on the agenda was the new role of planning under the treaties.

The first CSD was held on 10 April 1992 under the Portuguese Presidency at the Centre Borschette. It is perhaps significant to mention that for some participants this must have been their first experience of such meetings. By that time, though, there had already been consultations between the members of the Northern Group.

The Dutch noted at the meeting that the troika (of which they were still members) had barely met for five minutes. Also, the Dutch were surprised to find the Presidency and the Commission invoking terms of reference other than their own, which failed to mention the rotating Presidency. Obviously, the position of the CSD was far from settled. After the pronouncement of the agenda, the Portuguese chief delegate, already chairing the meeting, was duly elected chairman. This was followed by an exchange of views on the work of the CSD.

After the chair had emphasized the pioneering role of the CSD in anticipating important developments and in promoting economic, social and also what he called territorial cohesion, various delegations took the floor. This began with France announcing an imminent conference on urban networks amongst other plans. The UK delegation reported on a commissioned five-country comparison of planning systems in the EC (Davies *et al.*, 1989; eventually, the *Compendium* would be based on a brief prepared by its senior author). For political reasons, the UK delegation kept its distance from European planning. Professionally, UK planners made a significant contribution, though. As Chapter 8 shows, the arrival of a new government would eventually lead to an explosion of UK interest, allowing UK planners to fully bring their expertise to bear.

Other items on the agenda were the Commission's work programme beyond *Europe 2000*, the forthcoming ministerial meeting in Lisbon and a commissioned study on 'Urbanisation and the functions of cities in the European Community'. The British author gave an introduction, which voiced criticisms and made policy recommendations. Spain, Italy and Ireland reacted defensively, saying that, before accepting such studies, the Commission ought to give member states the opportunity to comment.

Regional policy was outside the competency of the CSD, at any rate. Clearly, its beneficiaries were apprehensive that such studies, and the work of the CSD in general, might impinge upon Community regional policy. This was to become a recurring issue.

The two remaining points on the agenda were the implications of Maastricht (which the Dutch had wanted to discuss first and foremost) and suggestions for follow-up meetings. The new director at DG XVI in charge of spatial planning (the previous member of the Delors cabinet mentioned in Chapter 1) spoke last of all. The Dutch noted that he, rather than the Presidency, gave the summing-up. He saw Maastricht as providing a stimulus for exploring the territorial dimension of European policies. He professed not to be overly-concerned about the status of the CSD. Legitimacy would flow from the good work of the Commission and the support it would receive from the CSD. Clearly, the Commission continued to see the CSD in a complementary role to its own.

The Dutch records note, with exclamation marks, that in future the Northern Group needed to hold preliminary consultations concerning the agenda. The Dutch were unhappy about the direction in which the CSD was moving.

LISBON: INFRASTRUCTURE AND THE NEED FOR A VISION

Understandably, Portugal's concern was the spatial dynamics of European integration. As the relevant volume of the *Compendium* explains:

> All Portuguese regions have an Objective 1 status. The financial support has mainly been geared towards the construction of major nation-wide infrastructures and equipment, which have a strategic role in regional development. (…) These projects have an obvious spatial structuring impact. In particular, transport policies are currently trying to address the whole issue associated with spatially uneven development (CEC, 2000d: 23).

The Portuguese therefore made infrastructure the focus of their Presidency, in particular the trans-European networks (TENs). As the two previous Presidencies had done, they presented a document to the meeting in Lisbon in 1992, which argued for the TENs to be based on a spatial perspective. Indeed, the very first paragraph of the document had as its title: 'The context: the necessity for a concept of spatial development on a Community scale' (Portuguese Presidency, 1992: 1). It gave reasons to explain why a coherent approach was needed, the conclusions of the Maastricht Summit being one of them. *Europe 2000* received credit for providing the necessary information. The document continued:

> However it is not enough to register changes taking place. It is necessary to
> seek to obtain a minimum anticipating ability so that it is possible to intervene
> at the right time and with the appropriate actions (ibid. 2).

The TENs would contribute to economic and social cohesion and improve the
competitiveness of Europe and the quality of services across the continent. In addition, they would accommodate the predicted growth in intra-community trade. So
the document identified the TENs as 'one of the major instruments for spatial
development on a European scale' (ibid. 3).

The document recounted the problems that the TENs were designed to rectify:
inadequate infrastructure in border regions and the 'marginalization' of peripheral
areas, especially in the countries of the so-called 'second circle', Ireland, Portugal,
Greece and Denmark. These countries were inadequately linked with the rest of the
Community. TENs also had a role in relieving congestion in core areas, but, like the
document of the Italian Presidency two years earlier, the underlying conceptualization
of the Community territory was based on a one-dimensional centre–periphery model.
However, attention was also given to the danger of so-called 'grey areas' where traditional infrastructure continued to be of importance. Invoking the term
'inter-peripherality' to describe it, the document also discussed the 'tunnel effect' of
TENs between stations in France. It was mainly for these reasons that the document
pleaded once again for the introduction of 'the spatial dimension into the guidelines
for the trans-European networks' (ibid. 9).

After the Structural Funds, the focus was now on the TENs. It was suggested
that 'the CSD could contribute towards making concerns about spatial questions an
integral part of other Community policies' (ibid. 16). The document listed four topics
for discussion, with each one divided into many sub-questions:

1. Granted that there was no need for a masterplan, what were the priorities for
    spatial development actions at Community level and what instruments should
    be used?
2. How could the instrument of TENs be used in achieving spatial development
    goals?
3. How can city networks be developed?
4. What principles should apply to the Observatory network?

There was great interest in the TENs. The proposed policy was to be based on
Article 129b of the new Treaty of Maastricht, which also meant that there was the
prospect of funds becoming available. The Commission uttered a warning, though.
The effects of investments in infrastructure were long term. Towns and cities and
urban networks were in need of immediate attention. The Delors II Package with
concrete proposals on the TENs was still some way off.

The Portuguese had not put the topic of a spatial vision as such on the agenda, but in his opening speech the minister addressed the need for one, as stated in their document. The theme was picked up again during the discussions. The Dutch, as the organizers of the last meeting the first to take the floor in Lisbon, were outspoken on this issue. Support was also voiced by France, Denmark and Germany. There had been a preliminary meeting with France, so this was no surprise. Denmark and Germany sat in the Northern Group, alongside The Netherlands (and Britain). Both Denmark and Germany were involved in the formulation of a vision for the Baltic Sea area, a test bed for the ESDP in more than one respect. Albeit more implicitly, Spain and Portugal also addressed the topic of a spatial vision. There was agreement that such a spatial vision needed to be broader and deeper than *Europe 2000*. The Germans' idea was that this vision should form the basis for co-ordinating Community policies. What the Presidential Conclusions specified was that a spatial dimension was fundamental to any policy designed to promote economic and social cohesion. They therefore recommended the development of:

> a coherent vision of the whole of the Community's territory, by amplifying the
> *Europe 2000* programme. The goal is to introduce this territorial dimension into
> the various Community policies and to have a permanent framework of refer-
> ence for Community, national and regional interventions and actions
> (Portuguese Presidency, 1992: 5).

Even though it was not officially on the agenda, much attention was given to the relationship between spatial development policy and European regional policy. Commissioner Millan related this to the status of the CSD. Obviously, a link with regional policy would make it easier to formalize the CSD, but regional policy and spatial planning were two different areas. The Dutch supported him in this. Other delegations were in favour of forging a closer relationship. Luxembourg also wanted to see a relationship established with environmental policy and proposed to factor environmental concerns into the eligibility criteria for the Structural Funds. All delegations acknowledged the importance of the TENs in spatial planning.

With regard to the status of the CSD, contrary to what the Dutch had assumed, it transpired that Article 10 provided insufficient grounds for formalizing it. Article 10 was only sufficient for research. According to Millan, the problem was the rotating Presidency, a thorn in the Commission's side. The Conclusions of the Portuguese Presidency made it clear, however, that the ministers attached great value to the CSD.

CONCLUSIONS

Unperturbed by its uncertain status, the CSD picked up steam. Given their disposition at the time towards planning and even more so towards Europe, nobody expected the UK to call a ministerial meeting. However, the earnest hope of many, in particular the Dutch, had been that the Danish would call a meeting. However, Danish planners were absorbed in work on the *Vision and Strategies around the Baltic Sea 2010* (Fourth Conference of Ministers for Spatial Planning and Development, 1996) and on a national planning document, *Denmark Towards the Year 2018* (Ministry of Environment and Energy, 1992) modelled on the Dutch *Fourth Report*. Both documents explored the implications of European integration (Jensen and Jørgensen, 2000: 35).

More importantly, perhaps, national planning in Denmark was in the process of being absorbed into the Ministry of Environment and Energy. According to the Danish *Compendium* volume, the aim of the Spatial Planning Department created within this ministry was to use spatial planning to 'strengthen the overall implementation of Denmark's environmental policies, and to stimulate development through planning' (CEC, 1999d: 32). The upshot was that Danish planners were unable to organize a meeting.

It may not have been politic to do so anyhow. Denmark had its doubts with regard to the Treaty of Maastricht. However, the Danish did inject environmental concerns into the proceedings. In a document laid before the CSD, they put 'spatial balance' forward as a key concept. It amounted to a decentralized urban system based on three basic principles; these were identified as urban spread, the development of corridors and the appropriate use of energy and transport. With its connotation of uncontrolled urban growth, the term 'urban spread' was rather unfortunate. What the Danish had in mind was something more in line with polycentric development, as described in *Urban Networks in Europe*. In their interventions, most CSD delegations paid tribute to the work of the Danish; even without organizing a ministerial meeting, the Danish made a difference.

Since the Danish will not figure again, it is apposite to relate here that Denmark was the first country to apply the principles of the ESDP to their own policy. Concurrently with the *First Official Draft*, to be discussed in Chapter 7, they published a document entitled *Denmark and European Spatial Planning Policy* (Ministry of Environment and Energy, 1997) applying its principles to their country.

At the CSD, routines were established. Discussions ranged from Commission initiatives, such as *Europe 2000+*, to reports from the member states and the work of the CSD itself. The Observatory and the *Compendium* were recurring items on the agenda, as was the status of the CSD, deadlocked over the issue of the rotating chair. The Commission regarded the CSD as an arena for consultations with member states. Other players had other designs. On substantive matters, apart from the successful introduction of environmental considerations, there was little progress.

The need for some form of spatial or territorial planning seemed unquestionable. Every document since Nantes had confirmed it. It was also clear that this should not amount to a 'European masterplan', but instead should be a framework, or a spatial vision underlying Community policies. *Europe 2000*, *Urban Networks in Europe*, and the document of the Portuguese Presidency made this point, too. In the eyes of north-west European planners, there was no doubt that there were still too many discussions about cohesion, based on a 'one-dimensional' view of Europe. At the same time, however, it had been recognized that core areas were in need of attention. Fortunately, the unresolved competency issue did not lead to stalemate.

CHAPTER 5

LIÈGE TO LEIPZIG – DAVID AND GOLIATH WORKING IN TANDEM

Somebody needed to take the first step towards a European strategy. The impetus came from an unlikely source: the Walloons who were holding the Presidency in the name of Belgium in 1993. Independently, the Germans then made plans for adopting a strategic document during their Presidency. These respective meetings at Liège and Leipzig represented stepping-stones on the way towards the ESDP.

The chapter starts with Liège, very much the result of personal initiative. It then goes on to discuss the meeting on Corfu, where an agreement was forged on procedures, known as the 'Corfu Method'. This forms the cornerstone of what Bastrup-Birk and Doucet (1997: 311) describe as the 'acquis' of generally accepted CSD methods. (This is taken from the acquis communautaire, the body of European law which, once adopted, everybody has to adhere to.) The chapter finishes with Leipzig. It may not have been all that the Germans had hoped for. They had prepared what they saw as a draft ESDP, called Spatial Planning Policies in the European Context (Beratungsgrundlagen in German). Eventually, their achievement was an agreement on the preliminary 'Leipzig Principles'. However, looking back it is now clear that the latter are constitutive for the ESDP.

LIÈGE: A BREAKTHROUGH

The Walloon region of Belgium is not a member state, of course, so the fact that the Walloon minister Robert Collignon chaired the fifth meeting of ministers requires an explanation. It lies in the 'federalization' of Belgium, which entails the transfer of planning powers to the Flemish, the Walloon and the Brussels Capital Region. As far as issues within their competency are concerned, these regions conduct their own foreign policy. However, the European Community only recognized member states, so the regions took turns in representing Belgium. Fortuitously, coming into force on 1 November 1993, the Treaty of Maastricht allowed politicians 'of ministerial rank' from sub-national levels of government to represent member states, so even if this had been a formal Council of Ministers, it would have been acceptable.

The Walloons styled Liège as an 'Informal Council of Ministers responsible for Regional Policy and Planning' rather than as an informal meeting. It was possible that Commission officials had encouraged them, seeing this as a stepping-stone in the process of achieving a formal Council. However, whether it was called a council or a meeting was of no consequence. The gathering was still informal; it didn't have the authority to make formal decisions or even to adopt resolutions. Clearly, though, the Walloons had made this change to enhance the status of the meeting. After all, the Walloon Prime Minister at the time was a committed European who wanted to make an impact. Wallonia was comprised of old industrial regions in need of diversification, which were recipients of Structural Funds. With the Programming Period 1994–1999 about to commence, the Structural Funds were due for revision. This added to the significance of Liège.

Day one was devoted to regional policy, which gave planners an excellent opportunity to prepare for day two, which featured spatial planning. The task fell to a small group of planners. In proposing the preparation of a strategic planning document, their concern was twofold: to make progress in Europe, and also to give Walloon planning a boost. The Walloon region currently has a structure plan ('Schéma de Développement de l'Espace Régional', or SDER). It presents the Walloon region as part of a northern European megalopolis (not unlike the 'Green Heart' in The Netherlands), more precisely as a sort of 'inner periphery', with all the problems attending this status (Granville and Maréchal, 2000).

In Liège, however, the actual work was delegated to a relatively junior person without prior exposure to European planning. This transpired to be a lucky strike. Unencumbered by much awareness of sensitivities, he worked through the dossiers, concluding that what was needed was a political breakthrough. This resulted in a document of the Walloon Presidency entitled *For a Significant Step Towards Co-ordinated Planning Policy for Europe*. It proposed the preparation of a *Schéma de Developpement de l'Espace Communautaire (SDEC)*, literally a 'Scheme for the Development of the Space of the Community'. The English title, now well-known, was amended to the 'European Spatial Development Perspective' (ESDP). A more accurate rendering of the French might have been 'Outline Plan for the Development of Community Space', but apparently in British eyes neither 'Plan' nor 'Community' were acceptable. As indicated in a previous chapter, in German, also, the meaning differs from the French. The German for SDEC became 'Europäisches Raumentwicklungskonzept', the acronym being EUREK. Literally speaking, *Konzept* (sometimes inaccurately translated as 'concept', as in *Spatial Planning Concept for the New Länder*) means draft, but in this case a more appropriate rendering would have been 'conceptualization' or 'vision'. The Germans also refer to a *Leitbild*. *Raumentwicklung* means 'spatial development' and has a more action-oriented connotation than the term used in the German planning act, which is *Raumordnung*. The reader will remember that the latter stands for a regulatory form of planning. Much like the English version, the German translation does not refer to Community space either. The Dutch version, *Europees Ruimtelijk Ontwikkelings Perspectief (EROP)*, is fairly similar to the German, but it invokes the term 'perspective', like the English version.

In a literal as well as in a metaphorical sense, the distance from the capital of Wallonia, Namur, to the Commission headquarters in Brussels is not great, and the Walloon official in charge of preparing this document had consulted with Commission officials. By then, Commissioner Millan had become sceptical about spatial planning. A Scottish Labour politician, thus not affiliated to the Conservative government, Millan considered spatial planning to be rather abstract and vague, and decidedly French in origin. The long-time Director-General of DG XVI (the son of Basque refugees from the Spanish Civil War domiciled in Paris) was sceptical, too. Hix (1999: 263) points out that senior officials in DG XVI 'tend to be from regions that receive substantial resources under the Structural Funds, such as the Spanish Basque and Scotland, and are consequently connected to networks of subnational elites'. That may be so, but it had been the Spanish government and not the Basque Autonomous Community that had put this candidate forward for the position of Director-General. Later on, when the Spanish began to have doubts about the ESDP process, the Director-General's scepticism also grew.

The officials most directly concerned were firm believers, however. They were the two Frenchmen mentioned previously. The first, a former member of the Delors cabinet, held the position of Director of Division A. The second, coming from DATAR, by way of the Chérèque cabinet, was directing the actual work. A third person involved was the Head of Unit A1, a Greek national with a degree from University College, London. (Under the rules governing the appointment of *experts nationaux détachés*, the Dutch planner had returned to the National Spatial Planning Agency where he held the position of international co-ordinator, involving himself actively in the process from the Dutch end.) Unit A1 comprised those who were working on the ESDP. The sceptical Director-General called them the 'poets of DG XVI'. As far as the ESDP was concerned, the 'poets' represented the Commission.

The Walloon planner had got along well with Unit A1. Presumably, it had been on the basis of these discussions that the proposal for what was to become INTER-REG IIC came to be included in the Walloon document. This was done against the wishes of Commissioner Millan, who preferred Pilot Actions under Article 10 of the ERDF regulations to planning work. Taking advice from Brussels, the Walloon official had also gone on a *tour des capitales*, consulting the Germans, French, British and Dutch. As will be remembered, most of them were already enthusiastic about a spatial vision. Although they had every right to be surprised at the official's visit (there had been no mention of this at the last CSD meeting prior to the Walloon Presidency), most could be counted upon to be pleased. The British were naturally more reluctant, given the Conservative government's stance on planning and European integration. However, the package deal proposed by the Walloons included elements that appealed to the British, so eventually they, too, would acquiesce to the ESDP.

What, then, was the package deal? There were four parts to it. As indicated, one referred to what was to later become known as the Community Initiative INTER-REG IIC, which concerned transnational planning. This would also apply to co-operation across maritime borders, the factor which pleased the British. The second was the principal suggestion of preparing an ESDP. The third was an invitation to the Commission to submit proposals concerning the competency issue. This was linked to the status and the further elaboration of the ESDP, the roles of various actors and the status of the CSD. The fourth part of the package was an invitation to the Commission to formulate rules for cross-border consultation on relevant national and regional planning issues.

The document of the Walloon Presidency gave a concise summary of the philosophy behind these proposals. It started by asking rhetorically whether it is possible for anybody to question the fact that planning should have an international dimension. What followed was an account of the previous meetings, emphasizing that no policy maker could ignore *Europe 2000*, but that the latter document had neither defined goals nor proposed a strategy. After all, planning was not a Community competency. (Clearly, by that time the German view on this had prevailed.) However, since the ratification of the Treaty of Maastricht, only days before Liège, the situation had changed. Pointing to the new titles XII, XIV and XVI on trans-European networks, economic and social cohesion and the environment, the document underlined that they all entailed policies with a spatial impact. In addition, with the completion of the Single Market Programme on 1 January 1993, a Europe free of customs barriers had become reality. There was also a trend towards more cross-border and international co-operation. All this required an earnest consideration of the substantive and procedural aspects of the spatial strategy to be pursued.

The document then set out the lines to be followed. To avoid the single market becoming a failure, problems in border regions had to be tackled. Spatial integration was a necessary complement to economic integration. Co-operation between regions and member states was the key and Community support for it a must. A tailor-made Community Initiative was worth considering. However, what kind of strategy should be followed? Would it be a strategy along the lines of the one set out in *Europe 2000+*, drafts of which were already circulating? Was there perhaps a need for a truly communautarian spatial planning strategy? According to the Walloon Presidency, the answer was clear. *Europe 2000+* needed to be augmented with a yet more strategic document for the consideration of the Council of Ministers. It was to be prepared by the CSD, in consultation with local authorities, regions and member states.

In the first place, the strategy was to co-ordinate, and make compatible, the various spatial options of Community sector policies. Beyond this, the proposed document should present general goals and principles, illustrating them with an inspiring synthesis. The intended document would thus become the federalizing document *par excellence* of European spatial policy.

The proposal continued with a discussion of procedures. Given the possibilities of the new Maastricht Treaty, it divined that formulating the proposed synthesis did not require a new Community competency. Under the subsidiarity principle, spatial strategies were the responsibility of national and regional authorities. It was perfectly legitimate though for them to join forces internationally. However, in doing so, they needed to go beyond mere recommendations. If making recommendations were all that the intended synthesis document aspired to, one might as well call the whole exercise off.

The forceful Walloon position statement listed the range of players who were involved. There was of course the Commission, whose continued support was essential. This went further than any comment made previously by a member state (or made thereafter, for that matter) about Community involvement. Without actually using the term, the Walloons proposed a 'third way', 'neither supra-national, nor purely inter-governmental', as Bastrup-Birk and Doucet (1997: 311) would put it later. Under the heading 'The decision-making framework at the European level', the document said:

> The scope and the concrete effects of the ESDP must (…) be specified with as much care as the contents. Should its status be purely indicative? In certain respects, that should be the case, as far as it is not called upon to develop new Community norms *sui generis*. All the measures of a normative nature that it would contain would only be the transcription of spatial implications of regulations and directives adopted under the framework of official Community policies. However this transcription would in itself allow the ESDP to acquire indirectly a certain binding character (Walloon Presidency, 1993: 8).

The above passage attracted little attention and was subsequently forgotten. It represents the only example of recognition by a member state of an implied Community competency. Clearly, not all member states envisioned a purely inter-governmental ESDP.

A passage further down enforces this impression:

> The Commission must continue to play its key role taking into account any redefinition of its tasks in the field of planning. It would seem logical, during the drawing-up of the ESDP, that the Commission sets up, within its administration, a structure able to co-ordinate the spatial aspects of various sectoral policies (ibid.).

One can understand why some still regard Liège as the high point of the ESDP process, when the prospects of a reasonable form of Community planning were optimal.

As was to be expected, ministers gave a sympathetic reception to the proposal for an ESDP. They decided that the work should be entrusted to the CSD, and the document should set broad guidelines for co-operation between member states, also providing their response to *Europe 2000+*. Clearly, the Walloons envisaged this being done in co-operation with the Commission.

As far as the content of a future ESDP was concerned, the Presidency had proposed guiding principles, such as sustainable development, prudent and rational use of land and a balanced development of the territory of the Community. During the discussions, ministers paid a great deal of attention to the concept of networks, meaning both infrastructure and the 'soft' networks of research institutions. Concepts spanning the continent, like the 'Blue Banana', were eschewed. Denmark and also Ireland emphasized environmental issues.

It is often said that the decision to prepare the ESDP was taken at Liège. The Conclusions of the Presidency merely relate that the ministers had considered the possibility. First, as is well known, an informal council cannot take decisions. Second and more importantly, the Greeks opposed it, regarding an ESDP as an unnecessary duplication of *Europe 2000+*. The British were also against it, due to their publicised aversion to planning, and the Irish were hesitant in approving it. These problems were not resolved until the next CSD meeting when the ESDP process started in earnest.

The final decision to launch INTERREG IIC was not made until Millan left the scene, two years later. The overloaded agenda meant that the fourth proposal concerning cross-border consultations was struck off the list, and the third one, concerning the competency issue, proved to be as problematic as ever. The Walloon Presidency may be considered a glaring success despite this. The Dutch delegation was pleasantly surprised by the quality of the work, as was the Commission. Before Liège, the Belgians, including the Walloons, had been an unknown quantity.

Note has been taken on page 64 of the role played by the junior Walloon official, clearly the right man in the right place at the right time! The Walloon Presidency was certainly a success for him. Commission officials who had had dealings with him invited him to fill the vacancy left by the Dutch *expert national détaché*, and he was slated to become one of the most seasoned European planners. At present, he is Programme Manager of the INTERREG IIIB programme for north-west Europe.

A TUG OF WAR UNTIL CORFU

Long before the Walloon Presidency, the Germans had started preparing for their turn in the second half of 1994. Everybody, not least the Germans themselves, expected the process to take a major leap forward.

As indicated, Germany took the initiative because there was fear that the Commission was arrogating planning to itself. Even the German parliament had become restive about *Europe 2000*. Just to remind the reader, the German counter-strategy was to prepare the ESDP as an inter-governmental document.

By late 1992, the Germans had laid out their strategy. In March 1993 they asked the Commission for a meeting. At that time, Walloon intentions were still unknown. As indicated, even at the CSD meeting immediately prior to their assumption of the Presidency, there had been not a word about these intentions. Instead, the German plans for the second part of 1994 were aired. According to the German records, the announcement had drawn scant attention. The three partners of the Northern Group had, of course, already been informed. Of the rest, Spain had asked to be kept posted. The only reaction had come from the representative of DG XVI, saying, true to form, that member states should leave the work on a strategic planning document to the Commission.

Eventually, the German meeting with the Commission, represented by the Director-General of DG XVI and some of his officials, came to pass in September 1993. The Commission delegation professed to be positive, encouraging the Germans to consult member states. The competency issue was put in parentheses. In all likelihood it was only after this encounter that the Germans heard about the Walloon ideas. They must have been taken aback, but the Germans harboured no ill feelings. David and Goliath were moving in the same direction. After Liège, the Germans would continue simply to carry the torch lit by the Walloons.

The problem though, as indicated, was that the Greeks holding the Presidency between the Walloons and the Germans were unenthusiastic about the ESDP. This provided the Commission with a new opportunity. Within DG XVI the feeling continued to be that the Commission should insist on its right of initiative; rather than being an exponent of inter-governmentalism, the CSD needed to be reconstituted in line with its original conception, as a committee advising the Commission. Under the rules, it will be remembered that such a committee was to be chaired by the Commission. By the time the last CSD meeting was held under the Walloon Presidency, the Commission had taken the initiative, distributing a questionnaire concerning the form, function, strategies, goals and content of the ESDP. Working with such questionnaires was common practice in these kinds of situations. However, in taking this step, the Commission placed itself at the centre, taking ownership of the ESDP. The Germans were unhappy, not only because of their well-known predilection for an inter-governmental ESDP, but also because they had prepared a discussion document of their own, called *Spatial Planning Policies in the European Context*. Some member states were already in possession of this document, which amounted to a draft ESDP, but others were not. CSD reactions to the document were negative, not solely due to its contents but rather because the Germans had given the impression of wanting to run the show.

Working for the Commission in his new position, the Walloon planner pursued a more balanced approach, combining inter-governmental and communautarian elements, as had been the case in the document of the Walloon Presidency. The tug of war between these two positions dominated the process until Corfu. The German Standing Conference of Ministers (the MKRO) played a role in this. It had adopted a resolution calling for the institution of a Council of Ministers with complete responsibility for planning. Apparently the MKRO considered this a good way of bringing inter-governmental planning into practice. The MKRO invited Commissioner Millan to enter into discussions with them. This meeting did not come to pass until early 1994; rather than Millan going to Germany, the MKRO went to Brussels.

In anticipation of the informal ministerial council scheduled to take place in the Spring on Corfu, the meeting in Brussels provided the occasion for a great deal of manoeuvring. Commissioner Millan announced that the Commission would produce a document for Corfu dubbed *Outline 2000*. Based on the replies to the questionnaire distributed to the CSD delegations, *Outline 2000* would go beyond surveys and put forward concrete recommendations on how to promote spatial development, also paying regard to the subsidiarity principle. In its resolution, however, the MKRO made no mention of *Outline 2000*. It stated rather that a spatial development perspective 'should be debated by the member states, co-ordinating with the Commission in the Consultation Committee on Spatial Development' (Ministerium für Umwelt, Raumordnung und Landwirtschaft des Landes Nordrhein-Westfalen, 1994: 9). The report to the assembled German ministers (on which this resolution was based) was more direct. This document (only available in German) also failed to mention *Outline 2000*, but referred instead to *Spatial Planning Policies in the European Context*. The latter was intended to form the basis of the work during the German Presidency of late 1994. The MKRO emphasized that defining planning goals was the prerogative of member states and their regions, a position that everybody in Germany shared then, and still shares now.

In the meantime, in preparing their Presidency, the Germans had requested the assistance of a Dutch expert. The assumption had been that this invitation would be reciprocated, allowing a German expert to come to The Hague, but this never came to pass. At any rate, the Dutch expert spent three days a week in Bonn, a rare example of close bilateral co-operation. At that time, generally speaking the atmosphere at the CSD was not overly co-operative. Each and every move was seen as strategic; planning cultures varied enormously, and international work was still unfamiliar. The position of the CSD remained unclear, too.

The situation made Denmark and The Netherlands weary. Their delegations were impatient to get the practical work underway. On the strength of the assumption that it was possible to separate 'technical' from 'political' matters, a working group was proposed. The Commission wanted the troika to be the working group. Contrary to what its name suggests, this troika had a fourth member, the Commission, which also provided the secretariat. In fact, as a permanent member, it held a strong position. Having been disappointed by the Commission's attitude towards the terms of reference, the Dutch resented the idea of the troika being the working group. They believed that the working group should consist of one representative from each of the member states on the troika. In the end, the issue was fudged by the fact that members of all delegations were allowed to join meetings of the troika working group. Its efficacy deteriorated as the working group ultimately met in the same form as the CSD. The fundamental problem of lack of mutual trust remained.

The troika working group had one achievement to its credit, which was the introduction into the proceedings of the sustainability principle. Summarizing member state reactions to the questionnaire, the Commission had already found that this principle formed something of a common denominator. With the troika members Denmark, the UK and Greece participating, the Commission prepared two documents for the working group on the elements and content of the ESDP. These arguments found their way into the Corfu paper and have formed part of the ESDP philosophy ever since.

Meanwhile, the Commission and the Germans soldiered on along their separate paths. Member states were critical of both. The Commission had paid insufficient attention to their answers to the questionnaire, whereas the German approach was considered to be reflecting a domestic agenda. The Commission wanted the Greek Presidency to prepare a document for Corfu, as had been the case previously. The Germans suggested instead that the replies to the Commission questionnaire should be incorporated into their paper *Spatial Planning Policies in the European Context*. Other delegations, in particular the Danish, reminded the rest of the CSD that collectively they were responsible for preparing the ESDP. When the joint document was drawn up, it naturally drew on both documents.

On Corfu the Germans felt that they were receiving nothing in return for the trust they had extended to the Dutch. However, looking back, Corfu was important, and for two main reasons. First, on Corfu the CSD working method crystallized. Up until then, the respective Presidencies had been responsible for making proposals and drawing conclusions. On Corfu it was agreed that submissions to the ministers required the consent of the whole CSD. This principle was to become known as the 'Corfu Method'.

The second reason for Corfu's importance was the fact that the Germans started to forge good working relations with the Commission. Corfu was also a success, because the Greeks had become more enthusiastic. The Minister of the

Environment had assumed responsibility for representing Greece, and he was positive about the exercise.

At the Corfu meeting, the first document which followed the Corfu Method was formulated. It was one that all the delegations had been involved in preparing, with groups of member states each working on certain topics. The substantive findings were not half as important as the feeling of common ownership. The outcome would form an input for the Leipzig informal council. The Corfu paper also laid down the *General Contents of the European Spatial Development Perspective* (Table 5.1). It was thus on Corfu that the outlines of the ESDP emerged, but it should be remembered that the Commission had played a role in formulating them.

Table 5.1 The Corfu paper: general contents of the ESDP

Parts	Sections
I. Introduction	1. Why an ESDP? 2. Main points of the ESDP
II. Present situation and existing trends	
III. What strategy for the European territory?	1. Essential characteristics of this part 2. Basic objective: economic and social cohesion 3. A general concept: sustainable development 4. Spheres of activity
IV. Orientations	Various categories of areas 1. Orientations defined by member states 2. Orientations with regard to co-operation between member states 3. Orientations with third countries 4. Orientations with regard to Community policies 5. Synthesis map

LEIPZIG: ON THE ROAD TO COMPLETION?

The first idea had been to hold the informal council under the German Presidency in Bonn, but on reflection one of the new *Länder* seemed more appropriate, and so the federal planners approached Mecklenburg-West Pomerania, economically the least developed. However, Saxony was able to provide better support, and so Leipzig was chosen.

The significance of this choice was linked to relations between federal ministries. Originally the idea had been to organize a meeting jointly with the Ministry of Economic Affairs responsible for regional policy. However, in taking their misgivings about a potential Commission role in planning straight to Parliament, the planners had outmanoeuvred other ministries. The Ministry of Economic Affairs was opposed to planning, irrespective of whether it was a Community or an inter-governmental function. Now it was faced with resolutions of Parliament which supported the planners in promoting inter-governmental planning (underscoring the role of federal planning in the process). The Ministry of Economic Affairs therefore did not see eye to eye with the planners, and so it was decided to hold an exclusive planning meeting. However, there was no financial support for such a meeting from central funds earmarked for the German Presidency, and the planners had to fund it out of their own budget. Given these constraints, Bonn would have been just about feasible, but another venue was not, which is why additional funding was necessary; this clinched the deal for Leipzig.

Originally, Leipzig was to provide the occasion for ministers to accept a draft ESDP. However, Corfu had shown that the ESDP needed to be a joint product of the CSD and the Commission, with the Commission occupying, if not the leading role, then at least a central position. So the Germans waited for the Commission to come up with proposals. However, the Commission was occupied with the completion of *Europe 2000+*, due to be presented at Leipzig along with the draft ESDP, and so its proposals were slow in coming.

However, the Germans did not take objection to this. They set out to improve their relations with the Commission further. Towards the end of July, a small working party of German and Commission officials thrashed out a draft text. It still needed the approval of other delegations, and so the Germans opened bilateral consultations. A practice of frequently exchanging drafts developed, which has been a characteristic of the ESDP process ever since.

Eventually, the Informal Council of Ministers responsible for Spatial Planning convened on 21 and 22 September 1994. For once there was enough time for planning: three sessions, five hours all told, as the Dutch records comment with obvious satisfaction, more than the two-hour sessions on Saturday mornings usually reserved for it. Sixteen countries (including the four accession countries, Austria, Finland, Norway and Sweden, as they were then known) were represented by a total of twelve ministers. The Netherlands, Denmark and Spain were represented at Director-General level and Greece at Director level. There was a dinner, which allowed ample time for informal discussions, attended by almost everybody. The chairperson, Minister Irmgard Schwaetzer, otherwise keen on European planning, was the only one missing. She had to deal with a crisis in parliament, which had also caused her to arrive late for the opening.

There were four documents on the table. First, there was the submission of the CSD called *Principles for a European Spatial Development Policy*, agreed following the 'Corfu Method', and second, the Communication of the Commission entitled

Europe 2000+: Co-operation for European Territorial Development. There were two further documents concerning the *Network of Spatial Planning Research Institutes in Europe* and *Co-operation in the Field of Spatial Planning and Urban Development Policy with the Reforming States of Central and Eastern Europe*. The first document was the most relevant one for the ESDP process.

The first session went surprisingly well. Just prior to it, the UK had informed member states, via their embassies, that it would reject European political spatial development principles. In the end though, only the first out of five principles had to be amended. Originally it read: 'Spatial development can contribute in a decisive way to the achievement of the goal of economic and social cohesion. It will also contribute to the implementation of Community policies which have a territorial impact'. An accompanying footnote dutifully stated: 'UK reservation on all references on economic and social cohesion and other Community policies'.

The British minister present (a New Zealander, in fact, who one surmises had no warm feelings for European integration, having weakened British bonds with the Commonwealth) merely proposed to replace '... and social cohesion. It will also contribute to the implementation ...' with: '... and social cohesion, but without constraining the implementation of Community policies'. Perhaps this was the result of German lobbying. At any rate, Commissioner Millan gave a sigh of relief and concluded that, with the clarification of the first principle thus achieved, all principles had been accepted.

In parentheses, the final text uses yet another formulation, splitting the first principle into two. One refers to the basic goal of economic and social cohesion and the other to existing Community competencies remaining unaffected. The six principles read as follows:

1. Spatial development can contribute in a decisive way to the achievement of the goal of economic and social cohesion.
2. The existing competencies of the responsible institutions for Community policies remain unchanged; the ESDP may contribute to the implementation of Community policies, which have a territorial impact, but without constraining the responsible institutions in exercising their responsibilities.
3. The central aim will be to achieve sustainable and balanced development.
4. It will be prepared respecting existing institutions and will be non-binding on member states.
5. It will respect the principle of subsidiarity.
6. Each country will take it forward according to the extent it wishes to take account of European spatial aspects in its national policies.

The outcome of the deliberations was a sixteen-page document that has been constitutive for the ESDP ever since. It put flesh on the bones of the previous 'Corfu paper'. These sixteen pages (excluding maps which illustrated the text without actually visualizing the spatial structure of Europe) were translated from German into English and French, and all three versions were published between two covers (BMBau, 1995).

The document started with the principles above, indicating how they represent a political agreement 'for European Spatial Development in co-operation between all the member states and the Commission' (ibid. 37). Table 5.2 shows the structure of the document. Compared to the 'Corfu paper' it was more logical in that, after mentioning the political principles in the introduction, it then started to lay out the fundamental goals for European spatial development policy. In the remainder, some items were emphasized, like the so-called 'spheres of activity', and others, like the description of the present situation and of existing trends, were touched upon only briefly.

Chapters A and B elaborated on the principles. Drawing on previous discussions, the single market, together with the planned enlargement of the European Union, were the main reasons for having an ESDP. The latter should aim

Table 5.2 The Leipzig document: 'Principles for a European Spatial Development Policy'

Parts	Sections
Political principles	
A. Introduction	
B. Fundamental goals	1. Economic and social cohesion 2. Sustainable development 3. Operating objectives for spatial development 4. Reinforcing the coherence of the European continent
C. Spheres of activity	1. Towards a more balanced and polycentric urban system 2. Provide parity of access to infrastructure and knowledge 3. Wise management and sustainable development of Europe's natural and cultural heritage
D. Guidelines for the implementation of spatial development policies in the European context	1. The role of the individual member states 2. Co-operation between member states 3. Co-operation with third countries 4. Co-ordination of Community policies 5. Informal Councils of Ministers 6. Transnational actions in the field

at ensuring the coherence and complementarity of the member states' spatial development strategies and at co-ordinating the spatial aspects of Community policies. Thus, by concentrating specifically on spatially relevant issues, the ESDP should provide significant added value for the European Union, for its economy, the quality of life of its citizens and for its sustainable development (ibid. 39).

It was clear that since Nantes, the debate had moved away from French-style *aménagement du territoire*, which Delors had in mind, to favour an approach more like that of The Netherlands and Germany.

Notwithstanding Dutch efforts in The Hague to give equal emphasis to the competitiveness of the EU, Chapter B was mainly about cohesion. It took note of Commission documents, like the *Fifth Periodic Report on the Social and Economic Situation and Development of the Regions of the Community* (CEC, 1994b) stating that disparities between regions 'have deepened in terms of employment but decreased in terms of infrastructure and stabled (*sic*) in terms of GDP per head, with a clear improvement for the Irish, Portuguese and Spanish regions' (BMBau, 1995: 43). However, *Europe 2000+* (CEC, 1994a) was quoted as warning 'that a series of factors (...) might increase disparities between central and peripheral regions'. The ESDP should counteract these developments.

Regarding sustainable development, reference was made to the famous Brundtland Report. According to the CSD, 'this fundamental concept implies not only economic development which respects the environment, but also balanced spatial development' (BMBau, 1995: 43). This reflected the Danish concept of 'spatial balance'. There were also references to the Treaty on European Union and to the White Paper on growth, competitiveness and employment (CEC, 1993). The document took note of regional disparities and, although it considered sustainability to be of universal applicability, it said that its 'application must be adapted to the particular situations of the regions' (ibid. 44). The document continued:

> Consequently, the ESDP should at the European level foster an outline consisting of three integrated components:
> - A polycentric urban system, as balanced as possible, discouraging excessive concentration around some large centres and the marginalization of peripheral areas
> - A network of environmentally acceptable and efficient infrastructure, strengthening the cohesion of the Community territory
> - A European network of open spaces for the protection of natural resources, with protection areas classified according to their different functions.
>
> (ibid. 44)

The document indicated that each of these three components 'should be as evenly distributed as possible (...) without neglecting (...) diversity'. These three components can be traced back to The Hague and Lisbon and to the influence of the Danish.

Chapter C of the document further elaborated upon these components, transforming them into the three 'spheres of activity' listed in Table 5.2. Eventually, they would become the main structuring device used in the policy chapter of the ESDP.

The section on the urban system reflected a view described as 'diversified Europe', where 'the regional and national urbanization patterns (...) differ enormously: from the very densely populated area (...) to thinly populated areas (...) many of which are located in the remote parts of the Union's territory' (ibid. 47). It then elaborated upon the European urban network, as discussed in The Hague. Once again, urban areas were recognized as being the engines of development. From the cohesion perspective though, the development of a 'relatively balanced polycentric urban pattern throughout the European territory' (ibid. 47) should be encouraged. This, however, was not to be understood as implying an even spread of urban development. Rather, the 'cities in various regions of Europe should be linked in urban networks'. In due course, '[t]he various existing systems on a national and regional scale should be connected, thus increasing the regional cohesion in Europe and preserving the natural and cultural heritage'. Therefore, it was not the size of a city so much as its functional specialization that determined its position within the urban network.

The section on the second sphere of activity, parity of access to infrastructure and knowledge, took a different tack. Once again it lapsed into taking a one-dimensional view of Europe. Trans-European networks were to 'contribute to improving the situation of peripheral regions', but the precondition was the availability of 'additional means to attract investment' (ibid. 50). Infrastructure was a means of linking the periphery to the centre. Where high-speed or express rail links were inadequate, air transport would have to augment them. The text also emphasized the integration of transport modes, in particular that of emergent 'European development corridors'. With transport intensifying and with the location behaviour of firms and households becoming ever more dynamic, a long-term spatial development policy was needed to safeguard open space, nature areas and sensitive landscapes, and a high quality of life for European citizens. As in Lisbon, the Leipzig document also called for the spatial dimension to form an integral part of the TEN guidelines.

'Infostructures' were thought to be gaining in significance. Benefits like tele-education, tele-training, tele-medicine and tele-servicing were expected to flow from ICT development (although the term ICT as such was not used). Infostructures were complementary to conventional infrastructure, and so regions blessed with the latter were expected to gain most. 'The spatial development policy should prevent this situation in which in the long term only some urban regions of the "core" of Europe as well as a few centres in the periphery will be in this position' (ibid. 56).

The third sphere of activity related to the natural and cultural heritage. All over Europe, vital nature resources were in need of preservation 'by linking them up to form ecological effective networks tied into all areas, especially into the high density industrial areas' (ibid. 58). This reflected the emergent discourse on a European ecological network. The concept was based on a perception of Europe as being highly diversified. A recurring problem was the lack of data concerning landscape types. At the European level, the 'Habitat' Directive and the CORINE programmes had already initiated research, but a spatial dimension still needed to be added.

The focus was not only on nature preservation. It was also on maintaining the living conditions of the local population. Due to changes in farming, the fear was that rural areas would become deserted, as had happened in France. This was also the subject of a paragraph on rural–urban relationships arguing for the 'system of villages and small urban settlements in sparsely populated rural areas ... [to] be stabilized as a backbone of supply and economic development and integrated into the regional urban network' (ibid. 48). Also, new environmentally friendly economic activities needed to be developed. By encouraging new methods of production, and by giving farmers income guarantees, the CAP could play a role in this.

Article 128 of the Maastricht Treaty defined a competency for the preservation of the cultural heritage. The Leipzig document noted that archaeological and architectural sites needed to be identified. The same was true for so-called 'cultural landscapes', these being constitutive of regional identities. Listing isolated monuments was insufficient. What was needed was a more integrated approach.

Lastly, Chapter D of the Leipzig document presented 'Guidelines for the Implementation of Spatial Development Policies in a European Context'. Because the three spheres of activity went way beyond the competency of the CSD, it was left to the member states and the regions to

> specify what national measures might be appropriate to contribute to the objectives of spatial development policies at the European level. On the basis of independent contributions (bottom-up approach), this will seek to promote a progressive improvement of the coherence of spatial development objectives of the individual member states and the common (i.e. reached by consensus) objectives for spatial development policy at the European level (ibid. 63).

This required transcending borders. 'This is the "rationale" for the European Spatial Development Perspective' (ibid. 63). Co-operation should take place on three levels: cross-border, inter-regional and transnational. Reference was also made to co-operation with third countries, with CEMAT operating as an institutional framework. Community programmes like PHARE and TACIS were also mentioned.

The paragraph on 'Co-ordination of Community Policies' stressed the importance of the 'spatial coherence' of sector policies. This was a challenge for the Commission. At the same time, the document states, '[t]he Community sectoral policies (agricultural, industrial, transport, environmental, research and technology policy, etc.) must take full account of the (…) ESDP' (ibid. 64). This seemed to be more binding on the Commission than on the member states, which was of course what the Germans, and other member states as well, had intended. The same section of Chapter D also proposed the identification of 'European action areas for integrated spatial development', in which pilot projects should be conducted. The Germans commissioned a French consultant to make further proposals.

France was to follow Germany in the Presidency, so the French minister took the opportunity to announce at Leipzig that, in March 1995, France would play host to the ministers and develop prospective scenarios, including the maps that so far were missing. These scenarios should provide a non-prescriptive framework for national planning policies, based on ideas drawn from member states as well as the Commission. Several ministers recommended drawing up a timetable. Optimistically, the German Presidential Conclusions announced that a first draft of the ESDP would become available in 1995.

With regards to *Europe 2000+*, the Commissioner and his team were congratulated on their effort. Due to extra time pressures, the maps and the Foreword were still lacking, but DG XVI had wanted to rush the draft through the last meeting of the College of Commissioners before the summer recess. At any rate, *Europe 2000+* was welcomed as it had provided the building blocks for the ESDP. Most of the ministers asked for regular updates. Millan, however, considered this document to be the last major effort of the Commission.

The last session, which dealt with co-operation with eastern and central European countries, was short. Member states from southern Europe vented their fear that this would distract from Mediterranean problems. The Scandinavian countries stressed the importance of co-operating with the Baltic States and the Russian Federation. The meeting welcomed a proposal for CEMAT to develop European spatial policy guidelines.

The Observatory network received more attention because there was disagreement about its form and structure. Should it become a Brussels institution with links to national institutes, or should the network be organized more loosely, thus preventing the Commission from playing a major role? Another tricky point was financing. According to Millan, Article 10 was not the appropriate source for financing activities of a permanent nature. The Commission was unable to foot the whole bill, most certainly not if its role was to remain a minor one. The Presidential Conclusions asked the CSD to further investigate the matter of financing the Observatory network.

CONCLUSIONS

The German hosts could look back to Leipzig with satisfaction. Their original hope of piloting a draft ESDP through had not been fulfilled, but they could be excused for thinking that the ESDP was close to completion. The meeting had run smoothly, there had been substantial progress, and the French would take care of the rest. There had been only one very minor incident. The Germans had footed the bill for the accommodation of the heads of delegations of member states, but the delegations of the Economic and Social Committee etc. insisted on the same generosity being extended to them. Once the meeting was over, the search for additional funding started, which only goes to show that organizing meetings requires attention to humdrum minutiae as well as the development of policy.

The German hosts had another worry. They discovered that the Ministry of Foreign Affairs, in its draft Report of the European Council to the European Parliament under Article D of the Treaty on European Union, had failed to mention Leipzig. They were also dissatisfied with the lack of attention given to Leipzig in the internal post-mortem on the German Presidency. This was but another reflection of the weak position of planning in relation to other departments, not only in Germany, but in many other EU member states as well.

On a more positive note, as their Presidential Conclusions had announced, the Germans promptly informed other ministers, the *Länder*, public associations, scientific bodies and the general public of the results of Leipzig. They printed 5,000 copies of the final document. Six months later, less than 10 per cent was still in stock, the rest having been distributed widely (100 going to each of the members of the MKRO for further distribution to *Länder* ministries, parliaments and so forth). This was the first ESDP document to receive such a wide circulation.

CHAPTER 6

STRASBOURG, MADRID, VENICE – IN THE DOLDRUMS

Although the Germans were still in the chair, the Commission ran the show after Leipzig, presenting a work programme for completing the ESDP. The Dutch noted that it made no reference to what the Spanish and Italians would be doing. Evidently, the Commission expected to be in charge.

The ESDP should have been completed by late 1995. However, a change of government meant an end to the French Presidency as an effective force. Also, the new Commissioner, Dr Monika Wulf-Mathies from Germany, made a vigorous entry, and Spain and Italy, holding the Presidencies after France, had doubts with regard to the ESDP. Lastly, the 1995/1996 Intergovernmental Conference cast its shadow on the ESDP process.

This chapter describes the situation in stages marked by the gatherings at Strasbourg, Madrid and Venice. The reader should note that these were once again called informal meetings, not councils. If this implied a lowering of ambitions, it was certainly not discussed.

FRENCH PANACHE AND A NEW LADY

As indicated, the French mounted a scenario exercise. To understand what this was about it is necessary to continue the story of French planning, already begun in Chapter 3. Chérèque had made room for the Euro-sceptic Charles Pasqua, who combined the interior with the planning ministry. (European planning became the responsibility of the Minister for European Affairs.) In 1995, the *loi Pasqua* was passed. It foresaw a national spatial vision defining the options with regard to *aménagement du territoire*, the environment and sustainable development. It was to be formulated bottom-up, involving nation-wide discussions and consultations (Alvergne and Musso, 2000: 51).

The CSD scenarios were to be formulated by the member states, also bottom-up. Being the first collaborative effort since Corfu, the exercise got the delegations going. Coached by the French, they set out to formulate trend scenarios for their national territories. The Commission was to formulate European scenarios based on the transnational studies for *Europe 2000+*. Making use of these inputs, the French were to compile overall trend scenarios and eventually also a policy scenario, called '*scenario volontarist*'.

The French expected more of the scenarios than most other delegations, who believed that the French had taken the process off on a tangent. A published Dutch account speaks of a 'tour de force' (National Spatial Planning Agency, 2000: 39). The Dutch would have preferred to continue formulating policy options.

Experts from the Federal Research Institute for Regional Geography and Regional Planning, which was the establishment that carried out most of the work for Germany, were more impressed (Sinz, 2000: 111). The scenarios held the promise of an analytical base for the ESDP, still sorely lacking. German experts made a major contribution to the exercise (BfLR, 1995).

With elections in the offing, the schedule was tight until the meeting in Strasbourg in early March 1995. The exercise produced a jigsaw puzzle of fifteen pieces, which reflected the disparate planning traditions of member states. At the final CSD prior to Strasbourg, the French presented three trend scenarios with a minimum of explanatory text. These were dubbed 'red', 'purple' and 'green', and coincided more or less with the three 'spheres of activity' from Leipzig, urban development, infrastructure and nature areas and open space (Figure 6.1). The cartography was highly professional. (The experts that did the scenarios would eventually work with the Dutch on the Noordwijk draft of the ESDP.) The CSD submitted the scenarios to the ministers.

At Strasbourg though, ministers took little notice of the scenarios; with the advantage of hindsight, however, the benefits are clear. Member states have become more familiar with spatial planning and since then their delegations have been much more active. At any rate, Wulf-Mathies, the new Commissioner, announced her support for spatial planning. Unlike her predecessor, Millan, the reluctant convert, she was very enthusiastic. A spatial framework for regional policies made sense to her. On her behalf, her cabinet had asked the Germans for background material on planning, which naturally they supplied.

By that time, DG XVI had built up a good track record. There was the enthusiastic team whom the reader has encountered before. However, top officials had briefed Wulf-Mathies about planning as opposed to Millan himself. She is now of the opinion that these officials had failed to warn her of the minefield represented by planning. After her term had ended, she also professed her disappointment about the fact that member states are always keen to receive financial assistance from the Commission, whilst being unwilling to acknowledge its role.

At the time, Wulf-Mathies wanted the competency issue out of the way. So she presented a paper on The Political and Institutional Aspects of a European Spatial Development Policy, inviting ministers to consider the options for the forthcoming Inter-governmental Conference. She asked rhetorically whether spatial planning should 'continue along the present informal path with the current interesting but limited results' or whether it should 'be extended and regularized, that is,

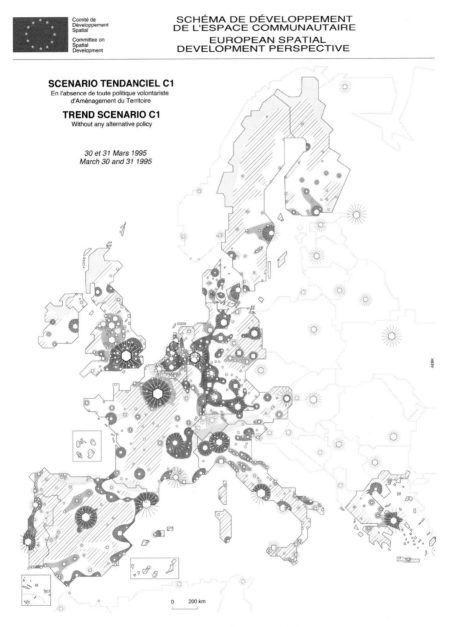

Figure 6.1 Trendscenario on urban development (Source: RPD)

institutionalized, so that we can move towards substantial practical measures, both in terms of existing Community policies and the primary responsibility of the member states'. She reviewed past achievements and spatial trends in the EU, which made the need for some form of spatial planning seem evident. A first step was to establish the Observatory. After all, 'as Leipzig has shown (…) the member states and the Commission are generally under-equipped for producing effective policy-making proposals because of the size and complexity of the challenges'. Invoking Article 10 of the ERDF Regulation, the Commission was ready to work with member states. The Commission used the floods along the Rhine and Meuse just weeks prior to Strasbourg, to become involved. To assist the stricken areas, the Community had made two million ECU available, and the member states concerned had no reason to object to this kind of initiative.

However, there were also the Community instruments for economic and social cohesion. 'The aim should be to exploit more fully the potential of Article 130b, both in respect of its primary goal of economic and social cohesion and in order to pro- mote balanced and harmonious development (Article 130a)'. More generally speaking, Article 10 of the ERDF and the objectives 1, 2, 5(b) and 6 of the Structural Funds could be used to implement ESDP priorities. The Commissioner proposed to add a third strand to INTERREG II, to support transnational planning. As the reader will remember, this idea had emerged in Liège, and it could be paired up with another idea from Leipzig, that of 'European Action Areas for Integrated Spatial Development' (Robert, 1995). Eventually, this third strand would be dubbed INTERREG IIC, now superseded by INTERREG IIIB (CEC, 2000b).

Turning to the ESDP, the Commissioner stressed the need for 'a European ref- erence framework for the spatial development of the Union, to ensure that both Community and national policies are made subject to the same pressing obligation to be mutually compatible'. Ministers should reflect upon 'how to make subsidiarity and the European spatial development dimension more consistent with each other, more effective and more complementary'. In doing so, they should make a political and institutional appraisal of the ESDP process so far, also taking into consideration the growing need for co-operation in the spatial development arena on a European level, both with regard to the fuller exploitation of Article 130b and closer strategic co-operation between member states.

Ministers were positive about INTERREG and about using Article 10 for pilot actions. There was a lot of money at stake here. With regard to the Observatory, ministers wanted to make an early start, and so they asked the CSD to make pro- posals before the summer. The important points to consider were its location, financing and who should be in charge, the member states or the Commission.

However, Wulf-Mathies later recalled having been taken aback by member state reactions to the competency issue. Clearly, her advisers had allowed her to go beyond the politically acceptable. Although a number of member states, including The Netherlands, had given at least some consideration to the idea of introducing spatial planning into a revised treaty, the Germans were the only ones to have explored the issue in depth. In the wake of Leipzig, the German Standing Conference of Ministers responsible for Regional Planning (the MKRO) had adopted another resolution based upon the earlier one they had adopted on *Spatial Planning Policies in the European Union,* the discussion document tabled by German federal planners mentioned on page 64.

The MKRO (1995) acknowledged the importance of close co-operation amongst member states and between the member states and the Commission, and advocated putting spatial planning policy into the European treaties. In doing so, however, the MKRO followed the bottom-up model that complemented the German system. The co-ordination of sector policies should be based on the objectives and principles formulated by the member states. The German Advisory Committee on Spatial Planning and the Academy for Regional Research and Regional Planning took similar views (Akademie für Raumforschung und Landesplanung, 1996). This position of including spatial planning in the treaty to curtail the Commission's authority, which initially appears counter-intuitive, became German policy (Faludi, 1997a). This fits into the broader picture. Germans see the treaties as vehicles not only for defining Community competencies, but also and particularly for limiting them.

After the elections the momentum of the French Presidency evaporated. France would not hold the Presidency again until after Potsdam. It seems apposite to briefly relate that in 1999 (without the overall strategy document foreseen in the *loi Pasqua* having seen the light of day) a new law was passed, *loi Voynet*, named after the Planning and Environment Minister Dominique Voynet. It foresaw nine schemes, one each per public service cluster, but the overall scheme was dropped. Instead, DATAR was asked to formulate a non-statutory vision of France in 2020, which it did (Guigou, 2000).

MADRID: ONE DECISION AND MANY UNCERTAINTIES

Madrid caused some political fireworks. Once again it was Wulf-Mathies who received most of the attention, but the attitudes of the hosts were also important. Spain was, and still is, the greatest beneficiary of the Structural Funds. Before discussing Madrid, the Spanish 'opportunity structure' needs to be analyzed.

SPANISH OPPORTUNITY STRUCTURE
Taulelle (2000: 65) claims that Spain saw spatial planning as a northern European plot to reduce its share of the Structural Funds. A similar view was expressed by the member state to succeed Spain in the Presidency, Italy:

> The Mediterranean countries, and Spain most of all, feared that the ESDP would
> become (notwithstanding the basic political agreements always confirmed by

the informal ministerial meetings) too rigid an outline to be used unilaterally by the Commission to define the allocations of Structural Funds on the occasion of defining the Rules for the forthcoming new programming period of the Funds (2000–2006) (Rusca, 1998: 40).

There is an element of truth in this. The reader will remember the Northern Group seeking to counterbalance the emphasis in the ESDP process on cohesion, something also evident in the Dutch work on *Urban Networks in Europe*. With Austria, Finland and Sweden having just joined the EU, all three net contributors and thus presumably in favour of streamlining the Structural Funds, the Spanish may have perceived an even greater danger to their allocation. In their book, two key German players, Krautzberger and Selke (1996: 33–4) commented on the impact of the introduction of Objective 6 of the Structural Funds for sparsely populated areas in two of them, Sweden and Finland. They believed that EC regional policy had been dominated by economic criteria for too long, but the fact that Objective 6 was based on spatial considerations portended a new policy. The Spanish were thus entitled to be apprehensive.

The Spanish 'opportunity structure' was also greatly shaped by the circumstances in Spain itself. At a German–Spanish seminar at Sevilla, Esteban (1995: 57) the Spanish CSD delegate described Spain since the adoption of the Constitution of 1978 as a quasi-federal state characterized by the presence of seventeen Autonomous Communities (see also the Spanish volume of the *Compendium*: CEC, 1999e). Esteban described the ensuing conflicts, with national government being in control of economic planning, including responsibility for infrastructure, whereas the Autonomous Communities had control over no fewer than twenty-two spatially relevant policy areas, including land-use planning, urban development and housing. Some further policy areas were a joint responsibility of the national government and the Autonomous Communities. Genieys (1998: 176) talks about a 'double level of institutionalization and representation' being an important aspect of the Spanish situation generally. Under these circumstances, of course, spatial planning was complex. Eser and Konstadakopulos (2000: 794) write about a 'territorial as well as functional fragmentation of competences'. At Sevilla, Esteban was more blunt, describing the situation as 'undoubtedly incoherent', reminding him as it did of the European Community:

> Spatial planning is (...) a matter in which the state has no competency. As annexed to this, the state is responsible for the formulation and implementation of sector policies. This means that the state cannot interfere with the setting of the framework (spatial planning), but it can nonetheless use certain instruments (sector planning) that are spatially relevant (Esteban, 1995: 59; authors' translation from German).

The main national concern was with transport planning. As Cádiz (1995: 80) reported at the same seminar, the overall transport plan had a wide remit, including the spatial and environmental impacts of proposed policies. Thus, the transport plan doubled up for a national planning framework. The situation was complicated further by the fact that the EC, too, was engaged in transport policy. This gave Esteban pause to reflect on European planning. One consideration was the absence of a Community competency. The second consideration was new: earmarking areas for housing and employment as it did, Esteban reckoned that planning might fall foul of the freedoms guaranteed to citizens under the European treaties! The third consideration was the importance of economic efficiency.

Clearly, this analysis by the Spanish CSD delegate left little room for the type of planning advocated by north-west Europeans. Indeed, Esteban concluded in his paper, written only months before Madrid, that the only viable option was cross-border planning.

> The quality and success of measures in this field are more a matter of good
> neighbourliness and of the urgency of finding solutions than of the fact that one
> is a member of one and the same community of interests, such as the EU
> (Esteban, 1995: 59; authors' translation from German).

The scepticism of the Spanish was apparent. They certainly let this be known. There are those who claim that

> Southern European states generally do not advance proposals of their own, nor
> do they obstruct proposals made by others. This acquiescence is a way to over-
> come national decisional paralysis, or better, let the EC overcome it (La Spina
> and Sciortino, 1993: 208, quoted after Lenshow 1999: 56).

Lenshow herself counters that, with regard to environmental government, this conclusion needs to be modified. She invokes Aguilar (1993: 231), saying that, especially where the notion of a complementary relationship between environmental and economic policy goals and interventions is concerned, Spanish attitude is defensive, and this also seems true of the ESDP.

PROGRESS ON THE ESDP

Spanish reluctance notwithstanding, work on the ESDP progressed. In May 1995, the CSD set up a task force to produce ESDP texts, structured according to the three spheres of activity, as defined at Leipzig. Taking heed of previous unsuccessful attempts to form flexible and efficient working arrangements, the task force comprised only one representative per delegation. Its brief was to prepare not only a draft ESDP but also a work programme for the Observatory.

The representatives of The Netherlands, Sweden, Finland and Luxembourg wanted to proceed with the formulation of policy options. Spain, Greece, Portugal and the UK wanted to dwell upon the trend scenarios. The southern view of planning was that of a technical exercise and the northern predilection was for a political document. For the UK there were, of course, ideological reasons which could stall the process.

If policy options were to be formulated, how to do this was another issue. One proposal was to set up six transnational working groups, in accordance with the transnational regions, as identified in *Europe 2000+* and/or under INTERREG IIC. The other was to form working groups for each of the 'spheres of activity'. These proposals came to nothing. At the next CSD in July, the first under the Spanish Presidency, questions were raised about the role of the task force. Once again the distinction between 'technical' and 'political' aspects transpired to be a difficult one to sustain, and without much ado the task force vanished.

At the same meeting, the north-west European delegations and the Commission, all of whom feared that the Spanish would bog down the proceedings, must surely have uttered a sigh of relief! This is because the Spanish announced that they wanted to continue with the trend scenarios and explore how to make the best use of Article 10 and INTERREG IIC. They proceeded in the same way as the French had done previously. Within two months member states were expected to give overviews of spatial trends and strategies, which should result in two documents, one on spatial analysis and one on policy options. Most member states viewed the Spanish intentions as positive.

In September 1995, a two-day CSD seminar was organized for member states and the Commission to present their results. Each delegation was expected to discuss the existing situation; spatial trends up to 2015; their planning strategy; the territorial impact of Community policies; the characteristics of the territory and spatial planning policy and conclusions with regard to Europe. Most participants enjoyed this exercise.

When the Spanish Presidency attempted to analyze the contributions, however, problems emerged. The Spanish had given little guidance to individual delegations, so member state inputs varied from two-page documents to well-considered reports. To cope with this diversity, in particular with regard to policy options, the Presidency divided the material according to the three 'spheres of activity', adding a fourth one: 'options in general and in relation to the socio-economic framework'. In addition, the Spanish proposed to classify policy options according to three criteria: 'geographical position' (central/peripheral), 'degree of integration into the European model of economic competitiveness' (high/low) and 'territorial inter-linking in the Union' (strong/weak). Later, a fourth criterion was added: 'potential for sustainable development' (Ministerio de Obras Públicas, Transportes y Medio Ambiente, 1996).

Generally speaking, the CSD thought that there was an overemphasis on the north–south divide. Besides, the Spanish document appeared to be departing from the Leipzig Principles, so the CSD withheld its approval. This was the first time since Corfu that a Presidency had been unable to obtain CSD approval. However, the four 'Madrid Criteria', as they were called, remained important, especially when it came to making maps for the Noordwijk document and formulating the 'Study Programme on European Spatial Planning' in 1998/1999 (Nordregio, 2000: 13–18).

At the ministerial meeting in Madrid in December 1995, as in Strasbourg, the submission of the Presidency drew scant attention. The Presidential Conclusions put a brave face on this, saying that ministers had welcomed it 'as a valuable input to the building of a shared vision'. As indicated, the bone of contention had been whether the time was ripe for policy options or not. The UK and the Presidency wanted to wait for more analyses to be carried out. Otherwise, most ministers were in favour of forging ahead with policy options. Nobody objected to policy options as such. The issue of whether to start formulating them would dominate the proceedings for a long time after Venice.

With reference to section D of the Leipzig Principles, the Conclusions stated that 'the options of the ESDP will not only include elements of national strategies'. Rather, 'also aspects closely related to transnational co-operation and Community policies ... [should] be incorporated in a European spatial planning vision which cannot be confined to the summing up of fifteen national visions'.

One firm decision was that a first draft of the ESDP should be completed within eighteen months and thus under the Dutch Presidency. Prior to the meeting, the Northern Group, now including France, had already come to this conclusion. The Commission gave its support, and other delegations could do little but approve. The Conclusions state that: 'The Italian and Irish Presidencies will stimulate the CSD's work in order to allow this deadline to be met'.

THE POSITION OF THE COMMISSIONER AND DG XVI

Commissioner Wulf-Mathies gave her second appearance, outlining the consolidated position of DG XVI. This prompted more discussion than the ESDP.

All delegations welcomed INTERREG IIC. Until 1999, the sum of 415 million ECU was set aside for this, along with 40–55 million ECU for Article 10 projects. This came in lieu of action areas proposed in Leipzig, on which the French consultant Robert (1995) had just compiled his report. That report was not opened up for official discussion but it was made available to delegates. On the whole, the action areas proposed in it were smaller than the INTERREG IIC programme areas. The latter are vast and between them cover the EU and beyond (Figure 6.2).

There was more business to do with the competency issue than anything else. In her intervention on 'The European Dimension of Spatial Planning', Wulf-

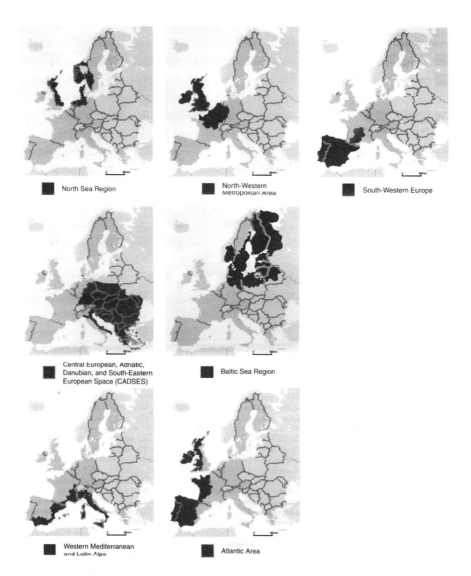

Figure 6.2 INTERREG IIC Areas 1997–2000 (Source: European Commission)

Mathies proposed to revise Article 130b of the EU Treaty to give the Community a role in spatial planning. She stated that, '[i]n view of the wording of Article 130b (…) the necessary competencies already exist at the Community level'. She held that:

> [t]he objective of strengthening of economic and social cohesion, formulated in Articles 130a and b of the Treaty, is the basis of the European dimension of

spatial planning (…) The structural action of the Community for reducing these [profound developmental gaps between the regions of the Community] has an important territorial impact.

In an effort to put the minds of the main beneficiaries of the Structural Funds at rest, the Commissioner emphasized that:

[t]he quantitative aspects of the Community's Regional Policy are discussed and arbitrated by specific bodies. On the basis of their decisions, to be taken as a starting point, European spatial planning can bring valuable and additional thoughts which focus on the nature of interventions and on their implementation methods, but not on their amounts (Wulf-Mathies, 1995).

The focus would be on qualitative instead of quantitative criteria. According to Wulf-Mathies, it was

necessary to agree on an approach making it possible to the various prospects concerned [with other policies having a territorial impact] and to examine them in the light of the common interest, by encouraging their coherence and co-ordination: it is what one can understand under the concept of spatial planning.

Although spatial planning would be related to regional policy, co-ordination with other Community policies was also being envisaged. She concluded by saying that this challenged European institutions, which is why it would 'be useful for a reference to be made in the Treaty'. Although Article 130s of the Treaty said something similar with regard to environmental policy, Article 130b was to be considered 'the most adequate to receive this complementary precision'.

The Commissioner and DG XVI were playing an interesting game. They were of the opinion that the Community already had a competency for spatial planning. The proposed treaty amendments were merely designed to clarify this. They would have expected France to be sympathetic to planning as an extension of regional policy. In Germany, Denmark and The Netherlands, spatial planning stood for something else, which was the co-ordinating of sectors. If anything, Dutch planners might have felt more comfortable if spatial planning had been attached to DG XI, the Directorate-General responsible for environmental policy (Fit and Kragt, 1994). However, as Wulf-Mathies' intervention made clear, DG XVI was moving towards spatial planning as the co-ordination of relevant policies, including those of the Community itself, so the ground was shifting.

What added to these complications was the fact that, as against the 1980s, member states were weary of Commission initiatives. The latter therefore had to put forward new proposals in the form of clarifications of existing provisions. Wulf-Mathies described the Commission's principal role as promoting the common European vision, in particular by supporting the development and updating of the ESDP. In parallel, it will develop a method of analysis and co-ordination for policies having an impact on the territory, making it possible to define the adjustments inherent to the envisaged exercise of co-ordination and of coherence. (...) Within the usual framework of partnership, finally, it will proceed to an operational implementation through its structural policies (Wulf-Mathies, 1995).

As in Strasbourg, member states were not on the same wavelength. Luxembourg, Sweden, Germany, The Netherlands and France were somewhat sympathetic to the position of the Commissioner. Portugal, Spain, Denmark, Greece and Italy kept a low profile. Ireland and the UK rejected her proposals. At any rate, it was clear that delegations had no mandate in the matter. In most member states, the position of spatial planning was (and still is!) weak. Besides, at the Inter-governmental Conference, momentous political issues were looming, like the EMU, enlargement and so forth. Governments had no time for minor but tricky issues like planning.

Out of the blue, Commissioner Wulf-Mathies came up with an alternative proposal that gained the support of the Presidency, suggesting that there had been prior contacts regarding this matter. It was to set up a 'high-level group' of personal representatives of ministers, whose task would be to identify and remove political obstructions that stood in the way of European spatial planning. The proposal came from the former member of the Delors cabinet responsible for spatial planning. It will be remembered that Delors had a predilection for *ad hoc* arrangements. Add to this the creative impatience that drove Wulf-Mathies, and the chemistry that produced this proposal becomes clear. To her the pace of work seemed painfully slow. It was difficult to attract public attention for planning issues. The member states were not helpful either. Some of them were positive, but often for reasons that had more to do with the domestic position of planning than with any empathy with the Commission. In this situation, a high-level group could have forced a breakthrough, Wulf-Mathies explained later. Reactions varied from cautiously positive to hostile. None of the member states could foresee all the ramifications, and so, although the Spanish Presidential Conclusions gave the impression of wide support, the high-level group was never formed.

The German delegation tabled a proposal. It was to reconstitute the CSD as 'a standing committee attached to the Council of the European Union', chaired, as indeed the CSD was, by the Presidency. The Germans did not like the CSD being treated as if it was a comitology committee. Naturally, the reconstituted CSD should continue to work on the ESDP. Besides, the CSD should 'give its views on the spatial implications of Community policies'. (See also Selke, 1999: 128.) However, this proposal received little attention, and the status of the CSD remained unresolved. The Observatory was not even on the agenda, and would not reappear before 1997.

VENICE: CONFIRMING THE DECISION TO GO AHEAD

In the wake of Madrid, there was much discussion as to whether the ESDP should indeed be completed under the Dutch Presidency. Apparently, the agreement to that effect at Madrid had been less firm than the Dutch might have hoped. Also, the competency issue was still unresolved.

The Italians continued along the lines of their predecessors. They also announced that they would hold bilateral meetings with member states and the Commission. Having been charged with presenting a draft ESDP by mid-1997, their forthcoming Presidency began to weigh heavily on the Dutch delegation. An internal memo to their Director-General proposed to make a de facto start with the work and to treat the ESDP as a priority issue for the National Spatial Planning Agency. It may seem surprising that within their own agency, Dutch international planners could not always count on receiving full backing, or even an enthusiastic reaction from Dutch sector departments.

The Dutch welcomed the bilateral meetings. Up until then there had been few informal contacts between them and the Italians. The Dutch stressed the need for continuity, and wanted to link the ESDP to INTERREG IIC. Also, they expected to be invited to troika meetings even before becoming official members in mid-1996, six months before their Presidential term would start.

At the CSD in February 1996, Italy announced that it planned to continue ana-lyzing spatial trends, placing emphasis on the impact of globalization on the development of cities and their cultural heritage. The Italians considered cultural heritage to be important to them, so this was a good example of combining national interests with the pursuit of topics in the ESDP. Member states were once again put to work. They were presented with a questionnaire and a summary of the Spanish policy options, adjusted to better reflect the Leipzig Principles. On this basis, each member state was invited to add policy options. The Italian Presidency would then analyze the results.

The Commission presented 'terms of reference' for writing the ESDP, some-thing which the Dutch had requested, albeit informally. The Dutch wanted to take on consultants, so terms of reference would be useful. In passing on the terms of refer-ence to a select group of delegations, proposing to have bilateral meetings with them, the Commission sidelined the Italian Presidency. The Italians responded by angrily accusing the Commission of persistent attempts to take the lead. Other dele-gations, including the French, shared the Italians' misgivings. In the end, it was decided to discuss the terms of reference in the presence of the Italians. Due to these manoeuvres, the Dutch work programme suffered delays. To the relief of the Dutch, though, at the next meeting the problems were ironed out. The Dutch were also forging links with the Irish, who were due to hold the Presidency after the Italians.

What remains is to report on the last German foray to get the CSD formalized. Since Leipzig, the Germans had been fairly passive. Formalizing the CSD seemed to be the only issue able to arouse their interest. At any rate, the Commission Legal Service countered that a Council working party in an area without a Community competency was unprecedented. In Madrid, Wulf-Mathies had argued that existing treaty provisions implied a Community competency for spatial planning. However, member states had refused to contemplate the minor modifications, which were designed to clarify this. The Commission's new position was to reiterate to the member states their own original message, which was that the Community did not have competency in the matter. As the reader will learn, in time this would have consequences for the Observatory, or ESPON, as well as for the CSD.

The German position received a more extensive hearing than before. The Dutch promised to consult their Foreign Ministry, but this did not appear to lead anywhere. The Dutch priority was to complete the job of producing the ESDP.

With regard to the practical work carried out under the Italians, there was a startling variety of contributions, which elaborated upon the French and Spanish trend scenarios. The Italian synthesis amounted to a list of over one hundred policy options, ranked in hierarchical order from the Community to the local level. It proved difficult to identify issues that were essentially European. There was little attention for cross-border developments and the relationships between regions.

The Italians also presented maps. However, these were inaccurate, and member states therefore paid little attention to them. (In the run-up to Noordwijk the Dutch would try to produce a new map based on the same data, but to no avail.) The attention paid to the spatial structure of member states, the problems they faced and the instruments they used was positive. This enhanced mutual learning.

The Dutch regarded the Italian synthesis as helpful. It gave an overview of policy options and of the issues member states found important. It was only with regard to Chapter 4 of the Italian document, 'Beyond Venice', that questions arose. This chapter was distributed at the CSD immediately preceding Venice, too late for delegations to be able to comment. At the troika meeting two weeks later, to which France and The Netherlands had also been invited, the text had been adjusted to the satisfaction of all delegations. Still, not all noses were pointing in the same direction. Beneficiaries of the Structural Funds continued to hold out for yet more analysis. Most of the others, along with the Commission, wanted to make an immediate start with the ESDP. More definite policy options could be formulated 'on the fly', as it were, and at any rate, the first draft was to be no more than a phase in an ongoing process, and thus subject to future improvement and elaboration. Clearly, differences in working styles continued to intrude.

This led to the meeting of ministers in May 1996 in Venice, which focused solely on one issue: should the Dutch be given the definite go-ahead for their work on the ESDP? The Dutch minister was unusually blunt, demanding a clear answer. Miraculously, member states who had previously been 'sitting on the fence', such as Great Britain, Portugal and Ireland, were now forthcoming. Germany, Sweden and Luxembourg were outspoken in their support. Reluctant converts to the ESDP, like Spain and Italy, saw no other option but to comply with the wishes of the rest.

At Venice, linking INTERREG IIC to the ESDP was another issue. The Dutch were particularly keen on this. Even before taking shape, the ESDP was already beginning to act as a framework for concrete policies on which the Commission, and the member states under the additionality principle, were proposing to spend money.

As the Conclusions of the Presidency at Venice show, the Italians continued to have some reservations. In Madrid, the Commission had been involved in formulating the Conclusions. The Italians were determined not to allow this to happen and, as it was their right, they wrote the Conclusions themselves. There was no mention in them of the decision to present the draft during the Dutch Presidency. Nor was the link that many delegations saw with INTERREG considered worthy of a mention. Rather, the emphasis was on urban development and on the preservation of the cultural heritage. Indeed, Job *et al.* (2000: 143) regard the Italian study on the protection of the cultural heritage in member states as having formed the basis for EU-broad protection of the cultural heritage. The survey concerned issues like a systematic notion of the protection, development, classification and quantification of the cultural heritage, and it identified differences and similarities between the individual countries (Presidenza del Consiglio dei Ministri, Dipartimento per il Coordinamento delle Politiche Comunitarie, 1996). However, with regard to the ESDP itself, the Italian position was unclear.

CONCLUSIONS

Contrary to expectations, Leipzig had not been followed by a speedy conclusion of the ESDP process. Prepared under tremendous pressure, the French scenario exercise threw the process off balance. The Spanish and Italian Presidencies preferred to dwell on trend analyses. With regard to the form the ESDP would take and the position of the CSD, there had not been much progress either. The only innovation was the link forged with INTERREG. However, by a small majority, those in favour of proceeding carried the day. The Dutch were only too eager to produce the ESDP. Others were finally content to let them go ahead.

Another result which added impetus to the process was the role assumed by the troika, with the Commission acting as the secretariat as always, and at the same time its only permanent member. The credit for facilitating this new role for the troika goes to the Italians. It had been their unprecedented initiative to extend an invitation to the French and the Dutch to participate in the last troika meeting prior to Venice that had started the process. Until then the role of the troika had been fairly marginal. Presidencies had preferred to operate independently. From then on, the troika became an effective force, working according to a programme that spanned several Presidencies.

The Italian Conclusions made explicit mention of the role of the troika, and within days of Venice the troika indeed met, once again in the presence of the Dutch. It agreed on a work programme for producing the ESDP. This programme was fairly detailed, itemizing things to be done, specifying methods of work and giving a timetable until 9/10 June 1997, the date of Noordwijk. Every member state would be asked to submit proposals to the Commission in its capacity as the secretariat of the troika. On this basis, the Commission would prepare a document. As the next chapter shows, based on the spirit established under the Italians, Noordwijk was slated to become a collective effort.

CHAPTER 7

NOORDWIJK – A COLLECTIVE EFFORT

Producing the ESDP became the priority of the CSD, and so from here onwards this account will be about working methods and will contain discussions of a more technical nature. During the process, each and every delegation wanted to have a say (National Spatial Planning Agency, 2000). The Dutch in particular had to take the intervening Irish Presidency into account, which enforced the need for co-operation. This chapter discusses the practical work, paying special attention to the problem of maps. It then describes the resulting document and the conduct of the Dutch Presidency at Noordwijk. By that time, it was apparent that there was sufficient momentum to bring the process to its conclusion. Nobody at the time could know that it would take a further two years to achieve this goal.

THE ROAD TO NOORDWIJK

The willingness of the Irish to place their Presidency at the service of the collective effort was remarkable. Irish planning expertise was limited, though. CSD delegates came from the Ministry of Finance responsible for European matters and from the Environmental Ministry. Indeed, with the exception of one official who participated actively, Irish input was limited. At that time, planning in Ireland was simply low key. 'There are no planning authorities, plan types or planning procedures of any significance above local authority level, although eight regional authorities offer a degree of co-ordination' (CEC, 1999f: 25). However, in the wake of the ESDP, Ireland has made a start with national spatial planning (Healy, 2000).

In Venice, the Irish had already been supportive. After Venice, the Irish Minister of the Environment confirmed the positive stance taken by the junior minister standing in for him at the meeting. This occasion, a visit of the Dutch minister to Dublin, was congenial. The Dutch wanted to make their *tour des capitales* early on, during the Irish Presidency, and this received Irish approval.

The previous chapter showed how the troika became more effective under the Italian Presidency. Right at the beginning of the Irish Presidency, the CSD welcomed most proposals concerning the troika. (By then, of course, the Dutch were members of the troika in their own right, and not just guests.) It was clear that Part IV of the draft ESDP would go no further than indicating ways in which the final version could be implemented. The priority was to formulate concise policy options for Part III. The Portuguese specified that they would like long-term scenarios to be included. Other delegations did not see the relevance of this, but the Portuguese were insistent. In the end, 'the development of long-term scenarios' would be discussed in section II.E.3 of the Noordwijk document.

The working arrangements were considered to be important. At the suggestion of the Commission, the troika proposed three principles:

1.   *CSD sovereignty.* It was through the CSD that member states and the Commission would finalize the content and procedures of the ESDP. This included the assessment and final approval of all draft texts, maps and diagrams.

2.   *A mandate for the troika.* The troika was to present drafts for the CSD to deliberate on. In doing so, it would draw on various sources and take special care to use a consistent style of writing. For this reason, it would hold frequent meetings. Also, a writing group of three to four members was to be formed, who would remain in close contact and have the purely technical role of editing the work.

3.   *Inputs.* A distinction was made between 'horizontal' elements of general concern (for instance, defining policy options) and 'thematic' elements with a more specialist character (for instance, the role of cities and the spatial impact of Community policies). Horizontal elements were the responsibility of the troika as a whole. Thematic elements were dealt with either by member states or the Commission, where necessary drawing on consultants. However, consultants could not report directly to the CSD. Co-ordination remained the task of the troika.

CSD trust in the troika was something of a novelty. In this respect, what was significant was the composition of the troika. Ireland and Italy could both be counted upon to ensure that the ESDP did not impinge upon the allocation of the Structural Funds. The Netherlands, later joined by Luxembourg, was willing to contemplate such a link. As always, the Commission stood for continuity. The troika was therefore well balanced. However, the balance may have been more superficial than real. The Dutch put a project team of no fewer than eight to work. Other troika members could not match this effort.

These were hectic times. Memos in the records show that the Commission, which along with the Dutch should have the most resources at its disposal, was late in committing itself. This placed the Dutch in an even more prominent position. They also had the most outspoken ideas on how the work should be organized. The Commission wanted all member states to submit texts for the troika to edit. The Dutch's interpretation was that the CSD had delegated this task to the troika. To achieve this end, a division of labour was proposed between the troika and a 'writing group'. The main principle was that all texts for the CSD needed the consent of the whole troika. Otherwise, the troika was in danger of forfeiting the trust of the CSD. In the interest of progress, the Dutch asked for intensive interaction by phone, fax or e-mail (the latter becoming more and more common). It was also necessary to create an informal atmosphere, with no hidden agendas. The credo became: 'First write, then discuss!'.

A subsequent troika meeting focused on content. The Irish chairman, seconded by two officials from the Irish Finance Ministry, emphasized the need for indicators and definitions to make spatial planning policy more operational. The Dutch delegation and the Commission were in favour of a list of definitions but did not relish indicators. The Italian delegation, just one person in fact, tried in vain to push for a more analytical approach. In the end, the troika reaffirmed the fact that the Noordwijk document would be no more than a first draft. The Commission suggested structuring the policy Part (III) around maps. The Dutch, however, were not in favour. It was agreed that troika delegations should submit their ideas for Part III on policy options. In addition, the Dutch asked the Commission to provide the troika with an advance copy of the *First Cohesion Report*, at that time awaiting the approval of the College of Commissioners. With regard to the division of labour, sections of Parts I and II were each assigned to one delegation.

The CSD that met the following October made three decisions. First, it reaffirmed its belief in the troika taking the lead, on the condition that it maintained a transparent style of working. Second, it approved the division of labour outlined in Table 7.1. A third decision was that, in writing the first draft, each troika member was now free to consult other member states.

Table 7.1 Division of tasks

Part I Aims and objectives	Commission
Part II.A Definitions and indicators	The Netherlands
Part II.B & C SWOT analysis	Italy
Part II.D Impact Community policies	Commission
Part III Policy options	The Netherlands
Part IV Implementation	The Netherlands

Because they were responsible for Parts III and IV, (a task that, as regards Part III, was shared jointly with the troika), the Dutch were asked to organize bilateral meetings. The intended length of the document was another point of discussion. Opinions differed, but in the end the troika resolved that it should total about sixty pages. Furthermore, it was agreed that in December the troika would submit drafts of Parts I, II.A, II.B and II.C and a working paper on Part III on policy options. The CSD wished the troika good luck in producing the rest of the document.

Luck was one thing that the troika needed, but another was time. In September the writing group started with Part III, which proved by far to be the most difficult. Initially, the group tried to make good use of the Leipzig, Madrid and Venice documents. It did not take long for them to discover that these were less consistent than they had hoped for, and so the discussion on policy options started all over again. The writing group also discovered that they had to learn each other's professional languages. For those involved this was frustrating. For instance, a discussion in Rome on policy options took fourteen hours, with less than half a page of text to show for the effort.

Prior to the meeting of the CSD in October, the Irish delegation had screened the basic documents for 'single-word terms' and 'word groupings', coming up with a list of about 150, which was dubbed the 'ESDP dictionary'. Despite strenuous effort, troika members failed to agree on the meaning of all of them, and so section II.A on 'Definitions, indicators and methodology', which included a whole list of concepts, never made it into the ESDP. During later stages though, the mutual learning which resulted from this proved to be invaluable. It is a common experience of international planners that they have to make initial investments in mutual learning (Zonneveld and Faludi, 1997: 10–11).

Much precious time had been lost though, and the December date for the completion of the draft was rapidly approaching. The writing group met no less than six times and the troika met three times. In early November a draft of Part I was ready which set out the approach. The idea was to write Parts II and III simultaneously to make them into a coherent whole, but this proved problematic. The troika then proposed to start with Part II, which contained a SWOT analysis (SWOT standing for Strengths, Weaknesses, Opportunities and Threats). After all, Part III should have flowed on from this. However, this proved to be unhelpful and at a troika meeting in early December the Irish Presidency proposed a new strategy. The priority was to complete Part III first, which elaborated on the three 'spheres of activity'. After this, the writing group had only a few days to prepare its document for the CSD.

Due to added time pressure, the process had not been as transparent as intended. The Dutch, who had organized bilateral meetings, and used them as a means of disseminating information on the progress of their work, had no clear idea of what kind of reception their work would have. However, to the relief of the troika, the CSD was quite positive with regard to Part III, but several delegations asked for a closer link to be forged with INTERREG IIC. The Germans wanted to include developments in central and eastern Europe and wondered at the reasons for departing from the Leipzig document. They also proposed to add the six Leipzig Principles to the Noordwijk document as an appendix. The most profound change was the introduction of a third fundamental goal, 'Competitiveness of the European territory', along with the goals of economic and social cohesion and sustainability.

Delegations gave detailed comments in writing. In addition, most delegations wanted to see maps. This had been envisaged, and already in November a cartographic group had been formed, with the writing group co-ordinating its work. Germany, France, Italy and Spain offered expert assistance. From among the troika members, only The Netherlands and the Commission participated in this group. Both had made their member of the writing group available for co-ordination, alongside one or more cartographic experts.

The first two meetings of the cartographic group took place in The Hague and Brussels respectively in January 1997. The focus of Part III was on the maps. Each 'sphere of activity' (balanced polycentric development, parity of access, natural and cultural heritage) should be accompanied by at least one map, which illustrated the various policy options. The idea was to merge maps illustrating individual policy options into one overall map per 'sphere of activity'.

However, not every policy option lent itself for cartographic representation, and there were also problems concerning the comparability of data. Because of the diversity of the European territory, raw data did not provide sufficient information about specific regions and how their situations were perceived locally. This was true of statistics relating to the size of cities, for instance, which did not indicate a lot about their function. The group therefore searched for appropriate 'cartographic criteria'. Here, the Madrid criteria and the Strasbourg maps served a useful purpose.

In discussing the policy options, the troika followed a suggestion by the Commission to hold multilateral meetings. Four sessions were held, with three member states in each. The CSD insisted that each working session should assemble member states from various corners of Europe. This enforced the idea of Noordwijk as a collective effort. The sessions gave an excellent opportunity for mutual learning. They were moderated by a Dutch consultant and took place in Commission premises in February 1997. Each one lasted for a day and was chaired by a Commission official. The groups were France/Greece/Sweden, Austria/Spain/Finland, Denmark/UK/Portugal and Germany/Belgium/Italy. Troika members attended all meetings. Luxembourg had become a troika member by this time, but the Dutch still chose to retain the Italian member of the writing group, which clearly indicated that the group had become a team.

For the multilateral sessions, the writing group had prepared various drafts. The focus was on policy aims and options and how to implement them and on cartographic criteria for the maps, then still under development. The sessions were to result in lists of priorities and new conclusions.

The following week, the troika met to evaluate the outcomes. The sessions had fallen short of expectations. These were stressful times. Handwritten notes in the files tell the reader, first, that there was little time to document progress properly and, second, that more questions were raised than answered. A major issue was the political message and to whom it was to be addressed. There were also discussions on spatial planning concepts, like the 'compact' and the 'sustainable' city, and how, if at all, these should be invoked. It also became apparent that a number of policy options lacked a spatial dimension.

Part IV on implementation was entrusted to a German consultant otherwise working for Luxembourg (an arrangement that is still pertinent at the time of writing). Part II became the work of Dutch consultants. The writing group focused on Part III, clearly the most pressing concern. After all, 26 March was the date of the next CSD, which was less than a month away, and the intention was that the full draft should be discussed.

With less than three months to go until Noordwijk, in March Parts II and III were discussed in two rounds. In general, the delegations were positive about Part II on spatial developments in Europe. After the introductory sections devoted to 'Driving forces', such as demographic, economic and environmental trends underlying spatial development, a 'Thematic geographical analysis' according to the three 'spheres of activity', and an analysis of the 'Impact of Community policies' followed. The final section, 'Geographical integration', was an attempt at synthesizing the previous two. Comments concerned the academic style, the weak links with Part III and the length of the section; fifty-four pages in total. Its length was intentional, as a letter from the troika to the CSD explained. The troika had wanted to be clear about all territorial issues. The text would be edited and reduced in length later.

To keep Part II as concise as possible some delegations proposed to put the more detailed analysis of spatial trends into an appendix. Eventually, the Potsdam document would feature a part B with the analytical material, but in March 1997 this was not accepted. The most frequent criticism was that Part II lacked coherence and direction, and its central political message was lost.

Whereas most delegations restricted their comments to ideas as to how to proceed, Portugal, Spain and to a lesser extent Italy also focused on contents. They were still not wholly convinced by the idea of an ESDP as it stood. Thus, Portugal complained that, by carefully weighing the advantages and disadvantages against each other, the document failed to convey a clear message with regard to marginal areas. They proposed rhetorically to ask the unemployed for their opinions on the matter. They were also unhappy with section II.E, the synthesis, which overemphasized the centre–periphery structure of Europe. This must have been a surprise. After all, the Portuguese had always stressed their peripheral position. The Spanish agreed with the Portugese and they, along with the Italians, cast doubt on the manner in which some issues had been framed. They also wondered whether sufficient attention had been paid to the outcomes of previous Presidencies. The section on TENs was regarded as too negative; it had been written from a north-west European perspective, and they questioned the assumption that education, training and infrastructure provisions were sufficient to counter marginalization.

There were also criticisms with regard to Part III. The introduction was too long. The next sections elaborated upon the three 'spheres of activity' and the fourth section, III.D, on 'A territorial framework for policy application'. It made the distinction between geographical categories, such as 'outer peripheral areas with long coast lines including islands' and 'the larger central European area', where the ESDP could be applied differently, according to whether the focus was on the European, transnational or regional/local level. Since this last section was based upon the next section, II.E on 'Geographical integration', the delegations proposed to merge the two. Few comments actually concerned the three sections devoted to the 'spheres of activity' as such. Some delegations mentioned topics they wanted to see included and others clarified their reading of certain policy issues.

A fundamental comment on the notion of 'competitiveness' came from the Spanish delegation. As the reader will remember, the competitiveness of Europe had been introduced as an issue by the last Dutch Presidency in The Hague. After simply receding into the background, it was then re-inserted by them as the third fundamental goal in Part I. Their intention had been to counteract the emphasis on cohesion. As north-west Europe was the most competitive part of Europe, the topic was particularly relevant for this region. As a concept, cohesion fulfilled a mainly similar role, for the member states in southern Europe.

The potential implication of 'competitiveness' as an ESDP goal was Community funding for north-west Europe. At least, that was how Spain viewed the issue. The Spanish delegation therefore proposed to modify the concept into 'balanced competitiveness'. The adjective was meant to signify that competitiveness as a concept did not only apply to the core of Europe. In these discussions, the Commission was acting as an intermediary. The CSD accepted the Spanish proposal, and so the Noordwijk document describes one of the three overall goals as that of 'balanced competitiveness of the European Union'. Some readers may feel that this is a meaningless concept, but this kind of compromise is inevitable in international co-operation.

By March, the CSD had been presented with a set of maps for Parts II and III. It had been intended that the maps would go further than descriptions in conveying some sort of vision for the future. Naturally though, the way in which the territories of various member states had been portrayed in the maps had drawn many comments, leading to numerous proposals to include specific features of one or more member states. It had become difficult to reduce the complexity of the maps. The following section will discuss the 'problem of maps' in greater detail.

A lot of attention was given to the headings of parts and sections. The multilateral sessions had led to many of them been revised. For instance, the heading of Part III, 'Policy Orientations for the European Territory', had been changed into 'Policy Priorities for the European Territory'. This apparently small amendment incurred the wrath of many. 'Priorities' suggested a firmer agreement than had actually been achieved. So the heading became 'Policy Aims and Options for the European Territory'.

All delegations were asked to submit written comments. On the whole they were between three and six pages in length and of quite a detailed nature, including text proposals. Two members of the troika, the Dutch polyglot planner from earlier chapters and a Commission official, neither of whom had been on the writing group, retreated for the weekend to the home of the Commission official to edit the March draft.

The final CSD took place on 6 and 7 May, after which delegations once again sent in their comments. In general these were positive. The issue was whether Part IV should be included, which gave no more than the bare bones of the follow-up of the ESDP. Although people could find little reason to object to what it said, Part IV was still quite sketchy, and the fear was that it might be misinterpreted. Eventually, though, the text went forward.

THE PROBLEM OF MAPS

Up until the very last moment, maps remained controversial. One suggestion at the multilateral sessions had been to leave out the maps in Part III. No agreement had been possible on the use of symbols, something that had been under discussion since the cartographic group had started work. For Part II existing maps would have to do. These were sent to the CSD at around the time of the March meeting. The CSD argued for more selectivity. For the meeting in May one new map was added, and the Dutch Presidency announced that it also wanted to include sketchy diagrams, not maps (Figure 7.1). Implying that the Dutch were already aware of the likelihood of heated discussions, they added: 'Everybody knows, however, how difficult it is to reach an agreement on such illustrations for policy relevant parts of the ESDP'. Further down the Dutch note added: 'Attached you will find two examples of illustrations for Part III.A–C that are now in the process of being finalized. For now they just give an *impression of the types of illustrations you can expect*' (italics original). This was followed by an apology, as certain materials contributed by member states had not yet been included. All in all, the cautious tone illustrated the tensions which surrounded the issue of maps, particularly where they concerned policy. In the end these illustrations did not make it into the Noordwijk document, but there is some resemblance to the icons in the policy chapter of the Potsdam document (see Figure 9.1).

The premonitions of the Dutch proved to be correct. Member states had different perceptions of the spatial structure of Europe and of their positions in it. The representation of the size and position of towns and cities was criticized. The Belgian and UK delegations felt that there was insufficient consensus on the meaning of the

Figure 7.1 Dutch proposal for a cartographic illustration (Source: National Spatial Planning Agency archives)

terms 'metropolis', 'agglomeration', 'gateway', 'rural area' and 'urban network'. To make things worse, the delegations found many inaccuracies. According to the British, for instance, important ports were missing, and according to the Belgians a number of so-called 'main transport axes' were not as important as the draft map made them appear.

Naturally, delegations focused on the representations of their own territories, which they then compared with those of others. Thus, the Belgians insisted that, next to the Randstad and the Ruhr area, the Flemish Diamond had to be included, whereas the French wondered aloud whether British cities like Belfast, Cardiff, Edinburgh and Berwick-upon-Tweed really deserved the label 'cities of international importance'. In the end, the maps were not included. Instead, four non-committal maps were put in the appendix, with the ominous proviso on each of them (Figure 7.2):

> This representation is only an illustration of certain spatial elements referred to in the text of the 'First Official Draft' of the ESDP. [...] They in no way reflect actual policy proposals and there is no guarantee that the elements displayed are exhaustive or entirely accurate (CEC, 1997b).

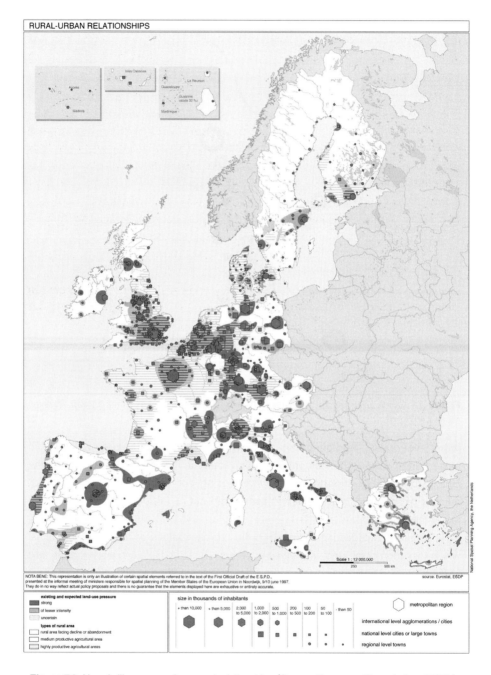

Figure 7.2 Noordwijk map on urban–rural relationships (Source: European Commission, 1997b)

Perhaps the best illustration of the difficulties surrounding maps is the tale of Figure II.1. This went through various permutations. The Dutch must have sensed what was coming. An early draft, which can still be found in the archives, bears the ominous note 'Migraine map' scribbled in pencil. The next version (Figure 7.3) gives a seemingly innocent view of Europe, showing the distances between Greece, Ireland, Finland and Spain, the seas and mountain ranges, which form barriers in-between, as well as the core of Europe, indicated by an elliptical shape. Southern Europeans were not amused. The map reflected a centre–periphery model of Europe (an early version in the files even carried this title), a juxtaposition of strong and weak regions. In the beginning it had of course been the southern Europeans who had identified disparities as the central issue. However, to represent this in map form was controversial. The compromise was to leave out the elliptical shape representing the core of Europe. This version can be found in the Noordwijk document.

Another map called 'territorial framework', on which the cartographic group had spent most of its energy, was rescinded altogether (Figure 7.4).

Zonneveld (2000: 278–9) describes it in some detail. It differentiated between urban and rural areas with a stronger and weaker economic structure. Zonneveld says that this was seen as 'stigmatizing those regions and member states which were

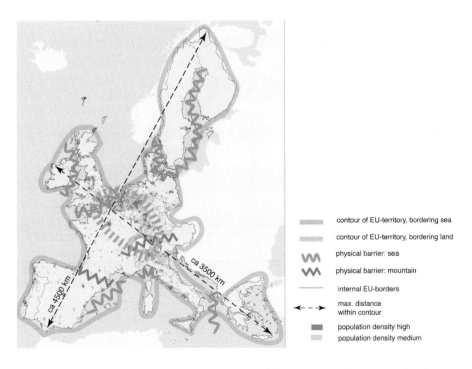

Figure 7.3 Original Figure II.1 with the core of Europe (Source: National Spatial Planning Agency archives)

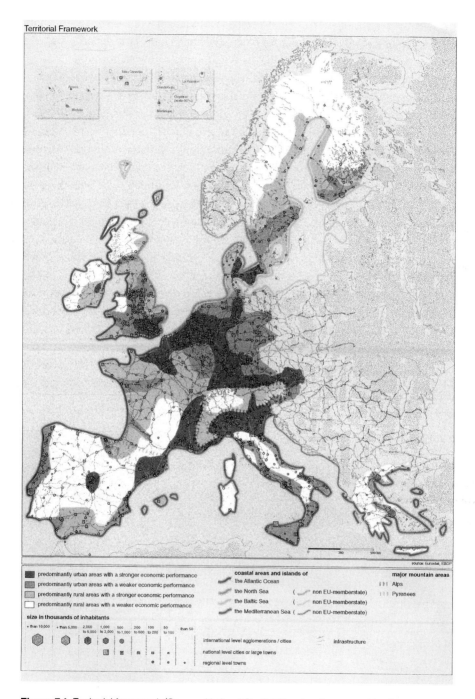

Figure 7.4 Territorial framework (Source: National Spatial Planning Agency archives)

not part of the European core'. As with Figure II.1, this was a concern. Nevertheless, the map almost made it into the Noordwijk document: all the comments made on an earlier version had been assimilated. In the end though, the Spanish delegation were determined to veto the map. At that time, with the restructuring of the Structural Funds on the agenda and the influence the ESDP might have on them uncertain, the Spanish delegation had no mandate to negotiate on this point. The Dutch were disappointed at the rejection of the map, not only because of the effort they had put into producing it, but more so because they believed that spatial planning was difficult to accept without these sorts of maps.

THE 'FIRST OFFICIAL DRAFT' OF THE ESDP

Much of what is in the Noordwijk document (CEC, 1997b) corresponds with the document of Leipzig, as discussed in Chapter 5. The two documents have the same structure and address the same issues (Table 7.2). However, comprising eighty six pages, the Noordwijk draft is more elaborate. Also, the Leipzig document had been

Table 7.2 The Noordwijk document: the 'First Official Draft' ESDP

Parts	Sections
I. The spatial approach at the European level	1. The basic goals 2. Its raison d'être 3. A document on policy options 4. The status of the ESDP 5. An approach to spatial policy in Europe 6. Promoting co-operation
II. Spatial issues: the European dimension	1. Introduction 2. Fundamental starting points for a spatial approach 3. Spatial issues of European significance 4. The impact of Community policies on the European territory 5. Further work on the spatial analyses
III. Policy aims and options for the European territory	1. Towards a more balanced and polycentric system of cities and a new urban–rural relationship 2. Parity of access to infrastructure and knowledge 3. Prudent management and development of the natural and cultural heritage 4. Framework for integrated spatial policy
IV. Carrying out the ESDP	1. The first phase of implementation 2. Holding the debate

addressed to the CSD and the ministers while the *First Official Draft* addressed a more general audience (Figure 7.5).

Part I of the *First Official Draft* explained the basic political goals, rationale, status, focus and contents of the ESDP. The rationale was the same as before, but the two basic goals of Leipzig had been supplemented with a third goal, that of balanced competitiveness, which is on a par with the other two. The single market had been the chief reason for formulating a spatial planning strategy, and it was still

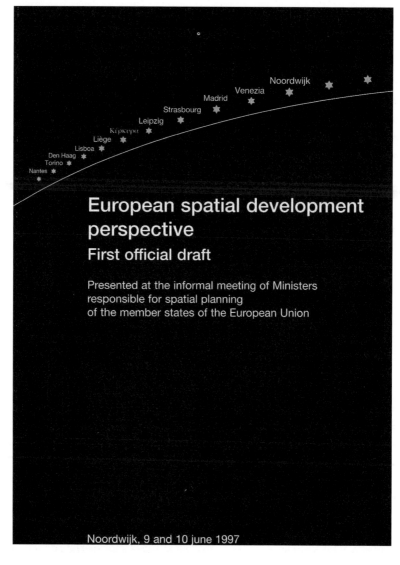

Figure 7.5 The Noordwijk document: the 'First Official Draft' of the ESDP

being invoked as a rationale for the ESDP. It is clear that not all regions were deriving equal benefits from it. Thus the 'spatial approach' aimed at: 'a better balance between competition and co-operation so that the whole European territory can reach the optimum level of competitiveness' (ibid. 2). In other words, the objective was to contribute to the fundamental goals of the EU Treaty by approaching them from a spatial or territorial point of view. The ESDP was intended:

> to be the expression of a shared vision of European territory as a whole, a
> common reference framework for action, and to guide the relevant authorities in
> policy formulation and implementation. It is also intended to be a positive step
> towards commitment to, and participation in, an on-going political process of
> discussion and guidance for decision making at the European level (ibid. 3).

Its influence would be long term. Concerning its status, the Noordwijk document emphasized that it was not binding; it was flexible towards existing authorities and it did not aim at a new Community competency. Nevertheless, the ESDP 'can serve the purpose of a better co-operation between member states, as well as between them and the Commission' (ibid. 5). In fact, the underlying idea was for territory to become a common denominator of what was called a new 'social contract'. Co-operation was the keyword throughout.

Part II gave an analysis of the European territory. A short introduction explained the philosophy behind it, making reference to three paramount elements:

> Firstly, European issues are above all, but not solely, those that occur at the con-
> tinental and transnational levels. They also include issues manifesting
> themselves at the regional and local levels … The common interest provides the
> European dimension … Secondly, the issues refer not only to problems and
> threats arising from certain weaknesses, but also to opportunities arising from
> certain strengths of the territory. Thirdly, a spatial approach is essentially a
> dynamic, forward-looking approach. The issues identified arise, therefore, mainly
> from emerging trends and not solely from existing situations (ibid. 9).

A short section gave the basic geographical characteristics of Europe. Figure II.1, which had been problematic, was included in this part. As indicated, it did not show the core of Europe. However, Europe's core was described verbally. 'The shape alone, with its fragmented character due to mountains, peninsulas and islands, gives rise to an inherent centre–periphery dichotomy.' Furthermore, a verbal conceptualization of diversity was given: 'striking climate contrasts from North to South and the related diversity of landscape and natural vegetation add to the basic picture of European geography' (ibid. 10). Three trends that affected the future spatial development of Europe were then identified: demographic trends and urban development, trends in the European economy and long-term environmental trends. Part II continued by discussing spatial issues of European significance, more or less on the lines of Leipzig, *Europe 2000*, *Europe 2000+* and the various Presidency documents. On a general level, an understanding of such issues was shared. Changes in urban structures, in the role and function of rural areas, in transport, communication and knowledge were discussed, as well as the pressures on Europe's cultural and natural heritage. All issues were accompanied by a SWOT analysis.

The text continued by analyzing the impact of Community policies on the European territory. Although this issue had been addressed many times before, this was the first attempt by DG XVI to provide an overview. The policies that were evaluated were agriculture, the structural and cohesion policies, the trans-European networks and environmental policy. As expected, the conclusion was that the policies were anything but neutral. In particular, the policies aiming at increasing European competitiveness focused on the more prosperous regions. A common feature of these policies was the absence of a spatial dimension in the decision-making process. Thus, there was a potential for the ESDP to help with improving co-ordination.

Part III started by explaining how the policy options had been formulated. Next to the three spheres of activity, four general criteria for identifying options had been specified: the options had to have a spatial dimension and a European dimension, they had to attract the interest of member states and, finally, they had to be feasible and potentially effective. As the ESDP itself recognized, since many options were quite 'sectoral', section III.D needed to give an integrated framework. A total of forty-six policy options was listed, divided into twelve sections. Examples are: 'Promotion of integrated spatial development strategies for clusters of towns, particularly in cross-border areas' (ibid. 55); 'Development of the European strategic role of global cities and of "gateway cities", with a particular attention to outer parts of the European territory' (ibid. 56). But there were also options like: 'Improvement of the level of general education and vocational skills as a part of integrated development strategies in regions where this level is low' (ibid. 64).

The section on the first sphere of activity, 'Towards a more balanced and polycentric system of cities and new urban–rural relationship', consisted of five sub-sections, three more than in the Leipzig document. They promoted networking and co-operation between towns and cities and making optimal use of complementarities. Greater attention was given to individual cities and towns, from the perspective of enhancing their attractiveness, whilst at the same time keeping an eye on sustainability. Also, partnerships between town and countryside were discussed, as well as the diversification of rural areas. All in all, the section's underlying philosophy was one of individual cities and regional urban networks assuming responsibility for their economic and social development. It also advocated using their endogenous potential and linking up with other cities and regions in order to share benefits. Clearly, what was prevalent was the conceptualization of a diversified Europe.

In fact, only 'gateway cities' (large seaports, intercontinental airports, cities where fairs and exhibitions were held, and cultural centres) were recognized as contributors to a more balanced economic development of the EU. With regard to this issue, a row erupted just before the document was due to go into print. Anticipating problems with the Ministries of Economic Affairs and Transport, the Dutch delegation wanted to tread softly on the issue, ensuring a more even distribution of large seaports throughout Europe. The Commission, however, wanted to go much further in securing a more even distribution, and so compromises had to be found. The Dutch delegation were right to anticipate trouble on their home front. In the spring of 1998, even the modest formulations in the Noordwijk document would incite strong reactions from other departments, who accused the planners of squandering Dutch national assets, such as the Port of Rotterdam (Waterhout and Zonneveld, 2000a, b). In the end the other ministries would get the upper hand and so only months before Potsdam, the Dutch delegation would be forced to backtrack on all previous pronouncements.

As opposed to the previous one, the section on 'Parity of access to infrastructure and knowledge' was based on a more centre–periphery, or one-dimensional view of Europe. It did not go beyond what had been discussed in Turin, The Hague, Lisbon and Leipzig. The accessibility of peripheral and ultra-peripheral areas, and also that of congested areas in the centre needed to be improved. What were referred to as 'infostructures' in the Leipzig document now fell under the heading 'Information society'.

With regard to the third sphere of activity, 'Prudent management and development of the natural and cultural heritage', there was more attention than had previously been given to the management of water resources. *Europe 2000* had already signalled the importance of water resources, but Leipzig had failed to pay much attention to this issue. Presumably because of the flood and drought problems in the mid-1990s, this issue now received more prominence. A distinction was also made between cultural landscapes on the one hand and cultural heritage in cities on the other.

Part IV, 'Carrying out the ESDP', was more like a work programme. Because of its non-binding nature, 'implementation on a voluntary basis will have to play a major role in the future' (ibid. 79). As will later become evident the makers of the ESDP would eschew the use of the concept of implementation, referring to the 'application' of the ESDP instead. At any rate, there would be numerous players involved. The ESDP process was an ongoing one, and its application should start straightaway:

> The transformation of the present 'first official draft ESDP' into a revised and democratically validated version of the 'first official ESDP' should build on three major interrelated inputs:

- a wide political debate;
- innovative and experimental actions;
- the establishment of a solid technical support.

(ibid. 79)

The last point referred to ESPON, the European Spatial Planning Observatory Network. The rest of Part IV elaborated on the organization of the wider political debate, to be discussed more fully in Chapter 8.

THE CONDUCT OF THE DUTCH PRESIDENCY

Naturally, the aim of the Dutch was to get the draft accepted. The strategy had been to defend Part III, which formed the core of the ESDP, at all costs. Parts I and II were considered unproblematic. Part IV was tentative and due to be completed under the Luxembourg Presidency, so changes to it were considered acceptable.

In her opening speech, the Dutch minister Margaretha de Boer emphasized the theme of competitiveness. She pointed out the importance of establishing a balance between healthy competition and free market forces on the one hand and co-operation on the other, thereby strengthening the complementarity of regions, towns and cities.

Rather than focusing on content, de Boer expressed more concern for the status of the Noordwijk document and how to continue with the process, in particular how and where the implementation of the ESDP could and should take place. The minister emphasized that the document did not replace existing policies. Rather, the ESDP ventured to generate new insights into how to improve the effectiveness of policies from a spatial point of view. In particular, the ESDP made no case for complicated planning procedures at the Community level, and it did not have a role in the pending revision of the Structural Funds. The minister saw INTERREG IIC as offering opportunities for realizing projects and for gaining experiences with respect to a territorial, multi-sectoral form of policy making at supra-national level. In achieving this, the role of sub-national authorities was important.

With the Dutch minister chairing the meeting, the task of leading the Dutch delegation fell to the Director-General, a seasoned participant well-known to delegates from the Dutch Presidency of 1991. She emphasized the fact that, despite the ESDP's non-binding nature, ministers and the Commissioner were about to enter a political commitment.

As is well known, Part IV had a different status to the first three parts. Nevertheless, the Director-General attached much importance to it. A measure of its effectiveness was the quality of the debate engendered by the ESDP and the extent to which it was able to generate consensus.

The German minister Klaus Töpfer was also positive about Part IV. It gave an excellent picture of the diversity among member states. Nonetheless, he made six suggestions for improvement. He wanted to strengthen the link between the ESDP and INTERREG IIC and to give consideration to the 'Observatory', an issue on which there had been no progress, despite firm commitments at Leipzig. A further three recommendations concerned the issue of making cross-border co-ordination of plans and policies mandatory, and a European 'Territorial Impact Assessment', as it would subsequently be called. This would enable neighbouring states to assess the potential cross-border impacts of any large-scale projects. Next came the well-worn issue of formalizing the CSD and the ministerial meetings. The final German proposal was that future discussions should include the twenty-five members of the Council of Europe, who were not members of the European Union.

The Spanish were in a contentious mood. At the CSD immediately preceding Noordwijk, Spain had even suggested that the ESDP be presented as a document of the Presidency, instead of as a CSD document, following the method established in Corfu. This would, of course, have put the whole exercise in jeopardy. At Noordwijk the Spanish asked point blank whether there would be a link between the ESDP and the review of the Structural Funds. Commissioner Wulf-Mathies replied that the ESDP would have no impact on the allocation of funds. The impact of the ESDP would be limited to the implementation of the policy concerning the Structural Funds. Eventually, as Chapter 10 will make clear, this would indeed be the case; the Commission would make frequent references to the ESDP when implementing its policies.

What was new and heartening was the attitude of the British after the election of a Labour government, only weeks prior to Noordwijk. The change in British atti-tude was so radical that, when asked about the effect of the change in government, the British chief delegate to the CSD related in an interview that he simply started saying the exact opposite of what he had said before. From this point onwards the UK was unambiguously enthusiastic about the ESDP, and Richard Caborn, a senior cabinet minister, cheerfully announced his intention of completing the ESDP under the UK Presidency in 1998. Others welcomed the British to the fold.

However, ministers had also agreed to hold the proposed far-ranging consul-tations on the ESDP. To organize these consultations and draw conclusions from them within the space of one year was indeed ambitious, so the reader will not be surprised to learn in Chapter 9 that finishing the ESDP took longer than anticipated.

The Conclusions of the Dutch Presidency started with the repetition of the belief that inter-governmental co-operation was what the ESDP was about. The ESDP had demonstrated that there was a spatial planning dimension to Community policies and also to policies at a European, transnational or cross-border level. Ministers had considered the ESDP 'to be a source of inspiration and ideas for policy makers'. They recommended it as

> a basis for political discussion on how European spatial policy can contribute to the integration of cohesion, sustainability and global competitiveness; as a framework for reinforcing the relationship between policies aimed at urban and rural areas; in introducing a more integrated, multi-sectoral approach to policies which influence spatial development at the cross-border, transnational and European level; as a framework for encouraging co-operation between European, national, regional and local administrations on matters relating to spatial development (Dutch Presidency, 1997).

Despite such compliments, ministers had also 'stressed that the ESDP is a non-binding reference document with no impact on the financial distribution resulting from Community policies such as the Structural Funds'. With a view to the future, the Commissioner and other ministers had promised to make the ESDP the subject of a broad political debate within member states, between member states at a transnational level and within the Commission. The intended drawing up of the 'formal ESDP document' (the reader should note that the ESDP had never been intended to become a formal Community document) was scheduled to take place prior to the end of the UK Presidency in 1998. It was therefore necessary to start the political debate immediately. The participants were not only the governments and administrations concerned; they also included NGOs and the business and academic communities. Whilst the consultations were taking place, the text and the maps should simultaneously be improved. INTERREG IIC was mentioned as a possible route for implementing the ESDP. Central and eastern European countries should also become involved. Finally, the Presidential Conclusions stressed the importance of updating the ESDP and deepening the current understanding of spatial trends. They welcomed a renewed initiative to set up the Observatory, expecting to receive proposals with regard to its organization and finance before the end of 1997.

CONCLUSIONS

Preparing the Noordwijk document had been a good experience. All delegations had been involved. The document carried sufficient conviction to satisfy everybody who wanted to go forward. With the UK throwing its weight behind the process, the future looked bright. Although for political reasons Britain had previously been hard to deal with, there had always been a great deal of respect for British professionalism. UK planning had strengthened its professional base during the Thatcher and Major years and there was much to be gained from the British input.

However, there was still the disaffection of Spain to deal with. In Spanish eyes, and in the eyes of other member states from southern Europe (see Rusca, 1998), the *First Official Draft* represented a north-west European agenda. Apparently, it had taken face-to-face discussions with the Dutch minister for the Spanish to approve the Noordwijk document. Spain would only relent after the Berlin Summit of March 1999, which settled the issue of the allocation of the Structural Funds.

The finale of the Inter-governmental Conference 1995/1996, which led to the Treaty of Amsterdam, followed shortly after Noordwijk. As will be remembered, both the Commission and the Germans had wanted it to address the competency issue, although for different reasons. The Commission had wanted to amend Article 130b and the Germans had hoped to include a protocol requiring the Community to respect the competencies and the spatial policies of the member states. Neither of them received a hearing at Amsterdam (Selke, 1999: 118–19, 128). The competency issue remained as unresolved as ever.

CHAPTER 8

GLASGOW AND THE CONSULTATIONS – TWO PARALLEL TRACKS

The UK Presidency had set its sights on concluding the business of the ESDP at a meeting in Glasgow in May 1998. Luxembourg's Presidency, in the second half of 1997, had given them six months breathing space. Such partnerships had become popular. However, it did not take long for British hopes of finishing the ESDP to evaporate. The next Presidency was being held by a new member state, Austria, a country with no real federal planning (CEC, 2000e; Faludi, 1998) and with no wish to preside over a large-scale ministerial meeting, so in the end the task fell to the Germans. Their role in finishing the ESDP will be discussed in Chapter 9.

Like Chapter 7, this chapter deals with practical arrangements and the daily work of international planners; it also describes the consultations. As one might have guessed, these consultations lasted quite a long time. The transnational semi-nars culminated in an ESDP Forum in Brussels, which took place approximately three months before Potsdam. Before venturing to describe the details, it is neces-sary to explore the opportunity structure of UK national planning.

THE UK OPPORTUNITY STRUCTURE

With planning an ideological issue in the UK, unlike that of any other country, the opportunity structure for UK planning is shaped by the predilection of the govern-ment in power. For example, under the Conservative government the UK took a back seat in the ESDP process. With the exception of the *Compendium* initiative, staying out of the way was probably the best course of action available to the British CSD delegation. With the coming of a Labour government into power, the opportunity structure changed radically, and UK planners were enthusiastic. However, this occurred at a late stage in the process, and they could do little else but bring their expertise to bear on the elaboration of the existing draft. It was too late to help shape the process, as such. Perhaps more significant than the making of the *Complete Draft*, which is the subject matter of this chapter, is the seriousness with which the UK treats the application of the ESDP, now that it has been completed.

Under the Conservative government, planning had been restricted to what the *Compendium* describes as the 'land-use management' tradition (with the UK being the main example) 'where planning is more closely associated with the narrower task of controlling the change of use of land at the strategic and local level' (CEC,

1997a: 37). Planning had not been a vehicle for social and economic policies, and the impact of Community policies on it was considered negligible (Tewndwr-Jones *et al.*, 2000: 658). However, whenever possible, local authorities had exploited opportunities for European partnerships (Eser and Konstadakopulos, 2000: 794). At any rate, availing themselves of the opportunities of the centralized UK system, the Conservatives had introduced so-called Planning Policy Guidance notes (PPGs; these differ somewhat in Scotland, Wales and Northern Ireland). They were used to ensure that even reluctant local authorities released sufficient land for development.

The Conservatives had been against the devolution of power to the constituent parts of the UK and/or to English regions. However, since the very beginning, the UK had been a recipient of Structural Funds. (Indeed, the Structural Funds had taken their present form precisely in order to give the UK some benefits from EC membership which it could not obtain under the Common Agricultural Policy, at that time the only large spender of funds.) Thus, following Community regulations, the UK was obliged to set up some form of regional organization, which in England took the form of Government Regional Offices. (For Scotland, Wales and Northern Ireland, such offices already existed.) A Regional Planning Guidance (RPG) was published for each region. As of April 1998, Tewdwr-Jones *et al.* (2000: 656–7) reported the existence of twenty-four PPGs (two equivalent statements for Wales and eleven in Scotland) and eleven RPGs in England alone.

Labour had promised devolution as part of its election campaign. When it came into power, the Labour government published *Modernising Planning*, a policy statement which emerged at the same time as the Glasgow meeting (DETR, 1998). Related aspects were constitutional reform (devolution of decision making and governance to the regional level) and strengthening relations with Europe. The system of PPGs and RPGs, inherited from the Thatcher years, was retained (Alden, 2000).

Richard Caborn (the Minister who had made such a splash at Noordwijk) felt that the European context had largely been lacking in UK planning, and that there needed to be 'a significant European dimension to our planning system' (Quoted from Shaw, 2000: 1–2). Nowadays, under *Planning Policy Guidance Note 11* (DETR, 1999) regional bodies, in preparing a draft RPG (which becomes a formal RPG upon approval by the Secretary of State of the Environment) must take account of the ESDP. In fact, in the absence of a national spatial development perspective, identified by the Royal Town Planning Institute as a shortcoming of UK planning (Wong *et al.*, 2000), the ESDP acts as a surrogate framework. As a result of this, the UK has given the ESDP a far greater status than many other countries. This explains the UK's enthusiasm towards the ESDP, ever since its publication. Professionalism has always been a top priority, which, as Healy (2000) observes, has allowed UK authorities to catch up swiftly with their European counterparts. Undoubtedly, more will be heard about UK contributions to European planning. At any rate, in research and as consultants, the British have always had a strong presence.

GLASGOW AND THE 'COMPLETE DRAFT'

Following Noordwijk, the course of action was quite clear: Parts II and IV needed to be completed and improved and Parts I and III had to be revised. In order to have several language versions available by May, the text had to be ready by February 1998. To expedite the process, the troika held another round of multilateral sessions in September 1997. The run-up to Noordwijk had produced a set of practical working arrangements, which subsequent Presidencies continued to practise.

The agenda for the multilateral sessions comprised four items. First, there was a Commission proposal on the post-Noordwijk process: the consultations within member states and the Commission and the wider public consultations. A second proposal concerning the 'mandate of the group of experts' came from the Dutch. After all, the writing group and the cartographic group had shown themselves to be examples of successful delegation in the run-up to Noordwijk. The third item on the agenda concerned ESPON, which will be discussed in Chapter 10. The fourth item related to the outcomes of a questionnaire sent to member states, which related to the implementation of the ESDP in Part IV.

During these sessions it became apparent that the debates in the member states would not be concluded in time for Glasgow. However, the revision of Part II and Part IV and the accompanying maps, undertaken by an 'expert group' consisting of one representative per member state, were in fact accomplished on time. From that point onwards, the post-Noordwijk process took on a different form than had been anticipated. First of all it comprised the work by the expert group, and secondly there were the parallel consultations, to be completed after Glasgow.

It also transpired that several Commission services had asked for a further elaboration of the text on the spatial impact of Community policies. The Noordwijk text, which concerned this issue, had been written by DG XVI, and was based upon the opinions of member states. Other Directorates-General had had no say in the matter and so, reiterating an old wish, member states urged the DG XVI officials to explore the issue in more depth, as they had already promised a long time previously. Eventually, at the ESDP Forum in Brussels in the spring of 1999, the Commission Services would indeed submit a *Report on Community Policies and Spatial Planning*, to be discussed on pages 131–133.

It was envisaged that this report, along with the enlargement of the EU, were both to be covered in the Glasgow document. This would be the task of the expert group. Contrary to the Dutch proposal, troika members formed a 'core group', which prepared documents and maps for the expert group. The further elaboration of Part III, dealing with policy options and the related maps, was seen as the task of the whole CSD. However, work on this could not start before the consultations had finished. Moreover, since the role of ESPON (expected to come into operation around June 1998, rather optimistically as it turned out) involved assisting with the maps, the work was postponed until after Glasgow.

Spain requested that there be short appendices, with information on the spatial planning policies of each country, including a SWOT analysis. Other member states were reluctant, suggesting that such national contributions could be used to update the *Compendium*, based as it was on the 1994 situation. (At that time the national volumes of the *Compendium* were not yet published. At the time of writing, the majority of them are out, and have been referred to throughout this book.)

Discussions at the multilateral sessions also covered the future of the process, in particular the anticipated revision of the ESDP. Representing a long-term strategy, member states thought that a revision once every five to ten years would suffice. Apparently, it was a foregone conclusion that the ESDP would be revised. (As Chapter 10 will show, this revision, and in particular the form it will take, is now uncertain.) The Commission, seeing the ESDP as always in relation to its own policies relating to the Structural Funds, proposed to revise it one or two years ahead of the final decision on Programming Periods. This would give the ESDP an opportunity to become what it was really intended to be, a framework for Community policies. It was decided that the first ESDP should be available in 1998 or 1999 and the revision in 2004 or 2005. To dispel any misgivings felt by the beneficiaries of the Structural Funds, the Commission was quick to reiterate that the ESDP would have no influence whatsoever on the distribution of funds, only on their application.

The minutes of the multilateral sessions relate that, along with the periodic review of the ESDP, member states also considered the idea of producing interim documents of a more operational nature to facilitate its continuous elaboration. Examples were the expected *Report on Community Policies and Spatial Planning* by the Commission and 'Spatial Planning Action Programmes', which set targets for spatial development and identify mechanisms for monitoring and evaluation.

An inconclusive discussion concerned the title of forthcoming ESDP versions. To avoid endless permutations of the term 'draft', and to strengthen its political appeal, it was suggested that the title should be combined with the year of approval, such as *ESDP 2005*. Not all member states were in favour of this, because it would create the impression of a final document rather than a step in a process. The title or subtitle should rather convey the idea of the ESDP being subject to periodic review, such as *ESDP: reference document for the period 2000–2006*, or *ESDP … To be revised in 2011*.

After the multilateral sessions the UK Presidency gave the ESDP an editorial overhaul. Beyond this, the limited mandate and the pressure of time meant that effort had to be focused on Part IV. One problem was that the continuation of the consultations beyond Glasgow meant that the discussions would be based on the outdated Noordwijk draft rather than on more recent versions. The analysis in Part II and the accompanying maps became the responsibility of the expert group, chaired by a senior official from Scotland.

The core group, who were doing the actual work, consisted of one Dutch and one British expert, a German expert representing Luxembourg and a Scottish chairperson. They were all relatively new to the process, with the exception of the Dutch cartographer, who had been party to the Noordwijk process. This group restructured Part II, proposing additional maps and diagrams. Meeting frequently, the members forged good personal relationships. (Prior to a meeting in Edinburgh the chairman entertained them at his home.) Just as in the run-up to Noordwijk, some members who had officially ceased to be part of the troika still continued working in partnership with them.

Within the expert group, co-operation was also smooth. However, until January 1998, due to reorganizations taking place in the governments of some member states, attendance was a problem. Be that as it may, having been out of the process for some time, a witness with experience of earlier unsuccessful attempts to form efficient working relations professed his surprise with regard to the new spirit of co-operation. The setting was informal, and English was the working language. People trusted each other, they were doing their homework and the whole exercise seemed very useful.

At a CSD in February 1998, the British announced their intention to present ministers with a coherent and comprehensive final draft. The member states commented upon the revised Part IV. At the next CSD in April, drafts of both Part II and Part IV were on the table. In general, delegations welcomed the suggestions with regard to the analytical Part II, acknowledging that the text had become more descriptive and less political and deterministic. The analyses of environmental trends were more detailed. The ambitions of Part II.D on the spatial impact of Community policies were more modest. Some delegations welcomed the rescinding of the SWOT analysis. The text was also less technocratic and academic and was more user friendly.

Nevertheless, delegations were critical of the text on Community policies. This had been the responsibility of DG XVI. The text had still not been endorsed by other Commission services and so it merely reflected the views of member states. A number of them, supported by DG XVI, were in favour of reinstating the SWOT analysis and improving the internal consistency of the text. Once again, Spain asked for national appendices. With regard to maps, not all member states were equally happy. After the meeting, the core group received comments in writing.

Although the UK Presidency could still envisage improvements, most member states were satisfied with Part IV, on the application rather than the implementation of the ESDP, a distinction that will be commented upon in Chapter 10. The exceptions were Luxembourg, Denmark and The Netherlands, who felt that the tone was not assertive enough. To stimulate discussion, a more ambitious approach was in order; consensus could be reached later. Obviously, discussion cultures continued to differ.

A recurring point was the position of Part III.D on a framework for integrated spatial policy. Most delegations wanted to move it to Part IV on the application of the ESDP. After all, an integrated framework would sit uneasily with the enumeration of 'policy options', which was what Part III was about. However, the Dutch and Belgian delegations thought otherwise. They saw such a framework as political, thus belonging to Part III. Eventually, in the Potsdam document, the figure illustrating the framework would end up in the chapter on application. Furthermore, there was to be a link with the INTERREG IIC programme. All this persuaded the Presidency that the text needed improving.

The CSD in May 1998 was unusual. Without prior notice, the UK Presidency had revised the document. The *Complete Draft ESDP*, or the *Draft of the Draft*, as the British called it, now consisted of six chapters. The British decided to rename the parts as chapters and to exchange Roman for Arabic numerals. In addition, Part II was divided into three chapters on trends, issues and the impact of Community policies. Parts III and IV thus became Chapters 5 and 6. Some sections were left out altogether and others added. Being native speakers, the British had also 'polished' the text, including the introduction, the spatial planning approach at the European level and the chapter on policy options, both the object of the consultations.

The Presidency had gone outside its terms of reference, and most delegations felt uncomfortable with the new structure and the changes made to various sections. The senior planner who was responsible later blamed this on the late circulation of the *Draft of the Draft*. A German source felt that the British had operated in splendid isolation, departing from the established mode of using either the expert group or the troika. The source did not know how right he was: the senior British delegate had edited the *Draft of the Draft* in person, in the 'splendid isolation' of the early morning hours of a weekend.

The *Draft of the Draft* was rejected and the original Parts I and III of the Noordwijk draft were reinstated, with the addition of the latest version of Part II, as approved by the expert group, and of Part IV, as submitted at the previous CSD meeting. Together, they formed the *Complete Draft ESDP*, in which the numbering of parts and paragraphs was identical to the Noordwijk document. The *Draft of the Draft* was described as a 'Committee document', and future Presidencies were invited to draw on it. As it happened, the Germans would follow the lead of the UK and divide Part II into several chapters. As indicated, in the Potsdam document Part II would become a kind of technical appendix entitled Part B.

With the exception of new paragraphs on the impact of two Community policies – research, technology and development and competition policy, the structure of Part II remained the same as in the Noordwijk document. Most of Part II.E on further analysis had been transferred to Part IV. The most profound changes concerned the maps. The diagrams relating to the SWOT analyses had disappeared. In parts the text had been re-edited to convey a more succinct political message.

The 'Introduction' and the text under 'Basic geographic characteristics of Europe' had both received a thorough overhaul. They now emphasized 'that spatial planning alone will not remove differences in the level of development between regions' (Meeting of Ministers Responsible for Spatial Planning of the Member States of the European Union, 1998: 7). 'Spatial planning seeks to integrate objectives relating to economic and social cohesion, sustainable development and competitiveness. Regional disparities ... are concerns of longstanding.' (op. cit. 7) The introduction discussed sustainability and competitiveness in more detail:

> Spatial planning provides an important means by which the objectives of sustainable development can be achieved through, for example, structuring the pattern of activities and transport links [Competitiveness] ... depends on regions having access to appropriate infrastructure, whether physical or electronic. But it also depends on people having the right skills and abilities and on people having good healthcare, housing and access to services (ibid. 8).

The reader should also note that Figure II.1 of the Noordwijk document had been replaced by two maps, one showing the physical characteristics of Europe, and nothing more, and one indicating the number of days per year with a mean temperature of +5°C and over, the range being from more than 300 to less than 120. The Swedish and the Finnish had pressed for this map to be included, which illustrated conditions in their part of the world. After all, cold temperatures resulted in 'major costs for ice breaking and winter road management, so that peripherality from markets is further hampered by transport problems at certain times of the year' (ibid. 9). Conversely, areas in the south of Europe suffered from water shortages, with detrimental effects on their regional development.

Only a few Noordwijk maps survived. Although both the core group and the expert group had put a lot of effort into making them, most of the new maps put before the CSD were judged too sensitive to be included. The maps in the appendix of the Noordwijk document disappeared without trace.

Table 8.1 Part IV of the 'Complete Draft ESDP'

IV. Applying the ESDP	1. Introduction
	2. Underlying principles
	3. Current and future action
	4. Conclusions

As indicated, Part IV went under the new title of 'Applying the ESDP'. This was the only part that really differed from the Noordwijk document (Table 8.1).

All was set for Glasgow. As on other occasions, the venue was of political significance. Once again, the meeting was a joint one with regional policy ministers. A sign of the importance attached to Glasgow by the hosts was the fact that the meeting was to be chaired by the Deputy Prime Minister, John Prescott. As it happened, at the last moment, Prescott had to stand in for Prime Minister Tony Blair at a US conference. A Scottish minister was briefed in the early hours of the morning and chaired the meeting with consummate skill, giving a very witty after-dinner speech at the end.

The meeting itself brought few surprises. All participants welcomed the *Complete Draft* (Figure 8.1).

Obviously, the time was ripe for a final ESDP. Austria and Germany were asked to prepare it. Portugal was the only delegation that remained reluctant, while Spain and Greece joined the majority in giving their support. Ministers stressed that the ESDP should be a non-binding reference document for the implementation and evaluation of Community policies. On her part, Commissioner Wulf-Mathies retorted that the ESDP should fulfil a similar role with regard to national policies. Ministers also agreed on the need to add a further part on enlargement. Italy and Greece also demanded a part on co-operation around the Mediterranean. The Germans pleaded for the formalization of the CSD and the informal meetings of ministers, this being an evergreen issue on their agenda. Surprisingly, they received support from the Dutch and French and also from the representative of the Committee on Regional Policy (now the Committee on Regional Policy, Transport and Tourism) of the European Parliament. Shortly before the Glasgow meeting this committee had tabled the *Report on regional planning and the ESDP* and adopted a resolution to be discussed further on page 135.

As it no longer had a Scottish Commissioner, Scotland was fearful that it might not fare so well in the forthcoming review of the Structural Funds. After the meeting, Commissioner Wulf-Mathies was flown to the highlands and islands that were in danger of losing their Objective 1 status. Eventually, they did, but not without a good transition package in place.

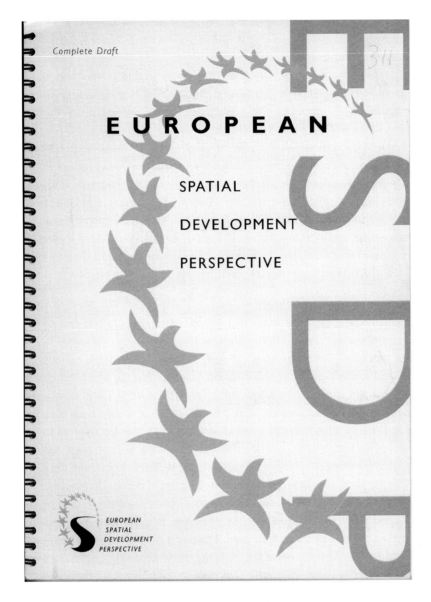

Figure 8.1 The Glasgow document: the 'Complete Draft ESDP'

THE SECOND TRACK

There were four types of consultations: national debates, discussions within Commission services, the transnational seminars and deliberations within European institutions: the European Parliament, the Committee of the Regions and the Economic and Social Committee. The European institutions had already each appointed a *rapporteur* and they wanted to participate in the transnational seminars. At Glasgow the Economic and Social Committee had been the only body not to be represented. In Potsdam all would be present.

The countries of central and eastern Europe needed to be informed, so the UK Permanent Representation in Brussels invited their representatives for a briefing. Later, ten accession countries and also Norway and Switzerland would give their reactions to the ESDP.

Other organizations were invited to give feedback. Those responding were: the Association of European Border Regions (AEBR), the Conference of Peripheral Maritime Regions of Europe (CPMR), the Assembly of European Regions, the *Deutsch-Französisch-Schweizerische Oberrheinkonferenz* and the Regional Committee Saar-Lor-Lux-Trier. There were also NGO reactions, from Birdlife International, for instance, reactions from regions like the Region Midi-Pyrénées, and professional associations, like the European Council of Town and Country Planners (ECTP) and the Association of European Schools of Planning (AESOP).

NATIONAL CONSULTATIONS

Few member states had experience of this type of consultation. The idea was to discuss Noordwijk with sector departments ('horizontal' co-ordination) and with regional and local authorities ('vertical co-ordination'). In addition, member states were supposed to organize public debates. How exactly this was to be done was unclear, but the debates were to involve research institutes and economic and social partners. Wisely, it was left up to member states to organize the rest. To offer some help, the joint work programme of Luxembourg and the UK referred to France, Germany, The Netherlands and Denmark as countries with relevant experience, adding that the respective delegations should share their insights with the CSD.

The national consultations cannot be covered in depth. Surely, any detailed analysis would show member states following different paths depending on historically rooted practices. To illustrate this point, the Belgian case may serve as an example. To be more precise, since spatial planning in Belgium is the prerogative of the Walloons, the Flemings and the planners of the Brussels Capital Region, the case discussed will be Flanders. The Flemish administration thought that the Noordwijk document was not a suitable subject for broad public debate. The debate was therefore restricted to the relevant sector departments, the Association of Flemish Provinces, the Association of Flemish Towns and Communities and the Association of Flemish Planners (Van der Lecq, 2000). It was understandable that those responsible were apprehensive of discussing the ESDP outside the circle of the CSD delegation. The uncertainty surrounding the whole exercise contrasted starkly with what the ESDP had hoped to achieve, and it did not help matters that the ESDP often made use of rather abstract terms. The vulnerable position of the

Flemish administration itself is also a factor to take into account in this case. The recently devised *Flemish Structure Plan*, a serious attempt to get spatial planning on the agenda, had elicited a mixed response. With only limited personnel capacity, yet another difficult discussion was something that the administation would want to avoid. Most other member states followed a similarly cautious approach, with little in the way of public debates. Only member states with well-organized planning communities, like The Netherlands and the UK for instance, held conferences to discuss the ESDP.

By the end of 1998 the national debates had come to an end and the results were forwarded to the Germans, who were due to assume the following Presidency. As Chapter 9 on Potsdam will show, by that time the Germans had already prepared a draft of the final document. The aggregated list of issues raised in the national reports exceeded thirty pages. Topics varied a great deal. Here the remarks have been rearranged under three headings: general comments, comments on the four parts of the Noordwijk draft and comments on the future.

Most general comments concerned the balance of emphasis between the three basic goals of the ESDP: (i) economic and social cohesion, (ii) sustainable development and (iii) balanced competitiveness of the European territory. Portugal, Spain, Italy and Greece wished to see economic and social cohesion placed above the two others in importance. The Netherlands, Belgium, Germany and the UK were in favour of integrating the three goals more closely.

The maps also received a lot of attention. Six northern countries and Portugal complained about the paucity of maps, which in their eyes had a detrimental effect on the readability of the document. The status of the four maps in the appendix of the Noordwijk draft was another issue. They had been omitted from the Glasgow draft, but the consultations were of course based on the Noordwijk draft.

With regard to the text, a number of member states thought that the Noordwijk document was too abstract, complex and ambitious. The UK in particular was of the opinion that it would not appeal to politicians and others who did not speak the planners' language. There were also complaints about insufficient coherence between parts of the text and about the overly academic nature of the language.

Part I came under similar attack. Although only five pages in length, it required close reading, including a certain amount of 'reading between the lines'. Five northwest European countries raised questions about the status of the ESDP. Although the national reports did not elaborate, what seemed mainly to be behind this were the reactions of the sector departments. In The Netherlands, for instance, sector departments had been highly critical for reasons connected with the pattern of relations between departments and the increasingly tense political climate surrounding Dutch spatial planning (Priemus, 1999). These departments had only been marginally involved in the process, forcing them to conclude that, by making this into a

European discourse, the National Spatial Planning Agency was seeking to increase its power over them (Waterhout and Zonneveld, 2000a,b).

Referring to the Leipzig Principles, the Noordwijk draft stated that the approach 'can only be indicative, not prescriptive. Nevertheless, it is expected to lead to tangible results for the European territory and provide stimulus for action' (CEC, 1997b: 4). Although to insiders this had been clear from the start, there was no explicit mention of the fact that the EDSP was not to be binding. Four member states therefore wished to see the position of the ESDP clarified, in particular with regard to Community policies and whether a Community competency was in the offing. Some of them added that they were opposed to such a competency and that member states and/or regions should remain responsible for spatial planning.

Other issues concerned only one or two member states. The Austrians, for instance, argued that the ESDP should address unemployment. Greece wanted to see a forecast of the potential spatial impact of the introduction of the Euro, whereas Spain and Belgium both argued for a new basic goal: increasing the quality of life of EU citizens. The UK wanted a clearer indication of the relationship with *Europe 2000* and the INTERREG programme.

Based on spatial trends Part II received numerous comments, many of a specific nature. Thus, Sweden drew attention to issues involving forestry, acidification and peripherality, whilst Austria wanted more information on the Alps. Italy would have liked to see the position of Mediterranean seaports addressed and Greece highlighted the position of its islands and coastal areas. A few points received broader attention. No less than nine member states suggested further work on the spatial impacts of Community policies, with special emphasis on competition policy. Greece and The Netherlands both addressed the CAP, and Germany and Denmark identified a divergence between the ESDP and Community policy with regard to the TENs. Also, member states from both northern and southern Europe requested that more attention be paid to rural areas. Peripheral countries like Sweden, Finland, Greece and Spain asked for a greater appreciation of the specifics of their geographical situation and the potential difficulties that they caused. A number of member states had problems with the analysis in general, deeming that it lacked detail and thus was likely to be misunderstood. Lastly, only Germany, Austria and Greece addressed the theme of enlargement of the EU, all being member states that one would expect to have an interest in it.

Part III received most of the attention. Once again, the majority of comments were of relevance to only a handful of member states, many of them expressing the same concerns as for Part II. No fewer than ten member states asked for a further elaboration of the policy options concerning rural areas. According to some northern European member states, the urban options were also in need of attention. There was broad support for the notion of a polycentric system of European cities.

There was support in north-west Europe for the concept of corridors. Specific

North–South and West–East corridors were mentioned, and there was an emphasis on multi-modal transport. Of course, other reports, too, made references to infrastructure and the trans-European networks, often in relation to peripheral areas. Only member states from the core of Europe addressed telecommunications and energy policy. Perhaps a trifle surprising was the fact that it was mainly north-west European member states that considered the part on the protection and management of cultural and natural heritage too weak. After all, Italy had been its main advocate, so one might have expected the Italians to focus once again on the cultural heritage. There was also much attention given to water management by four member states from north-west Europe. Finally, six national reports wanted unemployment, social problems, health care and criminality to be addressed as well, issues that on face value seem less relevant to planning on a European level.

With regard to Part IV, based on the implementation of the ESDP, as the Noordwijk draft still referred to it, no new issues emerged. A number of reports asked for more emphasis to be given to the role of the ESDP as a framework for Community policies. Cross-border and transnational co-operation were seen as important and in this respect reference was made to INTERREG. Some north-west European member states thought that the application of the Structural Funds should be informed by the ESDP, which other states predictably opposed. The principle of subsidiarity was stressed.

A further six member states saw Part IV as an opportunity to comment on enlargement. Sweden and the UK were the only ones with no land border with an accession state that wished to see more investigations carried out into the consequences of enlargement.

A number of comments related to the future. The early establishment of ESPON was the only point which received attention from more than half the member states. Other issues received only sporadic mention. Thus, a few member states raised the issue of the revision of the ESDP, to be carried out preferably before each round of discussions on the Structural Funds. Clearly, the national reports were repeating views already aired during the multilateral sessions.

Member states were united in their opposition to a Community competency. Spain and Denmark wanted to continue as before. Germany reiterated its well-known predilection for the concept of the CSD becoming a Council Working Party. Denmark and Germany thought that the Council of Europe should be involved.

THE WORKING PARTY OF THE COMMISSION SERVICES

For the purposes of consultation within the Commission services, an inter-service group had been anticipated. However, to establish one officially would have taken more than a year, so a more low-key approach was taken. A working group, composed of no less than nineteen representatives of various Directorates-General, held a couple of meetings to consider sector policies in relation to spatial development, as discussed in the ESDP. This in itself was unusual. Most of the time, consultations within the Commission take the form of written comments. Working groups are restricted to new and/or sensitive issues. In this particular case, a consultant prepared a text, which analyzed the spatial concepts implied by existing Community policies and the common ground between them. After the first meeting, participants gave written comments.

The tone of the *Report on Community Policies and Spatial Planning* was positive. The Foreword portrayed it as a first attempt to increase awareness within Commission services of the territorial dimension of their policies. So, the report did 'not constitute the end, but rather the beginning of a process aimed at examining territorial issues in a prospective manner and at strengthening co-ordination and co-operation' (Commission Services, 1999: 2). The approach differed from that of national reports in that it took a Community perspective. The document explored the difficulties of specifying the territorial impacts of Community policies. It classified the territorial concepts used in existing policies under five categories:

1. Delimitation of areas eligible for financial support and modulation of assistance;
2. Improvement of basic infrastructures;
3. Differentiation of policies and measures on the basis of territorial criteria;
4. Development of functional synergies;
5. Design of integrated policies.

These territorial concepts used – more or less explicitly – by the various Community policies can be confronted with those of the ESDP which are similar, if not identical in certain cases. Certain policy options of the ESDP refer to territorial categories or concepts for which specific objectives have been defined (cities and towns, rural areas, cultural landscapes and so forth). Other options favour synergy (accessibility and public transport, wetlands and utilization of water recourses etc) or integrated management approaches (e.g. city networks, water resource management, integrated conservation of cultural and natural heritage). It seems therefore not only possible, but even necessary to search for increasing coherence and convergence between these territorial categories and concepts (ibid. 12).

ESDP policy options related to the entire European territory. Moreover, they often coincided with Community policies. The two fundamental goals of the EU Treaty, economic and social cohesion and sustainable development, were well represented in the ESDP. So spatial planning might 'prove a remarkable instrument for strengthening economic and social cohesion' (ibid. 11). In certain cases, however, such as tourism, energy, and coastal and maritime areas, the ESDP provided insufficient support and orientations. 'This is an example of how future work needs to better define such territorial concepts and objectives with a view to assist Community policies' interventions' (ibid. 11). The report also identified a trend for Community policies to replace purely sectoral approaches with more integrated ones. In some instances a territorial approach was appropriate and even essential. In places, though, the Commission services felt that the draft was too abstract. They asked for more concrete alternatives to be illustrated by maps. However, the report related that the ESDP had already had an impact on the guidelines for the Structural Funds for 2000–6. With regard to enlargement, co-operation between the various Community policies for better 'territorial coherence' was to have an educational function for applicant countries. A recurring theme was that the Noordwijk document was not concrete enough and that it was necessary to do further work on a joint vision for the development of the European territory. The report emphasized the need for reliable data as a basis for formulating a vision and concluded that 'the moment appears convenient to begin … a work and medium-term co-operation process involving the various Community policies and the CSD' (ibid. 13). Clearly, the ESDP had succeeded in gaining the attention of the Commission services.

THE TRANSNATIONAL SEMINARS

As indicated, the transnational seminars were to be organized by DG XVI. Initially, DG XVI planned thirteen events, on the issues of enlargement, pressures of tourism in the Alps, transport links between Europe and Africa, environmental and coastal management and strategies for European seaports, amongst others. The idea had been for the seminars to take place before Glasgow, but this soon turned out to be unrealistic. Eventually, between April 1998 (barely a month before Glasgow!) and February 1999, nine seminars were held (Table 8.2).

Table 8.2 ESDP transnational seminars

Date	Place	ESDP theme
April '98	Berlin	ESDP launch – towards a policy strategy for Europe
May '98	Naples	Transport, telecommunications, perspectives for the periphery
June '98	Lille	Cities: the European urban system
July '98	Thessaloniki	Water management, floods, drought and sustainability
Sept '98	Manchester	Knowledge as a development factor
Oct '98	Salamanca	For a new rural–urban relationship
Oct '98	Göteborg	Environmentally sensitive areas
Nov '98	Vienna	Co-operation in the context of enlargement
Feb '99	Brussels	ESDP forum – closing event

Source: Williams, 2000

According to Williams (2000) they had the overall purposes of developing the ESDP through debate and advice on its different aspects from experts and governmental representatives, linking it to the transnational planning programmes under INTERREG IIC, and generating political momentum for the ESDP and support from a wide range of bodies including other Directorates-General of the Commission and the EU institutions, national and sub-national governments, non-governmental organisations, the Council of Europe and accession-countries (Williams, 2000: 360).

The starting and closing events were major affairs, which included speeches by ministers, the Commissioner and representatives of various European, regional and local bodies. To ensure endorsement of the ESDP, the speakers included representatives from other Directorates-General, the European Parliament and countries known for their scepticism. The closing event in Brussels had an audience of seven hundred, which included sector specialists and representatives of NGOs, as well as planners from all over Europe. The other seven seminars were conducted by DG XVI in conjunction with the CSD and national authorities. Attendance ranged from two to three hundred. The first day was mostly devoted to ESDP themes while on the second day INTERREG IIC programmes and/or Article 10 projects were discussed. The involvement of the public really depended on the local hosts. 'In some, participation meant little more than listening to a platform discussion, while in others, notably the Manchester seminar, sessions were given over almost entirely to discussion from the floor'. This led Williams to conclude that as a programme of public participation

> the seminars cannot be said to have reached all who may in due course need
> to pay attention to the ESDP, but they did reach many people who would nor-
> mally be outside normal EU policy processes and Brussels comitology. They
> were not simply intended as publicity sessions. The Commission wanted
> informed debate by participants with some understanding of the ESDP con-
> cept (ibid. 360).

The outcomes were summarized in a report, *The ESDP – a strategy for balanced and sustainable development of the European Union: Synthesis report of the Transnational Seminars*, which was presented alongside the report of the Commission services in Brussels. It gave the results and then, paragraph by paragraph, focused on the policy options (using the Noordwijk document as a basis). The comments more or less coincided with those in the national reports. Just like the Commission services, the transnational discussions had also been positive. They 'confirmed the need for new policy orientations for spatial development at the European Union level, especially with the view to the forthcoming enlargement, the closer economic integration which would follow from EMU and the continuing need for balanced and sustainable development' (DG XVI, 1999: 3). The ESDP itself was seen as helpful. Much attention went to polycentric development, 'which enables all regions to realise their economic potential while safeguarding their natural and cultural heritage' (ibid. 4). This should not lead to building 'cathedrals in the desert', but rather it was emphasized that the 'creation of a number of dynamic, economically-integrated areas, evenly distributed across the European territory and composed of metropolitan and rural areas and containing towns and cities of various size, can play a key role in improving spatial balance in Europe' (ibid. 6). Eventually, the concept of 'global economic integration zones' would be one of the innovations in the Potsdam document, although the abortive attempt by German federal planners to designate 'development regions' in the former GDR, reported on in Chapter 3, had foreshadowed this.

The transnational seminars had also put emphasis on the coherence between policies at various administrative levels and sectors, on economic and social cohesion, enlargement, globalization and balanced development and on the competitiveness of the EU as a whole. In addition, many of those attending had advised making the document more readable. As a final remark the report stated that it was 'worth stressing that the relevance and importance of the ESDP was not questioned and that its broad approach was generally endorsed by the vast majority of the participants' (ibid. 19).

THE EUROPEAN PARLIAMENT, THE ECONOMIC AND SOCIAL COMMITTEE AND THE COMMITTEE OF THE REGIONS

As Noetzel (2000: 10) points out, the position of the European Parliament has always been unambiguous in its support for European planning. As mentioned on page 126, on 2 July 1998 the Commission on Regional Planning therefore passed a resolution welcoming the ESDP. It drew attention to three previous occasions when it had discussed spatial planning (one of which is referred to in Chapter 4). The European Parliament, for instance, had always been in favour of Europe-wide regional planning policy 'capable of ensuring that the various Community policies complement, and are consistent with, the aim of achieving balanced and sustainable development throughout the territory of the Union, thus strengthening economic and social cohesion'. The resolution pointed out that the practical application of the ESDP was impeded by 'institutional weakness arising from the absence in the Treaty of specific Community powers in this area, the informal nature of the Council of regional planning ministers and the temporary nature of the Regional Development Committee' (obviously meaning the CSD). Furthermore, the Committee on Regional Policy, considering

> that there are no longer any possibilities for intergovernmental action and that it
> is therefore essential at the present stage to include regional planning in the

> Community sphere; accordingly strongly urges the formalization of the Council of Regional Planning Ministers and the establishment of the Regional Development Committee as a permanent body, with a delegation representing members of the Parliament's Committee on Regional Policy being invited to attend meetings of the Regional Development Committee. (Document No. A4-0206/98, Final Edition, Reports of the European Parliament, www.europarl.int)

The European Commission 'had immediate responsibility for and the opportunity of improving the complementarity and consistency of Community policies, in particular by establishing the internal mechanisms for co-ordination between its various departments and by incorporating a regional impact assessment in any measure that is adopted'. With respect to the reform of the Structural Funds, the Committee held that they 'must make it possible to incorporate in the programming the principles defined in the ESDP'.

The Economic and Social Committee was also supportive. It made a point, also raised by Greece in its national report, that quality of life had not been included as a goal. Furthermore, true to its brief, it regretted that employment policies had not been considered in conjunction with spatial coherence and that economic and social players had been insufficiently consulted. The Committee saw this as a consequence of the inter-governmental approach, expressing its hope that the position of spatial development in the totality of Community competencies would be considered. The Committee was in favour of formalizing the 'Council of Planning Ministers' and the CSD.

On 14 January 1999, the Committee of the Regions also passed a thorough and very detailed resolution on the ESDP. The outcome in brief is that the Committee demanded the instantaneous creation of a legal basis for the ESDP and also for ESPON, and that it wanted to bring the CSD under the umbrella of the Commission. This amounted to no less than the 'communautarization' of spatial planning. All three institutions, wedded to European integration as they are, favoured a more prominent role for Community institutions, including the Commission, in the ESDP process.

CONCLUSIONS

With the Glasgow document and the results of these consultations in hand, the German Presidency could proceed with putting the finishing touches to the ESDP. Participants were eager to turn their attention to other matters, like INTERREG, at that time already under active consideration, and also the various other kinds of follow-up. More than five years after the process had started, the ESDP had evolved from a distant prospect into a project that needed to be concluded speedily.

Chapter 9 demonstrates how the Germans were up to the challenge. Whilst they carried out their work, the competency issue simmered on. In late 1997, the Luxembourg Presidency had addressed it, whilst trying to get ESPON off the ground, and a CSD seminar in Vienna in 1998 had also discussed it. Chapter 10 discusses this in a separate section devoted to the competency issue. However, first the focus is on Potsdam.

CHAPTER 9

POTSDAM – THE CROWNING EVENT

On 10/11 May 1999 the ministers responsible for spatial planning met once again with Commissioner Wulf-Mathies to consider the *European Spatial Development Perspective: Towards Balanced and Sustainable Development of the Territory of the EU* (CEC, 1999a). As must surely have become evident from the preceding chapters, Potsdam was the result of years of dedicated work. The Leipzig Principles (Chapter 5) adopted in 1994, the *First Official Draft* (Chapter 7) from Noordwijk, adopted in 1997, and the *Complete Draft* (Chapter 8) from Glasgow, adopted in 1998, had been milestones in this process.

Like Chapters 7 and 8, this chapter deals with the work involved in each stage of the process, including some of the details that make up the daily life of an international planner. It is also about the document itself, giving special attention to the policy of strengthening the 'polycentric urban system of Europe', which is both complex and ambiguous.

PUTTING THE FINISHING TOUCHES TO THE ESDP

This time, it was Austria's and Germany's turn to form a partnership. The Austrian Presidency prepared the work programme for the end run. The work would be co-ordinated by Germany, together with the UK and the Commission. The Austrians themselves would focus on enlargement and on the future of the CSD, which would form the topic of the CSD seminar, discussed in Chapter 10.

The Germans were aiming to improve upon the existing text, taking account of the consultations. The British and others before them had successfully worked through the medium of the troika, and the Germans did the same. They wanted to make sure that the work would come to a successful conclusion. Only months before, when the British had taken an initiative of their own, they had been stopped in their tracks.

It is worth emphasizing that this time it was the Germans who produced the drafts. The troika merely acted as a sounding board. With the consent of the others, however, the Germans had invited the Dutch, no longer part of the troika, to participate in the work. Obviously, the Dutch had built up some credit by producing the Noordwijk draft.

In addition, a CSD working party, entitled 'Structure and Presentation', was to assist the troika. This working party discussed the layout, including the illustrations, and an ESDP logo. Originally this task had been delegated to a seasoned expert from the Federal Office for Building and Regional Planning, the institute that had previously been doing much of the European work for the German ministry under a different name. On his own initiative, this expert had invited colleagues from other member states to join him. In practice this meant the addition of a Scottish, an Austrian, a Greek and a Dutch expert to his group. French and Italian experts had also been invited but they did not attend. The people assembled in this group knew each other, and all spoke or at least understood German.

The bulk of the work was carried out between late August and the end of October 1998. It was a novelty because the Germans worked in German, English and French simultaneously. They had the services of a multilingual planning expert assisted by professional translators. Their ambition was to circulate a draft before Christmas. In addition to working on all these fronts, a German delegation attended all transnational seminars. There were also bilateral meetings with The Netherlands, France, Spain, Italy, Greece and Portugal. Naturally, the Germans also had to prepare the event itself.

Ministerial meetings are complex to organize. As early as 1997, the German planners had tried to get the meeting onto a list of no more than eight informal meetings that the German government regarded important enough to warrant central funding. They had failed to succeed. The next step followed in August 1998 when the venue was the subject of high-level exchanges with Bavaria. As had been the case in Leipzig five years previously, the meeting had to be paid for out of departmental funds, and so Bavarian willingness to share the costs had become important. By September, a two-day programme for a meeting in Munich had been agreed upon, featuring receptions, excursions, etc. By late October, it transpired that there were not enough conference facilities available.

Surely, a more important reason for the change of venue was the outcome of the federal elections. As reported in Chapter 1, the elections, combined with Bavarian scepticism with regard to the Commission's role in regional policy and planning, meant that eventually the venue became Potsdam.

The work itself progressed smoothly. Unlike the Dutch, who had worked with a team of eight, the Germans formed a team of only three to four, the aim being to work as efficiently as possible. There was also a monitoring committee, which held monthly meetings. It consisted of about twenty officials, most of them from various divisions of their own ministry, but some coming from other ministries to ensure the political acceptability of the text within the German administration.

The CSD group, 'Structure and Presentation', organized a CSD workshop in early October to discuss the illustrations accompanying Chapter 2. In parentheses, the reader will note that, just as the British had proposed, parts had become chapters and Roman numerals had made room for Arabic ones.

Surprisingly, Chapter 3, which featured the policy options, was no longer controversial. During one of their first meetings, the 'Structure and Presentation' group had agreed to rescind all the maps in this chapter. As earlier attempts had shown, maps had not been a great success. Instead, icons were developed, giving visual expression to the themes covered in Chapter 3. They will be discussed on pages 154–5.

In October 1998, a CSD was held with eleven accession countries in presence. Accession countries welcomed the Austrian's work on enlargement and emphasized transnational co-operation in the framework of INTERREG IIC. Greece, Germany, The Netherlands, Luxembourg and Portugal wanted information on the spatial effects of enlargement. Greece, Spain, Italy and also Cyprus emphasized the need for third-country co-operation around the Mediterranean. Bulgaria drew attention to the Black Sea area. The Germans reiterated their view that the Council of Europe could fulfil a role in involving the accession countries, something that had in fact already been decided at the Nicosia meeting of CEMAT the year before.

Apart from the Vienna Seminar (to be discussed in Chapter 10), there were no further CSD meetings in 1998. The Germans put the finishing touches to the work and shipped the draft to their colleagues in December, wishing them a Merry Christmas and a Happy New Year.

In early 1999 the final round of editing took place. To this end, two-day CSD meetings were held in January and in March. The December draft was given a favourable reception. Almost ten years of involvement in inter-governmental work had taught the Germans to think in truly European ways. In fact, this was the first occasion on which a country's assumption of a leading role had been met with general approval. Of course, the Germans were careful to take the consultations into account as much as possible.

The structure of the document had changed. To emphasize its political nature, the Germans had divided it into two parts. Part A was the political part, and Part B the analytical one. Almost the whole of Part II of the Glasgow document was assimilated in Part B of the Potsdam document. Part A needed to be short; initially, even the chapter on the 'Influence of Community Policies on the Territory of the EU' had been excluded. Eventually, this chapter was reinstated, however. As far as the rest of the document was concerned, member states and the Commission agreed with its new structure (Table 9.1).

A striking innovation was the reference in the December draft to the 'core of Europe' as a hexagon formed by London, Paris, Milan, Munich, the Rhine–Ruhr area and the Randstad. It will be discussed in a separate section below.

After the January CSD (attended by a representative of DG XI responsible for environmental policy), delegations submitted text proposals that the Germans incorporated into the draft, in preparation for the March meeting. The March draft

Table 9.1 The Potsdam document: ESDP

Part A. Achieving the Balanced and Sustainable Development of the Territory of the EU: The Contribution of the Spatial Development Policy
• Chapter 1. The Spatial Approach at European Level • Chapter 2. Influence of Community Policies on the Territory of the EU • Chapter 3. Policy Aims and Options for the Territory of the EU • Chapter 4. The Application of the ESDP • Chapter 5. The Enlargement of the EU: An Additional Challenge for European Spatial Development Policy
Part B. The Territory of the EU: Trends, Opportunities and Challenges
• Chapter 1. Spatial Development Conditions and Trends in the EU • Chapter 2. Spatial Development Issues of European Significance • Chapter 3. Selected Programmes and Visions for Integrated Spatial Development • Chapter 4. Basic Data for the Accession Countries and Member States

received another warm welcome. The Germans had asked delegations to submit concrete amendments, preferably in three languages, and to restrict themselves to what was politically acceptable. Sifting through the amendments and integrating them into the text remained the responsibility of the Germans.

During the March meeting something unexpected happened. Having read through the previous chapters the reader must now have a good grasp of the positions of various member states in relation to the ESDP. Therefore, it must surprise the reader to hear that this time it was the Dutch who raised objections. Albeit reluctantly, the Dutch delegation were compelled to express some reservations with regard to the spatial distribution of large seaports. They also had to stress that the status of the document was informal, with no influence whatsoever on sector policies. This had been the outcome of Dutch interdepartmental negotiations (Waterhout and Zonneveld, 2000a, b).

Of course, the German Presidency had been briefed beforehand, but few of the other delegations knew what had happened. In what has been described as an emotional reaction, and perhaps this may come as an even bigger surprise, Spain presented itself as an advocate of the ESDP. The world had turned upside down! Apparently, the Berlin Summit of March 1999 had settled the issue of the distribution of the Structural Funds for the Programming Period 2000–6, thus removing any danger of the ESDP impacting upon the Spanish allocation, and the Spanish delegation was now at liberty to speak from its heart, which it promptly did.

Having resolved the issue with his sector colleagues on a ministerial committee chaired by the Prime Minister, the Dutch planning minister at Potsdam was eventually able to take a more conciliatory position. This incident is remarkable in that it illustrates how a shifting 'opportunity structure' can influence events.

Delegations do not speak for themselves or their department or even their minister, but for their country and what is generally perceived as being in its best interest. It hardly needs to be emphasized that this will lead to discussion and conflict, often with unpredictable outcomes. This is what is meant by the reference to games of simultaneous chess in the Preface.

With the last CSD over, there were two more months to go until the meeting. By December, the interpretation of all official EU languages into German, English and French had been arranged. By way of exception, delegates unable to cope with any of these three languages would receive discrete assistance from interpreters who were to whisper into their ears. For reasons unrelated to the ESDP process, in which the issue had never arisen, languages had become a sensitive issue in the European Union.

The seating arrangements were another detail in need of attention. To stimulate exchanges between them, only heads of delegations would be seated around the conference table. In addition to the heads of delegations of fifteen member states and the Commission, this also included the heads of a number of European institutions. All in all, a table with twenty-four seats for the heads of delegations was required, with their retinues being seated behind them. The shape of the room and the position of the German Presidential logo on the wall meant that the German minister in his capacity as Chairman had to be seated at the long side of the table. Opposite the chair was the Commission's seat, with the member states in alphabetical order following suit.

Of course, these are only a few of the minutiae involved in organizing such meetings. To make sure that everything went smoothly, a computer programme was used that had been designed specifically for the purpose of organizing such meetings.

The printing of the document also had to be attended to. This expense was charged to the Presidency. The costs involved in such a meeting cannot be underestimated, particularly as in this case it included the printing of the provisional version of the ESDP in three languages. All funds came out of the budget of the Ministry of Transport, Building and Housing, of which planning had been a part since the election of October 1998. (The planners had to get used to a new house style 'on the fly', as it were, which obviously added to the complications of preparing Potsdam.)

Participants remember the meeting itself as something of an anti-climax. The German Presidency had made sure that there would be no hitches. The task had been made easier by the agreement on *Agenda 2000* reached at the Berlin Summit in March 1999. As indicated, any danger of the ESDP influencing the allocation of large sums of money had evaporated.

The Potsdam Document

The text has become more readable. The Potsdam document has a subtitle: *Towards Balanced and Sustainable Development of the Territory of the European Union* (CEC, 1999a) (Figure 9.1).

Figure 9.1 The Potsdam document: the ESDP

Besides, as the reader knows, it comes in two parts: Part A, and the more analytical Part B. The emphasis is given here to Part A, 'Achieving the Balanced and Sustainable Development of the Territory of the EU: The Contribution of the Spatial Development Policy'. The English version is no more than fifty-one pages long, a remarkable achievement for a text that has been many years in the making.

Chapter 1, 'The Spatial Approach at European Level', is the introduction presenting territory as a new dimension of European policy (Table 9.2). The opening sentence addresses the widespread feeling of unease with regard to the impact of European integration (and perhaps also spatial planning) on national, regional and local identity. Thus, in the spirit of the Leipzig document, the ESDP insists that variety needs to be retained. 'Spatial development policies ... must not standardize local and regional identities in the EU, which help enrich the quality of life of its citizens' (ibid. 7).

Since European integration, the significance of borders has decreased. Projects evolving in one country can have an impact on the spatial structure of others. Community policy, too, must pay attention to spatial factors, particularly now that European Monetary Union (EMU) is a fact, since it is no longer possible to compensate for productivity disparities by adjusting exchange rates. Spatial planning can help to prevent disparities from widening.

The authors of the ESDP show themselves to be well aware of the importance of a shared discourse. Complementarity can best be achieved when common objectives are held. This is why spatially transparent development guidelines are needed. Competition is one of the driving forces in the single market. However, as has been clear ever since Nantes, not all regions start from the same base line, and this is what cohesion policy is about. In an attempt to relate spatial development to well-established Community concerns, the ESDP asserts that spatial balance can contribute to a more even geographic distribution of growth. The key word is co-operation. Vertical co-operation between governmental and administrative levels is the way to resolve spatial issues in the EU. Horizontally, the ESDP helps with the co-operation between sector policies affecting one and the same territory. The claim is that this is 'how the subsidiarity principle, rooted in the Treaty on the EU, is realized' (ibid. 8).

Table 9.2 Chapter 1 – The Spatial Approach at European Level

1. The 'territory': a new dimension of European policy
2. Spatial development disparities
3. Underlying objectives of the ESDP
4. The status of the ESDP
5. The ESDP as a process

'Balanced and sustainable spatial development', an umbrella term since Noordwijk, is said to reconcile social and economic claims on land with an area's ecological and cultural functions, using a balanced settlement structure as the key. The ESDP refers to the three 'spheres of activity' identified at Leipzig:

- a balanced and polycentric city system and a new urban–rural partnership
- parity of access to infrastructure and knowledge
- sustainable development, prudent management and protection of nature and cultural heritage (ibid. 11).

The objectives must be reconciled, paying due attention to local situations. However, the makers of the ESDP in no way wish to provide a blueprint for action. This has been a theme throughout. The claim is rather more modest:

> In its aims and guidelines [the ESDP] provides a general source of reference for actions with a spatial impact … Beyond that, it should act as a positive signal for broad public participation in the political debate on decisions at European level and their impact on cities and regions in the EU (ibid. 11).

This leads into the first discussion of the competency issue. The text points out a fact which by now the reader is only too aware of: the ESDP is a document of the member states, formulated in co-operation with the Commission. As a legally non-binding document, it is a policy framework for better co-operation between Community sector policies and also between member states, their regions and cities.

Under 'The ESDP as a process', there is a list of the various milestones, described in much more detail in this book. This is followed by a brief account of the consultations. The next paragraph states that as a matter of course the ESDP will be subject to periodic review, a point that Chapter 10 will return to. The text adds that during this revision, the focus is likely to be on enlargement. (Enlargement is the subject of a separate chapter in the ESDP; see page 150.)

So the ESDP is being recognized for what it is, a document that must be followed through, if it wants to have any effect at all. To achieve success, member states need to co-operate with each other and the Commission:

> The translation of the objectives and options … into concrete political action will take place gradually. Initial proposals for the application of the ESDP … are presented in Chapter 4 … Other options and proposals will require further discussion and fleshing out at European level. This includes, in particular, the exchange of experiences and the monitoring and evaluation of spatial developments. The discussion on the future orientation of spatial development policy in Europe within the Committee on Spatial Development will also have to be continued after the ESDP has been agreed (ibid. 12).

Chapter 2 of the ESDP is about the 'Influence of Community Policies on the Territory of the EU' (Table 9.3).

On less than seven pages, it deals with seven areas of Community policy, singling three out as being of particular importance: the Structural Funds, the trans-European networks and environmental policy. These are discussed in Chapter 1 of this book. The text makes an attempt to indirectly root the ESDP in the European treaties, by pointing out various articles referring to cohesion and sustainability.

The chapter culminates in a section entitled 'For an improved spatial coherence of Community policies', inspired by the *Report on Community Policies and Spatial Planning* produced by the Commission Services (1999) and discussed in the previous chapter. The five spatial concepts, or 'spatial categories', identified as being used in formulating Community policies in that document are also listed. Also included is the recommendation to develop 'functional synergies' within the framework of Community policies. Last but not least, the text mentions the use of an integrated and multisectoral spatial development approach in the Community Initiatives INTERREG IIC and LEADER and in a Demonstration Programme on Integrated Coastal Zone Management (ICZM).

Chapter 3 of the ESDP presents policy options (Table 9.4). The authors of the ESDP would surely see this as a key achievement. This chapter has certainly required a lot of discussion. Like the Noordwijk document, this chapter is structured around the three 'spheres of activity', now presented as 'spatial development guidelines' for the territory of the EU:

1.   Polycentric Spatial Development and a New Urban–Rural Partnership
2.   Parity of Access to Infrastructure and Knowledge
3.   Wise Management of the Natural and Cultural Heritage.

Each of these is broken down into topics, which altogether number thirteen, one more

Table 9.3 Chapter 2 – Influence of Community Policies on the Territory of the EU

1. Growing importance of EU policies with spatial impact
2. EU policies with spatial impact
3. For an improved spatial coherence of Community policies

Table 9.4 Chapter 3 – Policy Aims and Options for the Territory of the EU

1. Spatial orientations of policies
2. Polycentric spatial development and a new urban–rural relationship
3. Parity of access to infrastructure and knowledge
4. Wise management of the natural and cultural heritage

than in the Noordwijk document. Under each topic the reader will find a number of policy options, the total number being sixty. As before, the policy options are of a highly diverse nature: 'Strengthening of several larger zones of global economic integration in the EU, equipped with high-quality, global functions and service, including the peripheral areas, through transnational spatial development strategies' (Policy option 1, to be discussed in a separate section on pages 152–6); 'Development of packages of measures which stimulate supply and demand for improving regional access and the use of information and communication technology' (Policy option 39); 'Maintenance and creative redesign of urban ensembles worthy of protection' (Policy option 58); and 'Promoting of contemporary buildings with high architectural quality' (Policy option 59). Obviously, the sixty policy options cannot be summarized.

An unusual feature of Chapter 3 is the use of icons. As indicated, in lieu of maps the final version of the ESDP uses icons to illustrate various policies, and the 'Structure and Presentation' group is responsible for their development. Thus, using the words of its creators, in the ESDP there is a common nose-shaped icon, which represents Europe as a peninsula of the Eurasian continent. This basic form is filled with various symbols to represent particular policies, such as 'polycentric and balanced spatial development', 'dynamic attractive and competitive cities and urbanized regions', 'indigenous development, diverse and productive rural areas', and so forth. These are the thirteen topics under which Chapter 3 presents the policy options. Figure 9.2 shows an example, the icon representing the 'polycentric developmental model'. Incontrovertibly, the icons are attempts to use spatial images. Whether they are a good way of portraying spatial concepts remains to be seen.

After an initial paragraph on integrated spatial development, Chapter 4, 'The Application of the ESDP', distinguishes between various levels of application, from the Community level to transnational, cross-border and inter-regional co-operation. There is a section on the application of the ESDP in the member states as well as on a pan-European level (Table 9.5).

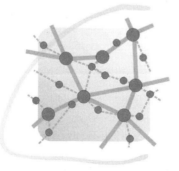

Figure 9.2 Icon in the ESDP (Source: European Commission, 1999a)

Table 9.5 Chapter 4 – The Application of the ESDP

1. Towards an integrated spatial development
2. The application of the ESDP at Community level
3. Transnational co-operation between the member states
4. Cross-border and inter-regional co-operation
5. The application of the ESDP in the member states
6. The importance of the ESDP for pan-European and international co-operation

The text also says that, in applying the policy aims and options, conflicts between sectors, spatial conflicts and timing difficulties are all factors that need to be considered early on. In a passage about arrangements for its further application, the ESDP says: 'This requires new ways of co-operation, which according to the ESDP's principles should be on a voluntary basis. The application of the policy options is based on the principle of subsidiarity' (ibid. 35). To this end, three planning levels are once again distinguished: the Community; the transnational/national and the regional/local level. However, the

> main focus of the ESDP's application as a European document is at Community and transnational levels. Priority should be given to issues which cannot be dealt with in an appropriate way by one or two member states but, instead, require the co-operation of several countries (ibid. 37).

The next paragraph is devoted to the application of the ESDP at Community level. The text reports on the formation of an inter-service group for investigating relationships between Community policy and spatial development. The recommendation is 'that the European Commission examine periodically and systematically the spatial effects of policies – such as the Common Agricultural Policy, Transport Policy and "Trans-European Networks", Structural Policy, Environmental Policy, Competition Policy and Research and Technology Policy – at European level' (ibid. 37). This is a German wish that has found its way into the ESDP. Germany publishes *Raumordnungsberichte* (Spatial Planning Reports) at irregular intervals, the last one having come out in 2000 (BBR, 2000). It is the stated German policy that the Commission should do the same.

Articulating the competency issue, the next passage deserves to be quoted fully:

> The meetings of the Ministers responsible for spatial development and those of the Committee on Spatial Development (CSD) play a central role in the application and further development of the ESDP. However, the informal character of these arrangements does not allow the taking of decisions or making of recommendations. For this reason, European institutions such as the European Parliament and the Economic and Social Committee support a formalization of

these arrangements, whilst maintaining the principle of subsidiarity. Member states have different opinions on this (CEC, 1999a: 37).

This is followed by the recommendation that 'Member States examine the suggestions of the European institutions (discussed at the end of the previous chapter) to formalise both the Ministerial meetings on spatial planning and the Committee on Spatial Development, while maintaining the principle of subsidiarity' (ibid. 37). The activity concerning the ESDP has reached its peak and, not surprisingly, the competency issue has reappeared as an item on the agenda. It will be discussed in the final chapter.

Further on in the document, member states are asked to 'regularly prepare standardized information on important aspects of national spatial development policy and its implementation in national spatial development reports, basing this on the structure of the ESDP' (ibid. 38). What follows are further recommendations concerning ESPON. It is evident that there is a desire for the work to continue.

A whole paragraph is devoted to transnational co-operation, actually alluding to INTERREG. It contains a statement of the underlying philosophy. There are also passages concerning cross-border co-operation. The next paragraph is about the application of the ESDP in member states, culminating in a passage about the inevitable 'Europeanisation of state, regional and urban planning'.

The last chapter of Part A is about enlargement (Table 9.6). It is the least well-developed, limiting itself to a short characterization of spatial development in the accession states and the specific tasks of European spatial development there. The brief chapter ends with a discussion of existing assistance programmes and a number of recommendations, including the option of integrating them with the INTERREG Community Initiative. In the meantime, the Commission has published a study on enlargement (CEC, 2000f) and enlargement also figures in the Action Programme agreed at Tampere (to be discussed in Chapter 10) and the *Second Cohesion Report* (CEC, 2001a). Understandably, the discussion of the impact of enlargement is particularly virulent in Germany and Austria, two countries that stand to derive overall benefits from enlargement, but where at the

Table 9.6 Chapter 5 – The Enlargement of the EU: an Additional Challenge for European Spatial Development Policy

1 A new reference territory for the ESDP
2 The main features of spatial development in the accession countries
3 Specific tasks of European spatial development policy in the future member states
4 The spatial impact of the enlargement on the regions of the EU
5 The policy aims and options of the ESDP in the light of the enlargement
6 Principles for integrating the enlargement tasks into European spatial development and planning

same time the distribution of the effects can be particularly uneven (Steiner, 2001: 22).

There is no doubt that the makers of the ESDP take its application seriously. This can be gleaned, not only from the document itself, but also from the Conclusions of the Presidency at Potsdam. The Conclusions were modest:

> The Ministers responsible for Spatial Planning in the member states of the
> European Union and the member of the European Commission responsible for
> Regional Policy emphasized in Potsdam that the conclusion of the political
> debate on the European Spatial Development Perspective (ESDP) was an
> important step in the progress towards European integration (Excerpt of final
> conclusions, reprinted in CEC, 1999a).

The reason for the absence of ceremony was the fact that ministers met informally, rather than as one of the incarnations of the Council of Ministers conducting Community business. There was, after all, no Community competency for planning. Like its predecessors, the Potsdam document raised this issue, as did the follow-up to Potsdam in Tampere, to be discussed in Chapter 10.

As the reader of this book is well aware, the Conclusions are the means by which the Presidency records the outcomes of these informal ministerial meetings. Having reassured the reader that the makers of the ESDP were in no way clamouring for greater responsibilities at the Community level, the Conclusions reiterate its character as a policy framework for the member states, their regions and local authorities and the European Commission. The Conclusions then specify the types of follow-up which are necessary, drawing on the chapter on application. Thus, the German Presidency and their successors, the Finnish, will forward the ESDP to the European institutions. In addition, the German Presidency will contact the accession states and others represented on the European Conference of Ministers responsible for Regional Planning (CEMAT). Other addressees are the sector planning authorities and the regional and local authorities of the member states. As a matter of course, representatives of third countries will be kept up-to-date at international meetings and conferences dealing with regional and urban development issues.

The Conclusions also report the meeting's consensus, that the application of the ESDP must now begin. The Finnish Presidency is invited to continue the ESDP process by proposing an Action Programme and by beginning a discussion on the form that future co-operation should take on issues relating to spatial development. The Conclusions stress that the ESDP should be taken into consideration in implementing the new regulations on Structural Funds and in revising the trans-European networks (TENs). The Commission is asked to report on the spatial impacts of Community policies. Also, it states that the European Spatial Planning Observatory Network (ESPON) should be speedily established.

The Conclusions also relate an agreement on the proposal made by the Presidency for a competition entitled the 'Future Regions of Europe'. Equally, the French proposal to mount a youth competition for secondary schools on the theme of European integration in their regions has received favour, as well as another French proposal to use the ESDP as a basis for preparing geography texts for secondary schools. Presumably, this will echo similar work conducted by the French for the Council of Europe, based on the strength of the argument that 'spatial solidarity cannot be appreciated without the ability to find a place in a complementary and articulate manner within various geographic scales' (Foucher, 1995: 5). These types of follow-up are part of contemporary policy making directed at improving communication, stimulating initiatives, and so on (Benz, 2001: 180–1).

Before the discussion in Chapter 10 of the Tampere Action Programme, where these proposals would be rendered more concrete, the last section of this chapter goes into more depth with regard to one of the central issues in the ESDP.

THE 'PENTAGON' AND THE 'POLYCENTRIC URBAN SYSTEM IN EUROPE'

The structure of the European territory and what to do about it has been a recurring theme throughout the ESDP process. This section looks into the treatment of this issue in the final ESDP. It also discusses its diagrammatic representation, or rather the lack thereof. Many would regard spatial concepts or images as an integral part of spatial planning. However, as far as imaging such concepts is concerned, the ESDP has encountered numerous difficulties. Initially, the conceptualization of European space seemed simple enough. It followed the core–periphery model, which has been identified as a view of 'one-dimensional Europe'. To counteract this trend, a more differentiated view has been put forward, referred to in this book as 'diversified Europe'. It pays more attention to the endogenous potential of regions, and also recognizes problems in the core. In the final ESDP, both models co-exist.

As indicated, the December draft of the ESDP had already described the core of Europe as a hexagon, called a 'zone of global economic integration'. The concept related to a theme that had cropped up before, the competitiveness of Europe. By designating the core area in this way, the Germans hoped to make the message easily understood. The area was therefore defined in such a way that it comprised 20 per cent of the Community territory, with 40 per cent of the inhabitants producing no less than 50 per cent of the GDP.

At the ESDP Forum in Brussels, the new German minister, Franz Müntefering, opened his speech with a reference to this core region. Of course, this concept may suggest a one-dimensional, core-and-periphery view of Europe. It is therefore remarkable that it has been included in the ESDP. The reason for its inclusion is that it forms part of a set of ideas that collectively satisfy all the parties concerned.

Before discussing this, it is important to add that in the final document, with Hamburg coming in lieu of the Rhine–Ruhr area and the Randstad, the hexagon has become a pentagon. Apparently, the 20-40-50 rule fits the pentagon better than the hexagon. Now 'pentagon' refers to an area delineated by the cities of London, Paris, Milan, Munich and Hamburg. (With German being the original language of the Potsdam document, the term used to designate this area was 'Städtefünfeck'. 'Pentagon' is quite simply the literal translation, obviously without any allusion to the US Defence Department. The French version refers to the core of Europe.)

The recent *Second Cohesion Report* (CEC, 2001a: 30) refers not to a pentagon but a triangle marked by North Yorkshire, Franche-Comté and Hamburg, but the analysis and the conclusions are essentially the same. For increasing competitiveness, global economic integration zones must be promoted. At first sight this is the opposite of what cohesion policies stand for. However, by encouraging areas outside the 'pentagon' to aspire to the status of global economic integration zone, in line with the idea of a 'polycentric urban system in Europe', the ESDP is marrying the opposites of promoting competitiveness as well as cohesion. (Perhaps this is what 'balanced competitiveness', the concept introduced at Noordwijk, is meant to signify.) Or, as the *Second Cohesion Report* has phrased it, while

> the concentration of economic activity in the stronger regions may lead to greater efficiency of production in the EU in the short-term, this may be at the expense of the longer-term competitiveness of the Union economy insofar as it damages their capacity to exploit comparative advantages. Moreover, the concentration of both businesses and people in particular regions conflicts with the objective of sustainable development (ibid. 29).

In all this, both the ESDP (CEC, 1999a: 20) and the *Second Cohesion Report* compare Europe unfavourably with the US where 'activity is more evenly distributed, despite its land area being twice as large as an enlarged EU and its population being much smaller (270 million inhabitants, 44 per cent less than in the EU)' (CEC, 2001a: 31).

Of course, how realistic this policy is has yet to be proven (Richardson and Jensen, 2000). In a searching review, Krätke points out that it

> is by no means certain that competitiveness on the world markets and the economic and social cohesion of the European regional system can complement each other without conflicts ensuing. It is more likely that a policy geared to strengthening world market competitiveness will lead in most cases to the ongoing development of the leading regional economic centres in Europe and

thus to a polarized spatial structure, which will tend to undermine the economic and social cohesion of the European regional system (Krätke, 2001: 112).

However, it is clear that the ESDP is a political document and the concept of a 'polycentric urban system of Europe' a compromise, and thus necessarily ambiguous. As with policy concepts in general, the criteria being applied to spatial planning concepts are different from the criteria being applied to analytical concepts, and the ability to form the basis for consensus is one that stands out amongst them.

This relates to the issue of mapping. It seems to be distinctly more difficult to reach compromise about cartographic concepts than about verbal ones. It will be remembered that the Dutch, keen on using maps to express spatial policy, have put forward a map showing the economic potential of various European regions, an initiative that has been rejected. The more innocent Figure II.1 in the Noordwijk draft was also controversial. Eventually, it made room for a representation of Europe showing nothing but the physical characteristics of the European territory, now included in the analytical Part B as Map 7: Physical Map and Distances (Figure 9.3).

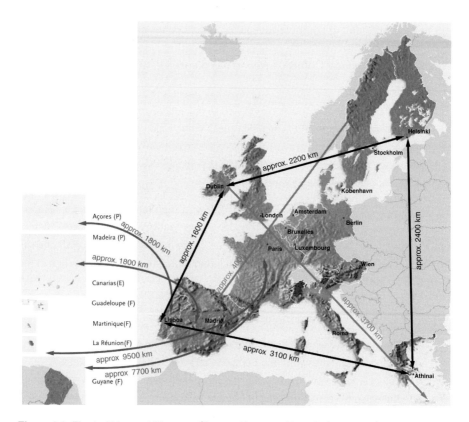

Figure 9.3 Physical Map and Distances (Source: European Commission, 1999a)

Significantly, the ESDP eschews showing the 'pentagon' on a map, even though this would have been easy, since there is nothing ambiguous about it. One of the authors of this book has done so in two alternative ways, one more abstract than the other (Faludi, 2000a, 2001a). More importantly, in a paper devoted to the ESDP, one of the key German players involved (Schön, 2000: IV) illustrates the '20-40-50 pentagon' in a way that would have fitted the format of the ESDP beautifully (Figure 9.4).

Remarkably, it shows the 'pentagon' to be almost exactly the same as the elliptical shape, shown by the Dutch to represent the core area of Europe, that had to be rescinded altogether from the Noordwijk document! (See Figure 7.3 in Chapter 7.)

Although the absence of policy maps makes the ESDP a curious spatial policy document, the reasons for this are clear. To represent areas on maps as the 'core', the 'periphery', 'developed', 'underdeveloped', or whatever attribute one might wish to give them, could be perceived as stigmatizing those concerned. In this respect, what is illustrative is an Austrian's reaction to the designation of the Alps in the Noordwijk document as a 'barrier'. This Austrian source pointed out that the Alps represent a home environment for millions of Europeans, and are not simply a barrier.

Another reason why policy maps have been eschewed is the fact that the ESDP's response to the existence of the 'pentagon' is subtle and does not lend itself easily to diagrammatical representation. It starts by positing that Europe, having

Figure 9.4 '20-40-50 pentagon' (Source: Schön, 2000)

only one global economic integration zone, as opposed to four in the USA, is dangerously exposed. Its competitive position depends solely on this one area, hence the ESDP's advocacy of the development of many more such zones. Now, there is an indication that two more areas have the potential to become global economic integration zones: the Øresund region and the region of Barcelona. However, this policy is tentative and it would be controversial to indicate just these two zones on a map, thereby excluding other contenders.

In addition, the ESDP takes a novel approach to promoting global economic integration zones. It does not follow classic regional policy, which results in claims for infrastructure investments linking peripheries to the core, and so forth. Rather, it adopts an endogenous development agenda, relying on local initiatives and networking. Naturally, this is flanked by regional policies and by the policy concerning trans-European networks, but one should not forget that the requirements of co-financing, 'additionality' and local empowerment make these, too, reflect the same agenda. The point being made here is that such policies do not lend themselves easily to being represented on maps.

Anyway, the use of spatial concepts and spatial images is one of the priority areas that the experimental SPESP (Study Programme on European Spatial Planning) has explored (Nordregio, 2000). Clearly, spatial concepts and images and their use on a European scale will remain on the agenda.

CONCLUSIONS

To take the ESDP further, a new partnership had been formed. By February the Finnish minister had visited his German counterpart to discuss the next meeting in Tampere in October 1999. By now, the hand-over from one Presidency to the next followed a well-practised routine. The Conclusions of the German Presidency invited the Finnish Presidency to do what had already been agreed at that meeting. The Finnish focus would be to make sure that the ESDP process continued. Chapter 10 will touch upon this.

The Germans also took action to inform those concerned about the ESDP. This included the CEMAT of the Council of Europe, with a membership at that time of forty-one, including the accession states. On 7 and 8 September 2000, the *Guiding Principles for Sustainable Spatial Development of the European Continent*, which emulated the principles enunciated in the ESDP, were adopted in Hanover (European Conference of Ministers Responsible for Regional Planning, 2000). At that time, Germany held the chair of CEMAT. (The next CEMAT meeting will take place in Slovenia in 2003 and will deal with the application of the *Guiding Principles*.)

The text of the ESDP was copy-edited and the document went into production. Like the Noordwijk draft, but unlike the Leipzig Principles and the Glasgow document, the final version is being published in all eleven Community languages at the expense of the Commission. The circulation of the ESDP is approximately 40,000 to 50,000. At the time of writing, various language editions are already available.

CHAPTER 10

'THE SHOW MUST GO ON'

A Dutch publication portrays the ESDP as 'no more than a snapshot in time'. It adds with some emphasis: 'The show must go on' (National Spatial Planning Agency, 2000: 12). Two more acts remain to be performed. They relate to the application and the revision of the ESDP. This chapter focuses on the application of the ESDP, meaning the extent to which it is already apparent how and by whom the ESDP is being applied. The revision of the ESDP still needs to be written. Revision touches upon the unfinished business of the competency issue. At present, the Commission is reassessing (and reasserting!) its position. This new twist in the evolving story of European spatial planning suggests the urgent need for a better understanding of what it is about. The Epilogue will make a plea for a greater emphasis on conceptualizing spatial planning, in the light of recent literature on European integration. This would help to solve the competency issue amongst other things.

APPLICATION ON COURSE

The fact that the makers of the ESDP have eschewed the mere suggestion of a European masterplan requires no further elaboration. The reader will remember Commissioner Millan disowning the idea in Nantes in 1989, and the present Commissioner, Michel Barnier, followed suit in mid-1999 during the hearings before the European Parliament prior to his appointment. Rather than as a masterplan, the ESDP has consistently been put forward as a framework. Such a framework achieves success when it does what frameworks are supposed to do: frame follow-on decisions. To find out whether the ESDP has in fact framed follow-on decisions, it is necessary to look beyond Potsdam.

Before doing that, it seems apposite to remind the reader of the ESDP's own specifications as to its follow-up. The Potsdam ESDP contains a chapter on this, like its predecessors. However, halfway through the process its makers ceased to refer to this as the 'implementation' of the ESDP, talking about its 'application' instead. Some may see this as a reason for dismissing the ESDP as a 'paper tiger', a view not shared by the present authors (see also Faludi, 1999, 2000b, 2001; Waterhout and Faludi, 2000). Rather, the switch from implementation to application signifies a rather intuitive understanding (since there has been no extensive discussion on this) of what adopting a strategic framework like the ESDP means. This is not the same as shaping development. Rather, a framework works indirectly, shaping the minds of the players involved in spatial development. Since such success is not always guaranteed, the successful application of a strategic framework requires its makers to think about further arrangements that need to be made, beyond the formal act of adopting it. This is why this section looks at what has happened since Potsdam, in particular the Action Programme adopted at Tampere and more generally at the development of Commission policy where it touches upon the ESDP.

THE TAMPERE ACTION PROGRAMME

In Tampere, Finland in October 1999, another informal meeting of EU Ministers Responsible for Spatial Planning and Urban/Regional Policy took place. It focused on the follow-up of the ESDP. (The substantive item on the agenda was the Urban Exchange Initiative, not covered in this book, which is the reason why ministers responsible for urban policy were invited.) The meeting adopted an Action Programme (Tampere Ministerial, 1999: 12–21) which listed twelve actions aiming to promote a spatial dimension in policies at Community and national level. They also hoped to improve knowledge, research and information on territorial development as well as to prepare for an enlarged territory of the European Union (Table 10.1).

The Action Programme takes a novel approach. Leading partners have committed themselves to co-ordinate the work on the various actions, with financing shared between all the partners involved. Responsibility for co-ordination and monitoring rests with the CSD. The period covered is 1999–2003. The actions will not be discussed in detail in this text. All that this is designed to demonstrate is that, as far as the policies of its makers are concerned, the application of the ESDP is on course. In the meantime, some of the actions have already borne fruit; Action 3 deserves a particular mention because it has formed the object of the first ministerial meeting since Tampere, held under the Belgian Presidency in Namur on 13–14 July 2001.

COMMISSION EAGERNESS

Naturally, the Commission is involved in the Action Programme and it is the lead partner for two of the twelve actions, addressing the spatial impacts of Community policies and enlargement. However, Commission commitment to the ESDP goes beyond these actions. The Community Initiative INTERREG has been set up of course for the purpose of applying the ESDP. For the period 2000–2006, INTERREG IIIB, as well as the Operational Programmes, are clearly intended to reflect the policy orientations of the ESDP.

In addition to INTERREG IIIB, the Structural Funds also have a role to play. The 'Guidelines for Programmes in the Period 2000–2006' state: 'The development strategy of each region must ... take account of the indicative guidelines [of the

Table 10.1 The Tampere Action Programme

Action	Lead partner and participants
1. ESDP policy orientations in SF mainstream programmes	All member states Portugal (experiences/prospects)
2. INTERREG III and ESDP demonstration projects	All member states Denmark (demo-projects)
3. ESDP policy orientations in national spatial planning	All member states Belgium (synthetic report)
4. Spatial impacts of Community policies	The Commission Portugal (ESDP/transport)
5. Territorial impact assessment	United Kingdom
6. Urban policy application and co-operation	All member states France (application experience)
7. Establishing the ESPON co-operation	Luxembourg Sweden (work programme)
8. Geography manuals for secondary schools	France
9. 'Future regions of Europe' award	Germany
10. Guide on integrated strategies for coastal regions	Spain
11. Pan-European framework for spatial development	Germany
12. Spatial impacts of enlargement on EU member states and non-member states	The Commission

ESDP] in order to include them in a broad overall view, not just of the country in question but the Union as a whole' (CEC, 1999g: 39). It will be remembered that, although financial allocations will not be affected, the implementation of policy under the Structural Funds will be guided by the ESDP. This was announced by Wulf-Mathies in Noordwijk in 1997, and apparently it is actually happening.

There is also a less well-known programme financed under Article 10 of the ERDF Regulation (the same one under which *Europe 2000* and *Europe 2000+* were funded). It is called TERRA and represents a laboratory for testing new approaches to and methodologies for spatial planning. Together with INTERREG IIC programmes, it is intended to assess the relevance of the policy options in the ESDP and as a 'means to demonstrating the importance of a multisectoral and integrated approach to spatial planning' (CEC, 2000b, 7). TERRA comprises fifteen projects, with sixty-three partners from eleven member states. It was conceived as a network 'in which all projects and individual partners were influenced by the ESDP and its development and by the interest in applying a modern spatial planning approach at the local level' (ibid 13). This relates to all three priority areas (obviously meaning the three 'spheres of activity') of the ESDP.

In addition, the Commission has published a Communication and a draft Recommendation on Integrated Coastal Zone Management (ICZM), which talks about 'territorial management' as the way forward, not only for coastal zones, but for other areas as well. Since this may be indicative of Commission intentions, it will be discussed in some detail. The Communication takes the reader on a comprehensive tour of current Commission policy:

> With the objective of encouraging balanced and integrated territorial manage-
> ment, the Commission will continue to encourage the application of the political
> conclusions contained in the European Spatial Development Perspective (ESDP)
> in the implementation of actions financed through the Structural Funds and par-
> ticularly through the Community Initiative INTERREG programme. *The
> Commission will work with the member states to support the application of the
> ESDP, including integrated spatial planning and management across adminis-
> trative, natural and socio-economic units.* In order to adequately address the
> specific needs of the coastal zone, in applying the ESDP, member states should
> include coastal waters (CEC, 2000c: 12; emphases in the original).

The Communication not only reviews relevant policy areas, but also refers to general mechanisms for internal co-ordination already in place, alongside current efforts '*to improve its procedures to ensure coherence between its various policies.* This horizontal process should improve, *inter alia*, collaboration on policies that influence coastal zones' (ibid. 18).

Coastal zone management is based on eight principles: a broad 'holistic' perspective (thematic and geographic), a long-term perspective, reflecting local specificity, working with natural processes, participatory planning, support and involvement of all relevant administrative bodies and the use of a combination of instruments. These are not specific to the coast, 'but rather are fundamental components of good governance' (ibid. 23; the theme of EU governance as such is the topic of a recent Communication COM(2001)428, designed to reform Community decision making; see CEC, 2001b). This is where the wider implications of the Communication on coastal zone management come to the fore:

> A broader adoption of such principles for good territorial management could
> improve conditions in individual parts of the territory, including the coast. It could
> also ensure that the many physical, institutional and socio-economic links
> between coastal zones and the other parts of the EU territory are not ignored as
> a result of separate planning and management activities specific to individual
> sections of the territory. Indeed, the EU is already promoting integrated territorial
> management on a broader scale ... The principles behind this ICZM Strategy
> closely parallel those of the European Spatial Development Perspective (ESDP),

and are also mirrored in the Commission's urban activities. The revision of the Structural Funds and the EU Agricultural Policies applied under Agenda 2000 are also moving towards a general implementation of the principles of good territorial management. However, the process of making these principles a foundation of governance will necessarily be slow because it involves a change of culture.

> This strategy therefore proposes some specific actions that can be applied directly to the coastal zones ... while a more general culture of territorial management is developing ... *The Commission will be studying how the Integrated Territorial Management approach can be eventually extended across the entire territory of the EU* (ibid. 23–4, italics in the original).

Interestingly, where the English version of this Communication speaks of 'integrated territorial management', the French version refers to *'l'aménagement intégré du territoire'*. Has the process returned to its starting point, with the invocation of this thoroughly French concept at the level of the Community?

Note also that the ICZM Demonstration Programme (1996–9) on which the Communication is based, has been a joint programme of DGs Environment, Regional Policy, and Fisheries. Based on information received from the DG Environment, it appears that the Communication itself (COM/00/547) was drafted by that DG in consultation with other services, and then formally proposed by the Commissioner for the Environment in agreement with the Commissioner for Regional Policy. Apparently, the 'horizontal approach' advocated in the Communication has already found its way into Commission practice.

Its implications for the future of the ESDP process are unclear, and whether DG Environment will take a greater interest in it is difficult to say. What is clear, though, is the commitment to pursue the ideas set out in the ESDP, in whatever form.

The same determination is evident in another Communication (CEC, 2000i), which refers to the ESDP in its margin. The topic of the Communication is 'Services of General Interest in Europe'. It identifies these services as key elements of the 'European model of society'. (Delors was also fond of talking about a 'European model of society'.) Under Article 16 of the Treaty of Amsterdam such services have a place among the shared values of the Union. Introduced at the behest of the *Assemblé des régions d'Europe*, the present Commissioner for Regional Policy, Michel Barnier, then French Minister of European Affairs, was instrumental in including this article in the Treaty (Husson, 2000: 85). Article 16 also refers to another concept, 'territorial cohesion'. Throughout the ESDP process, there have also been various references to territorial or spatial cohesion (sometimes also to spatial 'coherence') as a complement to the twin concepts of economic and social cohesion in the European treaties. Although relating solely to services of general interest, Taulelle (2000: 62) regards the presence of the concept of territorial cohesion in the treaties as significant for the development of European spatial planning.

Be that as it may, the Communication addresses the way in which these services impact upon territorial cohesion. The claim is that they contribute to the overall competitiveness of European industry and to economic, social and territorial cohesion, thus making them a Community concern. In paragraph 63 of the Communication, the Commission seems to be contemplating a kind of benchmarking:

> In order to facilitate the evaluation of services of general economic interest the Commission could envisage an examination of the results achieved overall in the Member States in the operation of these services and the effectiveness of the regulatory frameworks. Such an examination should take into particular account the interactions between different infrastructure networks, and the objectives of both economic efficiency, consumer protection and economic, social and territorial cohesion (CEC, 2000i).

Amongst 'other community contributions in support of services of general interest', the Communication mentions the ESDP. The whole concept reflects a French discourse. As reported in Chapter 6, France has abandoned the short-lived idea of a national planning scheme, as formulated in the *loi Pasqua* of 1995. Instead, the *loi Voynet* of 1999 has introduced nine 'schemes of collective services' (*schémas de services collectifs*). 'Collective services' include traditional public utilities, as well as sports facilities and amenities like open space and nature areas. After all, the Minister for Planning at that time, Dominique Voynet from the Green Party, was also responsible for the environment. The schemes will be based on long-term assessments of need (Alvergne and Musso, 2000: 52). After consultations, the state proposes to enter into covenants (*contrats du plan*) with regard to the level of services to be provided. The intended partners seem to be the so-called *pays*, territories characterized by their geographic, economic, cultural or social cohesion. A *pay* is not a new administrative unit, though; it is instead a framework for mobilizing public and private players into carrying out certain tasks. It is in this context that the notion of territorial cohesion is being invoked (DATAR, 2000: 25). From other sources (Husson, 2000) it seems that this concept relates to a concern to counteract the disruptive effects of globalization on local and regional communities.

The publication of the *Second Report on Economic and Social Cohesion* (CEC, 2001a), at around the same time as the manuscript of this book was completed, reinforces the impression that the Commission is reformulating the spatial planning discourse as a Community concern, under the flag of territorial cohesion. In its discussion of the core zone of Europe, Chapter 9 has already shown how this report has taken some key ideas of the ESDP on board. The passages quoted there are to be found in Section I.3, 'Territorial cohesion: towards more balanced

development'. It is clear that at long last 'territorial cohesion' and/or 'territorial management' are now forming part of the Community discourse and that the ESDP has
been an important source of inspiration. As will become evident further on pages
174–5, the White Paper on European governance strongly reinforces this impression. If, by virtue of its application in such a prominent sense and for no other
reason, the ESDP may already be considered a success.

REVISION A DISTANT PROSPECT

A conviction held throughout has been that even after the ESDP has been finalized,
the momentum must not be allowed to diminish. This is in line with modern views of
planning being a continuous process, the strategic variety in particular. Once implemented, a masterplan has served its purpose and may be allowed to lapse. Strategy
can only remain operative if it is regularly updated.

However, in 1998 the Commission representative at the CSD seminar in
Vienna (to be discussed) warned that revising the ESDP may not be a wise course of
action (Austrian Presidency, 1999), and others have adopted his viewpoint since.
Obviously, one needs to take into account all concerns about how revising the ESDP
could undermine its political legitimacy. However, there is a counter-argument. If revision should take place at around the time of the first round of enlargements as the
Potsdam document suggests, then time is pressing. Admittedly, there is no fixed
timetable for enlargement. Still, the first Luxembourg group of accession states
(Estland, Poland, Slovenia, Hungary and Cyprus) along with Latvia and Malta, are
hoping to join on 1 January 2003, by which time the EU wants to have everything in
order to be able to receive them (Deutscher Bauernverband, 2000: 119). These
expectations may be unrealistic, and dates from 2004 onwards are now being floated
as more realistic targets. (However, the Irish referendum of May 2001 which goes
against the ratification of the Treaty of Nice, designed to pave the way for enlargement, has shown once more how vulnerable the whole process is.)

A study published by the Commission (Biehl et al., 2000: 35–7) describes what
a revision of the ESDP would minimally entail, taking account of enlargement. It would
mean modifying or extending the ESDP 'in order to take account of the different conditions prevailing in the CEECs [Central and Eastern European Countries] and to
facilitate their accession'. Issues are that of diversity and heterogeneity, national cen-
tralization and regional decentralization, spatial planning versus regional policy (unitary
versus dual competency) and sustainable development versus regional policy.

The point about revising the ESDP is that, although preliminary studies on
enlargement do figure in the Action Programme, there are no arrangements regarding how to make an early start with the actual work. Judging by past experiences, it

would certainly be prudent to make the necessary provisions early on. If the character of the ESDP process to date is indicative of its future, then these provisions
would entail both the scheduling of ministerial meetings, and the formulation of a
work programme by the CSD, to be carried out by successive Presidencies over
several years, as is always the case with active Commission involvement. The most
probable explanation of why this has not happened is the generally unsettled nature
of arrangements for the continuation of the ESDP process. This points to what has
been described as the competency issue. Focusing on the practical work, Chapters
7–9 have bracketed the evolving debate on this issue. It is now an appropriate point
to review its progress.

UNFINISHED BUSINESS

Shortly after Noordwijk, two Commission officials (both of them *experts nationaux
détachés*, one a Danish national and the other an inhabitant of Wallonia in Belgium)
gave glimpses of the thinking within DG XVI (Bastrup-Birk and Doucet, 1997).
Unquestionably, the authors had the blessing of their superiors in publishing this.
They argued that strategic spatial planning was unlike land-use planning (for which
the Community had no competency, nor as the reader will remember did it ever want
one). For strategic spatial planning the Community could simply build on existing
competencies. The two authors also suggested that the Council of General Affairs
might adopt a resolution under what was then Article 235 of the EC Treaty, declar-
ing the ESDP a strategic reference document.

Nothing has come from this, but it shows that the Commission continued to
hold out for a formal role in the ESDP process. Since then, the competency issue
was central in Echternach in 1997 and the CSD seminar in Vienna in 1998. Most
recently, the Finnish Presidency put all the options on the table. This section discusses these events and their outcomes. Sadly, they do not point to a resolution of
the competency issue.

ESPON

As will be remembered, after The Netherlands it was Luxembourg's turn to fulfil the
Presidency of the European Union. Its history, geographic position and language mix
make the Grand Duchy highly open to international thinking. Its professional elite is
mainly educated abroad, giving it a good grasp of what is happening elsewhere. Of
course the personnel capacity is rather limited. One pragmatic solution to this problem
involved employing an expert from the University of Trier across the German border.

Draft national planning guidelines for Luxembourg, which were published concurrently with the Potsdam document, identify three levels of international co-operation. The European-wide level represented in *Europe 2000+* and the ESDP, of which the guidelines are an elaboration, is the first level. The transnational level is the second, featuring a 'Sarre-Lor-Lux+' Scheme prepared in the wake of Leipzig for the Grand Duchy, the Saarland, parts of the Palatinate and Lorraine and the Belgian province of Luxembourg. This scheme is structured according to the three 'spheres of activity' in the ESDP. Lastly, there is cross-border planning, sometimes under INTERREG IIA, involving co-operation with Belgium, Germany and France (Ministère de l'Aménagement du Territoire, 1999). Like other small countries (for instance Denmark; see Ministry of Environment and Energy, 1997, and Finland; see Ministry of the Environment, 1999; Lass, 2000: 32) Luxembourg is taking the ESDP seriously.

In 1997, rather than focusing on the ESDP (then in the process of being turned into the *Complete Draft* for the Glasgow meeting of 1998) the Luxembourg Presidency turned its attention to ESPON at the invitation of the CSD. A co-operation network of spatial research institutes to support the ESDP work had been a discussion point almost from the beginning (Williams, 1999). In 1997, 'European Spatial Planning Observatory Network' (ESPON; ORATE in French, NERPO in German) became its title. Luxembourg organized, if not a ministerial meeting, then at least a ministerial 'seminar' (the difference being one of protocol) in Echternach in late 1997. For this meeting it produced a 'Concept on the Establishment of the European Spatial Planning Observatory Network (ESPON)'. A 'task force' consisting of representatives from Germany, Italy, Luxembourg, Spain and Sweden continued this work until late 1998. By that time, it had become clear that ESPON would not be straightforward.

ESPON was to be a research network doing technical work, preparing the ground for periodic reviews of the ESDP. (In 1995, the intention had still been for the Observatory, as it was then called, to provide the groundwork for the ESDP itself, but then the opportunity lapsed.) Together with the permanent secretariat of ESPON, the CSD would be responsible for formulating the work programme. The permanent secretariat would also double up as secretariat for the CSD, a role that up until then had been fulfilled by DG XVI.

In proposing a test phase, the Echternach document laid the groundwork for the 'Study Programme in European Spatial Planning', which was to be co-financed by the Commission under Article 10 of the ERDF regulations. However, the Commission informed the task force that Article 10 was designed for pilot actions only and not for work of a more permanent nature. It was therefore the long-term financing of ESPON that formed the main object of deliberations. The task force followed the well-trodden path of multilateral consultations, at which the Commission's Legal Service gave a testimony.

The Legal Service ruled out the option of ESPON operating as a private-law association because this would not enable the Commission to participate. The options were: either a Council decision to be made under Article 235 (Article 308 at the time of writing) of the EC Treaty, based on the argument that, in the course of the operation of the common market, ESPON was necessary to attain one of the Community objectives or an agreement under international law. With regard to the second option, the Legal Service foresaw problems, which in effect confined the course of action to the Article 235 route. Article 235 entailed the Commission making a proposal to one of the various formations of the Council of Ministers, under its right of initiative. Acceptance would be contingent upon the consent of national ministries other than those responsible for planning. In fact, those other ministries (for instance transport, environment, economics or even the foreign ministries) would actually have to sponsor spatial planning. The reader will remember that it was the perennial conflict with precisely those ministries (in particular economics and finance) that had prevented the formalization of planning in the past, and there was nothing to suggest that the situation had changed.

During consultations, a member of the European Parliament suggested placing ESPON under the umbrella of technical support for innovative measures, as foreseen in the revised regulations on the general provisions of the Structural Funds.

In their 1998 report, the task force spelt out a number of home truths, with wider application than ESPON alone. The Commission did not wish to be accused of stretching its mandate. Member states would thus have to unanimously invite the Commission to create an initiative. It will be remembered that in the past whole policy areas were opened up by the use of Article 235 such as environment and regional policy. However, as is widely known, the general mood regarding European integration had become somewhat inauspicious, and a positive signal from member states would therefore be required to jolt the Commission into action.

At that time though, Spain was still a reluctant partner because of the potential link that it saw with the Structural Funds, and so the task force noted that Spain, as well as Greece, found the route via Article 235 difficult to accept. Therefore, without much enthusiasm, the task force investigated the inter-governmental approach. Initially, only the British were in favour, but eventually Spain and Greece joined them. The other member states saw this as a fallback position. In the end, notwithstanding some difficulties, the task force recommended taking the Article 235 route. Their optimistic hope was that a definite proposal with regard to ESPON would be on the table at Potsdam, together with the final ESDP. As will become evident, it would take until the tail end of 2000 for ESPON to be fully set up.

THE CSD SEMINAR

In late 1998, the Austrian Presidency organized a CSD seminar, which was to have a free-ranging discussion on the future (Austrian Presidency, 1999). This was the occasion mentioned earlier, during which a Commission representative warned against any premature talk about revising the ESDP. (It was also the occasion at which one of this book's authors met the full CSD!) At this seminar, concerns were expressed that the ESDP process should not fade into oblivion once the document had been adopted. The discussion was structured around four questions: What can a European and transnational spatial planning approach achieve, and with what instruments? Who really needs European spatial planning? Which political challenges are likely to arise over the next decade? What are the necessary (and feasible!) arrangements for European spatial planning? There were four keynote speeches followed by discussions. Since this meeting was not about policy, participants were encouraged to speak their minds.

The published proceedings provide evidence of searching discussions. Take for instance the following quote: 'We have been very focused on the ESDP text in the past; we missed the wider picture!' (ibid. 48). Also witness the quote: 'We must become more professional!' (ibid. 48). The position of DG XVI came to the fore as a fundamental issue. The report of the Austrian Presidency cast doubt on the restrictive interpretation of the Commission's role, as merely that of one partner amongst many. 'One should look for more positive words. EC/DG XVI has two important tasks: to ensure contacts with sectoral policies on the European level and to influence the agenda for the next Commission' (ibid. 48).

The Commission representative (an Austrian from the Organization for Economic Co-operation and Development, the OECD, who had joined DG XVI to replace the Greek national working on the ESDP) gave a glimpse into the internal workings of the Commission. He volunteered the information that the ESDP process had drawn the attention of the environmental Directorate-General (the same one that would prepare the Communication on integrated coastal zone management two years later) and the Secretariat-General responsible for tracking new European initiatives. The experience of writing the *Cohesion Report* (CEC, 1996) had demonstrated that various EU policies followed different approaches. The ESDP could be useful in this situation, but a problem was that DG XVI had little negotiating power. DG XVI therefore suggested that the ESDP should focus on truly European issues. The concept of polycentric development was identified as a winner. (As the reader knows already from Chapter 9, the Potsdam document would indeed put a strong emphasis on polycentrism.) Furthermore, the representative of DG XVI emphasized that an action programme (this was before Tampere!) should focus on the application of the ESDP.

The Austrian Presidency drew a number of conclusions from this. They believed, for instance, that 'a lot of further discussion will be necessary until we arrive at something like a common understanding' (ibid. 52). It was clear that opportunities for joint reflection were needed. INTERREG IIC was seen as a framework for experimenting with transnational co-operation and as such it was worth sustaining for the next Programming Period. As a last point the Austrians concluded that the 'genuine European dimension of European spatial policies has to be strengthened and a useful division of labour between the member states and the Commission has to be found' (ibid. 53).

THE TAMPERE PAPER

Contrary to the hopes of the task force on ESPON, at Potsdam there was no further discussion of the wider issues involved. That discussion was postponed until Tampere. In addition to the Action Programme discussed above, the Finnish Presidency prepared a 'Discussion Paper on Future Co-operation in European Spatial Planning and Development' (Tampere Ministerial, 1999: 22–9). The paper gave a comprehensive overview of the situation with regard to the status of the CSD and the ministerial meetings. It started by reflecting on the need for continued co-operation, referring to economic integration and to co-operation between member states and other interested parties, to enlargement, environmental challenges, technological innovation and the role of local and regional authorities in spatial development. All of this called for better co-ordination. Community policies, too, would continue to influence the development of the European territory. In short, spatial development would remain an important focus of attention.

From here, the paper explored the formation of what it called a European territorial identity. The current perception of the European territory was inadequate: it was still based on a centre–periphery model according to the Finnish, described by this book as a view of 'one-dimensional Europe'. Underlining the emphasis in the ESDP on polycentricity, the paper claimed that the European territory should be seen as having a polycentric and balanced structure supporting the competitiveness of the EU, whilst at the same time promoting sustainable development and economic and social cohesion. In short, the view of a 'diversified Europe' had carried the day.

However, the development of a European territorial identity was not a matter for member states alone. European institutions had expressed an interest, and the Commission would evidently have a role to play in promoting cross-border and transnational co-operation and in monitoring territorial trends and bringing a spatial dimension to bear on relevant Community policies. In addition, it was necessary of course to prepare for enlargement.

All this called for a spatial development perspective. Like the Action Programme, the paper paid tribute to the pan-European *Guiding Principles for Sustainable Development of the European Continent*, then under development, and asked for an assessment of the spatial impacts of enlargement. It then specified that EU institutions, member states and accession states should be involved in this. In addition, what was also relevant was the preparation of the next Programming

Period for the Structural Funds, starting in 2006.

The paper emphasized the innovative character of spatial planning. It could improve co-operation between sectors pursuing common territorial objectives at national and regional/local as well as at Community level. Invoking common territorial concepts would increase the effectiveness of interventions and reduce the risk of investment failures.

Spatial planning was also a tool for sustainable and balanced development. It should focus on the overall situation of the European territory, taking into account any opportunities arising from enlargement. It was evident, though, that spatial development required co-operation between public authorities on various levels.

Having made the case for European planning, the paper went on to explore the role of the Community. Basically, there was a need for stability and continuity, to enable the Commission to play a stronger support role, ensure close co-operation between Community services and facilitate the monitoring of spatial development trends by a network of research institutes. Some instruments were needed at Community level. Demonstrating its aversion to a communautarian form of planning, the Finnish paper indicated that the idea of a Community competency as such should be put to rest. However, it made eminent sense for the Community to monitor European territorial developments and to co-operate with member states in developing European spatial development strategies as well as in setting up a political platform to promote the spatial dimension of relevant Community policies. In fact, this amounted to a plea for the formalization of existing arrangements.

The paper went on to explore the problem of the hybrid character of the CSD, which contained elements of both an expert group, normally convened by the Commission, and a Council Working Party. It reminded readers that the Council and/or Parliament could create committees only within the framework of the EC Treaty. As the task force on ESPON had previously concluded, the way out would be the route via Article 308 (ex-235) of the Treaty. The Finnish paper repeated, though, that it was the Commission's responsibility to initiate such a procedure.

With regard to the suggestion made by certain delegations (referring of course to the Germans) to transform the CSD into a Council Working Party, the Finnish paper noted that this was a matter for the Council itself. Once again though, the initiative lay with the Commission. At any rate, once established, a Council Working Party would primarily have to react to Commission initiatives. It was clear that the future role of the ESDP and of European spatial planning touched upon issues of competency and subsidiarity. For the sake of progress, the Finnish paper invited member states and the Commission to debate the issues, expressing the hope that this could be part of the preparations for the next Intergovernmental Conference (the one to culminate in the Nice Summit at the end of 2000). One way forward would be to consider a limited competency for the

Commission to develop overall strategies for the European territory, to monitor trends and to engage in policy co-ordination at Community level, but not in matters relating to national competencies in land-use planning. Note that since then one of the key participants from The Netherlands, Martin (2000), has also mooted the idea of such a limited competency for the Community. The Finnish Report continued by saying that any decision with regard to the long-term future of the CSD would have to be left pending until this debate has been resolved. As an interim solution, the CSD should continue as an 'expert group' under the regulations pertaining to 'comitology' committees.

The Finnish paper considered it indispensable to monitor European territorial development trends. It referred to the 'Study Programme in European Spatial Planning', then already under way. Obviously, this was a test phase for ESPON. With regard to possible models for the latter, a solution for the short and medium term would be to set it up as a joint INTERREG III project involving all member states, with the Commission playing an active role. The maximum time span for such an undertaking should be the Programming Period 2000–6, with a possibility of reviewing its progress after four years. Whilst this was being done, there would be time for more permanent arrangements to be made. They would require a broad consensus on the objectives and role of European spatial development and planning. This was why it was necessary to contemplate a Community competency for the research and monitoring of European territorial trends.

The paper concluded by proposing a task force to continue the discussion. This task force should work in close co-operation with its counterpart on ESPON, led by Luxembourg. The paper expressed the hope of a concrete political decision taking place during the French Presidency in the second half of 2000. Curiously, these detailed proposals hardly received any mention in the Conclusions of the Finnish Presidency. The latter merely stated:

> The Ministers and the Commission agreed to continue their discussion on how the concrete framework for their co-operation could be improved. It was considered important to ask for the opinion of the new European Parliament, the Council and the Committee of the Regions on an appropriate future co-operation framework (Tampere Ministerial, 1999).

HE WHO PAYS THE PIPER CALLS THE TUNE

Shortly after the start of the Finnish Presidency, at a CSD in July 1999, the Commission spelt out its position clearly, and this had been declared in the Finnish paper. Essentially, the Commission had reiterated its opinion that the CSD was an anomaly. Bringing the CSD in line with comitology rules, in future it was to be regarded as an expert group, and so the Commission would only pay the expenses of one member per delegation instead of two, as had hitherto been the case.

Commission sources convincingly denied that this was done to put pressure on the CSD, in retaliation for the member states' lack of enthusiasm for a Commission role in spatial planning. For some time, the Legal Service had insisted that in view of new regulations governing 'comitology' committees, demanded by the European Parliament (Hix, 1999: 45), DG Regio (the new designation of DG XVI) needed to regularize the CSD position. With a view to safeguarding the completion of the ESDP, DG Regio had simply shielded the CSD from this regularization; now that the ESDP was on the books, this was no longer an option. Still, member state delegations might be excused for thinking that the Commission had decided to become tough.

At that time, Council Regulation 1260/1999 was also passed; Article 48 of this regulation established the Committee of Development and Conversion of Regions (CDCR) (CEC, 2000g: 69–70) as a management committee, giving opinions on draft measures submitted to it by the Commission representative. On other matters, mainly with regard to the Structural Funds, it was intended to operate as a consultative committee. This relates to Objectives 1 (Development and structural adjustments of regions whose development is lagging behind) and 2 (Supporting the economic and social conversion of areas facing structural difficulties). Unlike Objective 3 (Adapting and modernising policies and systems of education, training and employment), Objectives 1 and 2 focus on specified regions (CEC, 2000g, 10–15).

At around the same time, the revised ERDF Regulation (EC) 1783/1999 was published, allowing for the continued funding of innovative measures, for 'studies initiated by the Commission to identify and analyze regional development problems and solutions, particularly with a view to the harmonious, balanced and sustainable development of the whole of the Community's territory, including the European Spatial Development Perspective' (Article 4) amongst others, thus demonstrating once again that the Commission was alive to the importance of the ESDP.

In the meantime, at the end of 2000, DG Regio proposed to establish a sub-committee on spatial development under the Committee on the Development and Conversion of Regions (CDCR), the latter being set up under regulations adopted the previous year. Naturally, the Commission will chair this sub-committee, but it will have its own agenda, independently from the CDCR, with member states and the Commission both having an equal say. Some member states are hesitant, though. On an interim basis, the CSD continues with a brief to look after the co-operation between the accession states, neighbouring countries and Mediterranean countries and to assist with the orientations for ESPON. Whether it will continue to meet after the sub-committee has officially been formed remains a moot point.

There are more signals to indicate a firm commitment on the part of the Commission to make a success of the ESDP, whilst at the same time keeping the member states in reign. Thus, the Commission plans to bring out a communication on the application of the ESDP in the Objective 1 and 2 mainstream programmes. Also, ESPON will now materialize, with the Management Authority located in Luxembourg. ESPON will be engaged in thematic studies and work on cartography and statistical indicators. The Commission has given some orientations for the period 2001–6. There will be a mid-term review, just as the Finnish had proposed. Three or more member states can make joint proposals for co-financed projects. The Commission will adopt the programme, with the Management Authority in charge of co-ordination.

Most importantly, the Commission, in its White Paper on European governance, has placed the ESDP at the core of its future efforts to achieve more coherence, this being one of the five 'principles of good governance' that it wants to pursue:

> Policies and action must be coherent and easily understood. The need for coherence in the Union is increasing: the range of tasks has grown; enlargement will increase diversity; challenges such as climate and demographic change cross the boundaries of the sectoral policies on which the Union has been built; regional and local authorities are increasingly involved in EU policies. Coherence requires political leadership and a strong responsibility on the part of the Institutions to ensure a consistent approach within a complex system (CEC, 2001b: 10).

One can easily interpret this as referring to the need for some form of spatial planning, amongst other requirements. However, did the Commission not have other, more important issues on its agenda? Further down, where the Commission makes proposals for change, any remaining doubts disappear. Under 'overall policy coherence', the White Paper states:

> The territorial impact of EU policies in areas such as transport, energy or environment should be addressed. These policies should form part of a coherent whole as stated in the EU's second cohesion report; there is a need to avoid a logic which is too sector-specific. In the same way, decisions taken at regional and local levels should be coherent with a broader set of principles that would underpin more sustainable and balanced territorial development within the Union.
>
> The Commission intends to use the enhanced dialogue with member states and their regions and cities to develop indicators to identify where coher-

ence is needed. It will build upon existing works, such as the European Spatial Development Perspective adopted in 1999 by Ministers responsible for spatial planning and territorial development. This work of promoting better coherence between territorial development actions at different levels should also feed the review of policies in view of the Sustainable Development Strategy (CEC, 2001b: 13).

Note that a former member of the Delors cabinet and director of the Forward Studies Unit of the European Commission, later a director at DATAR and as such a member of the CSD, has been called to Brussels to work on this White Paper. Presumably this is why the ESDP has received the attention that it surely deserves. The stage seems set for a revival of Commission interest in spatial planning.

CONCLUSION

In the light of these developments, will ministers continue to meet and deliberate on CSD proposals and in time accede to a revised and, one hopes, improved ESDP?

In fact, since Tampere, there has been a lull in the proceedings. The Portuguese Presidency of 2000 passed without much incident, and the French, despite organizing a ministerial seminar in Lille, seemed to lack inspiration. (They have done good work, though, on the 'polycentric system of cities in Europe'.) As indicated, the Belgians have held the one and only classic ministerial meeting to date on the application of the ESDP in the member states, this being the specific action in the framework of the Tampere Action Programme, for which they are the lead partner. At the time of writing, the results of this meeting are not yet available.

Whilst the member states are adopting a position of 'wait-and-see', the Commission thus reasserts its position. It appears that European spatial planning will veer towards a form of *aménagement du territoire*, integrated in the Commission's regional policy and hopefully co-ordinated with other Community spatial policies.

Whoever is afraid of a dominant Commission may take comfort from the knowledge that the personal capacity devoted to this task continues to be pitifully small. In addition, using the 'comitology' system, the Commission has always been good at drawing on the resources of member states, and there is no reason to assume that this will not continue. Albeit in a different form, the co-operative relationship established within the CSD may thus continue although, to be sure, Presidencies will be far less important. The course will be set out by the Commission and not by the member states.

What this will mean for the revision of the ESDP remains unclear. Without the inputs of successive Presidencies that have propelled the ESDP process along, will revision be feasible? So far, nobody seems to have posed the question, let alone attempted to answer it. People are concerned with the business of the day, the establishment of ESPON and the re-positioning of the CSD in relation to the sub-committee of the Committee on the Development and Conversion of Regions, the CDCR. The Commission seems convinced that, even without the CSD, it can make good use of the ideas generated during the ESDP process. They appear to be thinking that in future they will have no need for the institutions that have produced these ideas, the informal ministerial meetings and the international network established around the national representatives on the CSD.

EPILOGUE

The ESDP process has generated the institutional capacity for a voluntary form of European spatial planning. Chapter 10 has shown that this institutional capacity is in danger of evaporating.

The situation being described results from the stalemate surrounding the 'competency issue'. Member state acceptance of a modest Community role in planning could have prevented this. However, these are inauspicious times to be advancing arguments in favour of greater integration. The issues are of course much wider than just the field of planning. As Chapter 2 has shown, there is much uncertainty about the meaning of European integration, let alone the current or future position of spatial planning, in the evolving context of EU governance (the topic of a very recent White Paper; see CEC, 2001b).

It is therefore necessary to place spatial planning in the context of general thinking about European integration. This is where the issues of sovereignty and subsidiarity are relevant. Conceptualizing European spatial planning in the light of the general literature on integration is a tall order and certainly beyond the scope of this book, which has merely been about the 'flow of policy' culminating in the ESDP. With the exception of a report by a working party of the Academy of Regional Research and Planning (Akademie für Raumforschung und Landesplanung, 1996; see also Faludi, 1997a) no sustained attempt has been made to position spatial planning in the context of general thinking about European integration.

Of course, this may turn out to be a fool's errand. The literature is complex. Much of it is about historic missions and major issues, such as the European treaties. Positions are presented as polar opposites, like that of 'functionalists' promoting integration on the one hand and 'realists' emphasizing the dominance of nation states on the other. One growing body of literature is different, though. It is not about 'grand theory' but about the actual workings of European institutions. This literature tends to take a middle ground and adopt concepts which planning writers are more accustomed to, like networks, discourses and governance. From this literature, what is needed is a reasoned agenda for a theoretical reflection on European spatial planning.

Once again, this is not the task of this book. This is merely suggesting that, in order to clarify further the enterprise of European spatial planning, such theoretical work would be needed.

The initiators of the ESDP process would probably be the first to agree. When embarking upon this process, there was no way that they could have appreciated what the outcome would be. Certainly, it has evolved a long way from the straightforward idea in the beginning of a spatial strategy to underpin the delivery of the Structural Funds. Rather than allowing the Commission to develop such a spatial strategy and put it before a Council of Ministers, successive Presidencies involved themselves instead. Obviously, some were more in sympathy with the Community and its regional policy than others. In view of the existence of different and, indeed, divergent planning traditions, it is clear that the process could never have been neat and cumulative but was necessarily somewhat messy, with ideas bouncing back and forth and simultaneously changing shape. The authors have set out to document the twists and turns of this learning process.

In all this, it remains clear that the process has not only been shaped by anonymous forces, but also and in particular by specific individuals. One outstanding task is to reflect on their attitudes and skills.

As experience cumulates, the preconditions of successful participation in international planning become clearer. Pallagst (2000: 97–108) gives a profile of successful national planning in a European context, and this will form the starting point for a reflection on the attitudes and skills of international planners. Concerning national planning as such, she refers to planning levels and their relations (subsidiarity, strengthening of regions and the capacity to participate in international co-operation) and to the approach (action-oriented, willing to take European perspectives on board and to form an overall national strategy). On the basis of the *Compendium*, she concludes that eight member states (Austria, Denmark, Finland, France, Germany, Greece, Ireland and The Netherlands) all have a national strategy or are in the process of formulating one.

Once again, Pallagst refers to planning systems and not planners. By showing the skills that planners have applied throughout the ESDP process, this book adds to her analysis. Many aspects of daily life are affected by European integration, and this applies with even greater force to politics and administration, including planning. In the past, foreign policy has been the privilege of diplomats. At present, players operating on all levels and in all branches of government engage in diplomacy. They receive delegations from abroad, organize international workshops, set up and participate in international projects (for instance in the framework of INTER-REG IIC/IIIB), negotiate with foreign investors, network with colleagues from abroad and lobby in Brussels. In fact, their geographic position and whether and how they are embedded in international networks is probably a stronger determinant of the external orientation of local and regional authorities than any formal competency, or the lack thereof. Witness Lille occupying a leading position thanks to an energetic former French minister becoming mayor. Located on the high-speed line from Paris to Brussels and to London, it has been selected as the seat of the secretariat of the INTERREG IIIB programme for north-west Europe, rather than London (where the secretariat of the INTERNET IIC programme for the 'Northwest Metropolitan Area' has been located).

Personal skills also have a role to play in all this. Using various terms, scholars talk about what is often described nowadays as 'governance', meaning the inter-related nature of European, national, regional and local levels. This cannot fail to have an impact on the day-to-day work of planners. Indeed, as will be remembered, the ESDP itself asks for the 'Europeanization' of regional and local planning (CEC, 1999a: 45).

Too often, Europeanization is seen as a zero-sum game, as if all that matters is minimizing the impact of European regulations (witness the widespread consterna-tion about the requirement of designating bird protection areas) and maximizing the receipt of European funds. However, Europeanization is also about new perspec-tives, about better being able to position oneself in European space.

The focus here has not been on the Europeanization of planning practice as such. Rather, the focus has been on the vanguard of international planners who are actively shaping the process. Going by the evidence of the ESDP process, what are their attitudes and skills? To start with, the researchers have discovered the 'roving band of planners' (Faludi, 1997b) involved in the ESDP to be highly dedicated pro-fessionals. One cannot help being impressed by their drive and initiative. Surely, after so many meetings the glamour of international travel must have worn thin, but their commitment has been unswerving and has included weekends. (Some of them have been involved since Nantes, over a period of more than ten years!)

Also, one cannot help being impressed by the sheer skill that this group of planners have exhibited. Their expertise not only concerns the professional aspects of their work, but also the conduct of negotiations, the preparation of meetings, down to the minutiae of making travel arrangements, budgeting and paying bills, as well as the development and maintenance of international networks, and so forth.

Since European integration has ceased to be the reserve of diplomats, this has obviously meant that other players have had to develop discretion and other diplomatic skills. For non-English speakers, despite translation facilities provided by the Commission for the CSD and by the member states organizing ministerial meet-ings, this in fact implies the ability to communicate in the idiom of Euro-English. It also implies developing a feel for other cultures and for the exigencies of interna-tional exchanges. Where ministerial meetings are concerned, protocol comes into it as well. Witness the arrangements for inviting, accommodating and seating delega-tions and for the conduct of meetings which, informal or not, mirror the proceedings of the Council of Ministers. These skills are not covered by a typical planning course.

The point is that as Europeanization intensifies, all these skills will be required, not only by the elite of international planners, but by ordinary professionals as well. If this is true, then this book will have relevance, not only for the initiates of European planning, but for all those practising the planning trade, and also for those studying to become planners in a world that is becoming more and more complex. Our hope is that this book will be attractive to each of the three concentric circles of the audience identified in the Preface.

Hopefully, this account of the ESDP process will have enlightened outsiders and reflected the truth to insiders. If it reflects a positive disposition towards the ESDP then, once again, so be it! No account can be entirely objective, and, as the Preface has already indicated, the authors are sympathetic to the idea of European spatial planning. We hope that it may continue, in whatever form, to share in the shaping of 'Europe's Experimental Union', the telling title of a recently published, penetrating analysis by Laffan et al. (2000) on Europe's future.

REFERENCES

Aguilar, S. (1993) 'Corporatist and statist designs in environmental policy: the contrasting roles of Germany and Spain in the European Community scenario', *Environmental Politics* 2 (2): 223–47.

Akademie für Raumforschung und Landesplanung (1996) *Europäische Raumentwicklungspolitik; Rechtliche Verankerung im Vertrag über die Europäische Union* (Arbeitsmaterial 233), Hanover: Verlag der ARL.

Alden, J. (2000) 'The changing institutional landscape of planning in the United Kingdom and European Union', paper for the annual conference of the Association of Collegiate Schools of Planning, Atlanta, Georgia, 2–5 November.

Allen, D. (2000) 'Cohesion and the structural funds: transfers and trade-offs', in H. Wallace and W. Wallace (eds) *Policy-making in the European Union*, Oxford University Press: 243–65.

Alvergne, C. and Musso, P.F. (2000) 'Aménagement du territoire et prospective: Chroniques d'un devenir en construction', *Territoires 2020: Revue d'études et de prospective* 1: 47–55.

Andersen, J.J. (1996) 'Germany and the structural funds: unification leads to bifurcation', in L. Hooghe (ed.) *Cohesion Policy and European Integration: Building Multi-Level Governance*, Oxford: Clarendon Press: 163–94.

Ash, T.G. (2001) 'The European orchestra', *New York Review of Books*, 17 May: 59–65.

Aspinwall, M. (1999) 'Planes, trains and automobiles: transport governance in the European Union', in B. Kohler-Koch and R. Eising (eds) *The Transformation of Governance in the European Union* (ECPR Studies in European Policy Science 12), London/New York: Routledge: 119–34.

Austrian Presidency (1999) *The Future of European Spatial Development Policy – CSD and ESDP after 1999*, Vienna: Federal Chancellery.

Bach, M. (1994) 'Technocratic regime building: bureaucratic integration in the European Community', in M. Haller and R. Richter (eds) *Toward a European Nation? Political Trends in Europe, East and West, Center and Periphery*, New York/London: M.E. Sharpe, Armonk: 83–95.

Bagnasco, A. and Oberti, M. (1998) 'Italy: "le trompe-l'oeil" of regions', in P. Le Galès and C. Lequesne, (eds) *Regions in Europe*, London: Routledge: 150–65.

Balme, R. and Jouve, B. (1996) 'Building the regional state: Europe and territorial organization in France', in L. Hooghe (ed.) *Cohesion Policy and European Integration: Building Multi-Level Governance*, Oxford: Clarendon Press: 219–55.

Banister, D. (2000) 'Sustainable mobility', *Built Environment* 26 (3): 175–86.

Bastrup-Birk, H. and Doucet, P. (1997) 'European spatial planning from the heart', *Built Environment* 23 (4): 307–14.

BBR (2000) *Raumordnungsbericht 2000*, Bonn: Bundesamt für Bauwesen und Raumordnung.

Benz, A. (1998) 'German regions in the European Union', in P. Le Galès and C. Lequesne (eds) *Regions in Europe*, London: Routledge: 111–29.

Benz, A. (2001) 'Mehrebenenkoordination in der europäischen Raumentwicklungspolitik', in K. Wolf and G. Tönnies (eds) *Europäisches Raumentwicklungskonzept (EUREK)*, Forschungs und Sitzungsberichte 216, Hanover: Akademie für Raumforschung und Landesplanung: 171–84.

BfLR (1995) *Trendszenarien der Raumentwicklung in Deutschland und Europa: Beiträge zu einem Europäischen Raumentwicklungskonzept*, Bonn: Bundesforschungsanstalt für Landeskunde and Raumordnung.

Biehl D., Hoffmann, H-J., Niegsch, C., Rathjen, J. and Korn, O. (2000) *Spatial Perspectives for the Enlargement of the European Union* (European Union: Regional Policy, Study 36), Luxembourg: Office for Official Publications of the European Communities.

BMBau (1995) *Grundlagen einer Europäischen Raumordnungspolitik – Principles for a European Spatial Development Policy – Principes pour une politique d'aménge-ment du territoire européen, Selbstverlag der Bundesforschungsanstalt für Landeskunde und Raumordnung*, Bonn: Bundesministerium für Raumordnung, Bauwesen und Städtebau.

Boardman, P. (1978) *The Worlds of Patrick Geddes – Biologist, Town Planner, Re-educator, Peace-warrior*, London/Henley/Boston: Routledge and Kegan Paul.

Breuilly, J. (1997) 'Sovereignty, citizenship and nationality: reflections on the case of Germany', in M. Anderson and E. Bort (eds) *The Frontiers of Europe*, London/Washington: Pinter: 36–67.

Brunet, R. (1989) *Les Villes européennes, Rapport pour la DATAR, Délégation à l'Aménagement du Territoire et à l'Action Régionale, under the supervision of Roger Brunet, with the collaboration of Jean-Claude Boyer et al.*, Paris: Groupement d'Intérêt Public RECLUS, La Documentation Française.

Bursen, P., Beyers, J. and Kerremans, B. (1998) 'The environmental policy review group and the consultative forum', in M.P.C.M. van Schendelen (ed.) *EU Committees as Influential Policymakers*, Aldershot: Ashgate: 25–46.

Cádiz, J.C. (1995) 'Der Infrastrukturleitplan', in Bundesforschungsanstalt für Landeskunde und Raumordnung, *Raumordnungspolitik in Spanien und Deutschland*, Bonn: Selbstverlag: 79–84.

Calussi, F.B. (1998) 'The Committee of the Regions: an atypical influential committee?', in M.P.C.M. van Schendelen (ed.) *EU Committees as Influential Policymakers*, Aldershot: Ashgate: 225–49.

CEC – Commission of the European Communities (1991) *Europe 2000: Outlook for the Development of the Community's Territory*, Luxembourg: Office for official publications of the European Communities.

CEC (1993) Growth, Competitiveness and Employment: the Challenges and Ways Forward into the 21st Century, COM (93): 700, final. Luxembourg: Office for official publications of the European Communities.

CEC (1994a) *Europe 2000+. Cooperation for European Territorial Development*, Luxembourg: Office for official publications of the European Communities.

CEC (1994b) *Competitiveness and Cohesion: Trends in the Regions – Fifth Periodic Report on the Social and Economic Situation and Development of the Regions in the Community*, Luxembourg: Office for official publications of the European Communities.

CEC (1996) *First Report on Economic and Social Cohesion 1996*, Luxembourg: Office for official publications of the European Communities.

CEC (1997a) *The EU Compendium of Spatial Planning Systems and Policies* (Regional Development Studies 28), Luxembourg: Office for official publications of the European Communities.

CEC (1997b) *European Spatial Development Perspective* (ESDP) – *First Official Draft*, Luxembourg: Office for official publications of the European Communities.

CEC (1999a) *European Spatial Development Perspective: Towards Balanced and Sustainable Development of the Territory of the EU*, Luxembourg: Office for official publications of the European Communities.

CEC (1999b) *The EU Compendium of Spatial Planning Systems and Policies: The Netherlands* (Regional Development Studies 28K), Luxembourg: Office for official publications of the European Communities.

CEC (1999c) *The EU Compendium of Spatial Planning Systems and Policies: Germany* (Regional Development Studies 28F), Luxembourg: Office for official publications of the European Communities.

CEC (1999d) *The EU Compendium of Spatial Planning Systems and Policies: Denmark* (Regional Development Studies 28C), Luxembourg: Office for Official Publications of the European Communities.

CEC (1999e) *The EU Compendium of Spatial Planning Systems and Policies: Spain* (Regional Development Studies 28M), Luxembourg: Office for official publications of the European Communities.

CEC (1999f) *The EU Compendium of Spatial Planning Systems and Policies: Ireland* (Regional Development Studies 28H) Luxembourg: Office for official publications of the European Communities.

CEC (1999g) *The Structural Funds and their Coordination with the Cohesion Fund. Guidelines for Programmes in the Period 2000–2006*, Luxembourg: Office for official publications of the European Communities.

CEC (2000a) *The EU Compendium of Spatial Planning Systems and Policies: Italy* (Regional Development Studies 28I), Luxembourg: Office for official publications of the European Communities.

CEC (2000b) *Structural Actions 2000–2006: Commentary and Regulations, Luxembourg:* Office for official publications of the European Communities.

CEC (2000c) *The EU Compendium of Spatial Planning Systems and Policies: France* (Regional Development Studies 28E), Luxembourg: Office for official publications of the European Communities.

CEC (2000d) *The EU Compendium of Spatial Planning Systems and Policies: Portugal* (Regional Development Studies 28L), Luxembourg: Office for official publications of the European Communities.

CEC (2000e) *The EU Compendium of Spatial Planning Systems and Policies: Austria* (Regional Development Studies 28A), Luxembourg: Office for official publications of the European Communities.

CEC (2000f) *Spatial Perspectives for the Enlargement of the European Union* (Regional Development Studies 36), Luxembourg: Office for official publications of the European Communities.

CEC (2000g) *TERRA: An Experimental Laboratory in Spatial Planning*, Luxembourg: Office for official publications of the European Communities.

CEC (2000h) *On Integrated Coastal Zone Management: A Strategy for Europe,* Communication from the Commission to the Council and the European Parliament, COM (2000): 547 final, Luxembourg: Office for official publications of the European Communities.

CEC (2000i) *Services of General Interest in Europe*, Communication from the Commission, COM (2000): 580 final, Luxembourg: Office for official publications of the European Communities.

CEC (2001a) *Second Report on Economic and Social Cohesion 2001*, Luxembourg: Office for official publications of the European Communities.

CEC (2001b) *European Governance: A White Paper*, Communication from the Commission, COM (2001): 428, Brussels.

Chicoye, C. (1992) 'Regional impact of the single European market in France', *Regional Studies* 26 (4): 407–11.

Churchill, W.S. (1997) 'Speech in Zurich, September 1946 (Document 10)' in: Salmon, T. and Nicoll, W. (eds) *Building European Union*, Manchester: Manchester University Press: 26–28.

Cini, M. (1996) *The European Commission: Leadership, Organization and Culture in the EU Administration*, Manchester/New York: Manchester University Press.

Cole, A. (1998) *French Politics and Society*, New York: Prentice-Hall.

Commission Services (1999) 'Report on Community policies and spatial planning. Working document of the Commission services', presented at the ESDP Forum, Brussels, 2–3 February.

Council of Europe (1984) *European Regional/Spatial Planning Charter* (Torremolinos Charter), Strasbourg.

Damette, F. (2000) 'Le SDEC: un travail à pursuivre', *Territoires 2020: Revue d'études et de prospective* 1: 67–73.

DATAR (2000) 'Les lois: quelques réponses à propos des lois Voynet et Chevénement', *Territoires 2020: Revue d'études et de prospective* 1: 24–30.

Davies, H.W.E., Edwards, D., Hooper, A.J. and Punter, J.V. (1989) *Planning Control in Western Europe*, London: HMSO.

DETR (1998) *Modernising Planning: A Statement of the Minister for the Regions, Regeneration and Planning*, London: Department of the Environment, Transport and the Regions.

DETR (1999) *Planning Policy Guidance Note 11: Regional Planning – Public Consultation Draft*, London: Department of the Environment, Transport and the Regions.

Deutscher Bauernverband (2000) *Situationsbericht 2001: Trends und Fakten zur wirtschaftlichen Lage der deutschen Landwirtschaft*, Bonn.

DG (Directorate-General) XVI (1999) 'The ESDP – a strategy for balanced and sustainable development of the European Union: synthesis report of the transnational seminars', presented at the ESDP Forum, Brussels, 2–3 February.

Dieleman, F.M., Dijst, M.J. and Spit, T. (1999) 'Planning the compact city: The Randstad Holland experience', *European Planning Studies* 5 (5): 605–21.

Dijking, G. (1996) *National Identity and Geopolitical Visions: Maps of Pride and Pain*, London/New York: Routledge.

Dinan, D. (1999) *Ever Closer Union? – An Introduction to European Integration*, Houndmills/Basingstoke/London: Macmillan Press Ltd.

Doucet, Ph. (1998) 'Pour une strategie officielle de développement territorial de l'Union Européenne', paper given at the Transnational Seminar, Thessaliniki, 2–3 July.

Drerup, D. (1997) 'German policy perspectives', in J. Bachtler and I. Turok (eds) *The Coherence of EU Regional Policy: Contrasting Perspectives on the Structural Funds* (Regional Policy and Development Series 17), London/Philadelphia: Jessica Kingsley Publishers: 337–45.

Drevet, J.F. (1995) *Aménagement du territoire: Union Européenne et développement regional*, Paris: Editions Continent Europe.

Drevet, J.F (1997) *La nouvelle identité de l'Europe*, Paris: Presses Universitaires de France, Collection Major.

Drevet, J.F (2000) 'Une Europe rassemblée ou intégrée?', *Futuribles*, 259: 23–36.

Dupuy, G. (2000) 'L'aménagement du territoire vu par un aménageur', *Territoires 2020: Revue d'études et de prospective* 1: 11–13.

Dutch Presidency (1997) 'Presidency Conclusions', presented at the informal meeting of ministers responsible for spatial planning, Noordwijk, 9–10 June.

Eising, R. and Kohler-Koch, B. (1999) 'Governance in the European Union: a comparative assessment', in B. Kohler-Koch and R. Eising (eds) *The Transformation of Governance in the European Union* (ECPR Studies in European Policy Science 12), London/New York: Routledge: 267–85.

Eser, T. and Konstadakopulos, D. (2000) 'Power shifts in the European Union? The case of spatial planning', *European Planning Studies* 8 (6): 783–98.

Esteban, F. (1995) 'Der Autonomiestaat: Raumplanungskompetenzen in Spanien', in Bundesforschungsanstalt für Landeskunde und Raumordnung, *Raumordnungspolitik in Spanien und Deutschland*, Bonn: Selbstverlag: 57–9.

European Conference of Ministers responsible for Regional Planning (CEMAT) (2000) *Guiding Principles for Sustainable Spatial Development of the European Continent*, adopted at the 12th Session of the European Conference of Ministers responsible for Regional Planning in Hanover, 7–8 September.

Evers, D., Ben-Zadok, E. and Faludi, A. (2000) 'The Netherlands and Florida: two growth management strategies', *International Planning Studies* 5 (1): 7–23.

Faludi, A. (1996) 'Framing with images', *Environment and Planning B: Planning and Design* 23 (2): 93–108.

Faludi, A. (1997a) 'European spatial development policy in "Maastricht II"', *European Planning Studies* 5: 535–43.

Faludi, A. (1997b) 'A roving band of planners', *Built Environment* 23 (4): 281–7.

Faludi, A. (1998) 'Planning by minimum consensus: Austrian "co-operative federalism" as a model for Europe?' *European Planning Studies* 6: 485–500.

Faludi, A. (1999) 'Eine Archivleiche? – Erwartungshaltungen in bezug auf das Europäische Raumentwicklungskonzept', *Raumforschung und Raumordnung* 57 (5–6): 325–7.

Faludi, A. (2000a) 'The European Spatial Development Perspective – What next?', *European Planning Studies* 8 (2): 237–50.

Faludi, A. (2000b) 'Die Anwendung des EUREK – oder: Wonach man strategische Plandokumente bewertet', in R. Noetzel and H. Schmitz (eds) *Europäisches Raumentwicklungskonzept – Entstehung und Anwendung* (Material zur Angewandten Geographie 37), Bonn: Verlag Irene Kuron: 33–46.

Faludi, A. (2001a) The 'European Spatial Development Perspective and the changing institutional landscape of planning', in A. da Rosa Pires, L. Albrechts and J. Alden (eds) *The Changing Institutional Landscape of Planning* (Urban and Regional Planning and Development Series), Aldershot: Ashgate: 35–54.

Faludi, A. (ed.) (2001b) Regulatory Competition and Cooperation in European Spatial Planning (Special Issue) *Built Environment*: 27, No. 4.

Faludi, A. and van der Valk, A.J. (1994) *Rule and Order: Dutch Planning Doctrine in the Twentieth Century*, Dordrecht: Kluwer Academic Publishers.

Faludi, A., Zonneveld W. and Waterhout, B. (2000) 'The Committee on Spatial Development: Formulating a spatial perspective in an institutional vacuum', in T. Christiansen and E. Kirchner (eds) *Committee Governance in the European Union*, Manchester/New York: Manchester University Press: 115–131.

Federal Ministry for Regional Planning, Building and Urban Development (1992) *Spatial Planning Concept for the Development of the New Länder*, Bonn.

Federal Ministry for Regional Planning, Building and Urban Development (1993) *Guidelines for Regional Planning: General Principles for Spatial Development in the Federal Republic of Germany*, Bonn.

Finka, M. (2000) 'Europäisches Raumentwicklungskonzept', in M. Finka and D. Petríková (eds) *Priestorov? rozvoj a plánovanie v kontexte euróskej integrácie* (Spatial Development and Planning in European Integration), Bratislava: ROAD: 430–41.

Fit, J. and Kragt, R. (1994) 'The long road to European spatial planning: a matter of patience and mission', *Tijdschrift voor economische en sociale geografie* (TESG) 85 (5): 461–5.

Fontaine, P. (2000) *Ein neues Konzept für Europa: Die Erklärung von Robert Schuman – 1950–2000*, Europäische Dokumentation, Luxembourg: Amt für amtliche Veröffentlichungen der Europäischen Gemeinschaften.

Foucher, M. (1995) *The New Faces of Europe* (A Secondary Education for Europe), Council for Cultural Co-operation, Strasbourg: Council of Europe Press.

Fourth Conference of Ministers for Spatial Planning and Development (1996) *Vision and Strategies around the Baltic Sea 2010: From Vision to Action*, Stockholm, 22 October.

Genieys, W. (1998) 'Autonomous communities and the state in Spain: the role of inter-mediate elites', in: P. Le Galès and C. Lequesne, (eds) *Regions in Europe*, London: Routledge: 166–80.

Gottman, J. (1961) *Megalopolis*, New York: The Twentieth Century Fund.

Granville, O. and Maréchal, L. (2000) 'La Wallonie au centre de l'Europe: comparisons interrégionales', *Les Cahier de l'Urbanisme* 27: 6–15.

Guigou, J.L. (ed.) (2000) *Aménager la France de 2020: Mettre les Territoires en Mouvement*, Paris: DATAR – La documentation Française.

Guyomarch, A., Machin, H. and Ritchie E. (1998) *France in the European Union*, Houndmills/Basingstoke/London: Macmillan Press Ltd.

International Industrial Relations Institute (1931) *World Social Economic Planning*, The Hague.

Hajer, M.A. (2000) 'Transnational networks as transnational policy discourses: some observations on the politics of spatial development in Europe', in W. Salet and A. Faludi (eds) *The Revival of Strategic Planning*, Amsterdam: Royal Netherlands Academy of Arts and Sciences: 135–42.

Healy, A. (2000) 'Europe: surge in popularity for spatial planning', *Planning* 1 (December): 11.

Héritier, A. (1999) *Policy-making and Diversity in Europe: Escape from Deadlock*, Cambridge: Cambridge University Press.

Hix, S. (1999) *The Political System of the European Union*, Houndmills/ Basingstoke/London: Macmillan Press Ltd.

Hooghe, L. (ed.) (1996a) *Cohesion Policy and European Integration: Building Multi-Level Governance*, Oxford: Clarendon Press.

Hooghe, L. (1996b) 'Building a Europe with the regions: the changing role of the European Commission', in L. Hooghe (ed.) *Cohesion Policy and European Integration: Building Multi-Level Governance*, Oxford: Clarendon Press: 89–126.

Husson, C. (2000) *L'europe des territoires ignores: Le concept de cohésion territoiriale*, Etude réalisée pour la DATAR dans le cadre d'un contrat avec les Entretiens Régulier pour l'Administration en Europe, Europa.

Hüttmann, M.G. and Knodt, M. (2000) 'Die Europäisierung des deutschen Föderalismus', *Aus Politik und Zeitgeschichte, Beilage zur Wochenzeitschrift das Parlament*, B. 52–53, 31–38.

Irmen, E. and Sinz, M. (1991) 'Regionale Entwicklungspotentiale und Enpass in den neuen Ländern', *Informationen zur Raumentwicklung* 11/12: 755–71.

Jensen, O. and Jørgensen, I. (2000) 'Danish planning: the long shadow of Europe', *Built Environment* 26 (1): 31–40.

Job, H., Weizenegger, S. and Metzel, D. (2000) 'Strategien zur Sicherung des europäischen Natur und Kulturerbes: Die EUREK Sicht', *Informationen zur Raumentwicklung* 3/4: 143–55.

John, P. (2000) 'The Europeanisation of sub-national governance', *Urban Studies* 37 (5/6): 877–94.

King, R. (1997) 'The Mediterranean: Europe's Rio Grande', in M. Anderson and E. Bort (eds) *The Frontiers of Europe*, London/Washington: Pinter: 109–34.

Knieling, J. (2000) *Leitbildprozesse und Regionalmanagement* (Beiträge für Politikwissenschaft 77), Frankfurt: Peter Lang.

Krätke, S. (2001) 'Strengthening the polycentric urban system in Europe: conclusions from the ESDP', *European Planning Studies* 9 (1): 105–16.

Krautzberger, M. and Selke, W. (1996) *Perspektiven der bundesstaatlichen Raumplanungspolitik in der Europäischen Union: Das Beispiel Bundesrepublik Deutschland*, Schriftenreihe für Städtebau und Raumplanung, Wien: Institut zur Erforschung von Methoden und Auswirkungen der Raumplanung der Ludwig Boltzmann – Gesellschaft, Technische Universität Wien.

Kunzmann, K.R. and Wegener, M. (1991) *The Pattern of Urbanisation in Western Europe 1960–1990*, Berichte aus dem Institut für Raumplaning 28, Dortmund: Institut für Raumplanung, Universität Dortmund.

Laffan, B., O'Donnell, R. and Smith, M. (2000) *Europe's Experimental Union*, London: Routledge.

Lagrange, R. (1997) 'French policy perspectives', in J. Bachtler and I. Turok (eds) *The Coherence of EU Regional Policy: Contrasting Perspectives on the Structural Funds* (Regional Policy and Development Series 17) London/Philadelphia: Jessica Kingsley Publishers: 330–6.

Lass, J. (ed.) (2000) *Compendium of Spatial Planning Systems in the Baltic Sea Region Countries, Visions and Strategies around the Baltic Sea 2010*, Gdansk.

La Spina, A. and Sciortino, G. (1993) 'Common agenda, southern rules: European integration and environmental change in the Mediterranean States', in J.D. Liefferink, P.D. Lowe and A.P.J. Mol (eds) *European Integration and Environmental Policy*, London/New York: Belhaven Press: 217–36.

Lecq, van der, R. (2000) 'The role of Flanders in the European spatial policymaking process. A search for possibilities to strengthen the ties with the European policymaking level', Master thesis, Brussels/Nijmegen: Ministry of the Flemish Community/University of Nijmegen.

Lenshow, A. (1999) 'Transformation in European environmental governance', in B. Kohler-Koch and R. Eising (eds) *The Transformation of Governance in the European Union* (ECPR Studies in European Policy Science 12), London/New York: Routledge: 30–60.

Lieshout, R.H. (1999) *The Struggle for the Organization of Europe: The Foundation of the European Union*, Aldershot: Edgar Elgar.

Marcou, G., Kistenmacher, H. and Clev, H.-G. (1994) *Deux conceptions différentes de l'aménagement du territoire : l'une privilégie l'action régionale, l'autre la planification physique*, Paris: Documentation Française.

Martin, D. (2000) 'Les Pays-Bas dans le territoire européen: un petit pays central face à l'internationalisation de l'aménagement du territoire', *Territoires 2020: Revue d'études et de prospective* 1: 80–91.

Meeting of ministers responsible for spatial planning of the member states of the European Union (1998) *European Spatial Development Perspective (ESDP), Complete Draft*, Glasgow, 8 June.

Milesi, G. (1995) *Jacques Delors: l'homme qui dit non*, Paris: 1st edition.

Minister of Housing, Physical Planning and the Environment (1991) *Urban Networks in Europe: Contribution of the Third Meeting of the Ministers of the EC Member States Responsible for Physical Planning and Regional Policy*, The Hague: National Physical Planning Agency.

Ministère de l'Aménagement du Territoire (1999) *Programme directeur d'aménagement du territoire – Project*, Luxembourg.

Ministerio de Obras Públicas, Transportes y Medio Ambiente (ed.) (1996) *Balance of the Spanish Presidency of the European Union with respect to Spatial Planning*, serie monograficas, Madrid.

Ministerium für Umwelt, Raumordnung und Landwirtschaft des Landes Nordrhein-Westfalen (1994) *Raumordnungspolitiken in der Europäischen Union: 23. Ministerskonferenz für Raumordnung in Brüssel*: Düsseldorf.

Ministry of Environment and Energy, Spatial Planning Department (1992) *Denmark towards the Year 2018: The Spatial Structure of Denmark in the Future Europe* (National Planning Report for Denmark), Copenhagen.

Ministry of Environment and Energy, Spatial Planning Department (1997) *Denmark and European Spatial Planning Policy* (National Planning Report for Denmark), Copenhagen.

Ministry of the Environment (1999) *Reform in the Land Use Planning System: The New Land Use and Building Act of Finland*, Helsinki.

MKRO (1995) 'Entschließung Anforderungen der Raumordnungspolitik an die Revision des Vertrages über die Europäischen Union (Regierungskonferenz 1996)', Ministerskonferenz für Raumordnung, *Gemeinsames Ministerialblatt* 46 (17): 337.

Morata, F. and Muñoz, X. (1996) 'Vying for European funds: territorial restructuring in Spain', in L. Hooghe (ed.) *Cohesion Policy and European Integration: Building Multi-Level Governance*, Oxford: Clarendon Press: 195–218.

Nadin, V. and Shaw, D. (1999) *Subsidiarity and Proportionality in Spatial Planning Activities in the European Union – Final Report*, London: Department of the Environment, Transport and the Regions.

National Physical Planning Agency (1991) *Perspectives in Europe: Exploring Options for a European Spatial Policy for North-West Europe*, The Hague: Ministry of Housing, Physical Planning and the Environment.

National Spatial Planning Agency (2000) *Spatial Perspectives in Europe, Spatial Reconnaissance's 1999*, The Hague: Ministry of Housing, Spatial Planning and the Environment.

Needham, B. and Faludi, A. (1999) 'Dutch growth management in a changing market', *Planning Practice and Research* 14 (1): 481–91.

Noetzel, R. (2000) 'Die Entstehung europäischer Raumentwicklungspolitik', in R. Noetzel and H. Schmitz (Hrsg.) *Europäisches Raumentwicklungskonzept – Entstehung und Anwendung* (Material zur Angewandten Geographie 37), Bonn: Verlag Irene Kuron: 9–16.

Nordregio (2000) *Study Programme on European Spatial Planning: Conclusions and Recommendations*, Stockholm: Nordregio R2000: 4.

Nugent, N. (1999) *The Government and Politics of the European Union*, 4th edition, Houndmills/Basingstoke/London: Macmillan Press Ltd.

Pallagst, K.M. (2000) *Raumordnung der Tschechischen Republik: Mittel und Osteuropa vor dem Hintergrung europäischer Raumordnungsbestrebungen*, Berlin: Berlin Verlag Arno Spitz GmbH.

Pond, E. (2000) 'Come together: Europe's unexpected new architecture', *Foreign Affairs* 79 (2): 8–12.

Portuguese Presidency (1992) 'The spatial development of Community territory – the case of trans-European networks', Meeting of ministers of the EC member states responsible for regional policy and physical planning, Lisbon, 15–16 May.

Poussard, A (1997) *L'Arc Atlantique. Chronique d'une Coopération Interrégionale*, Rennes: Presses Universitaires de Rennes.

Presidenza del consiglio dei Ministri, Dipartimento per il Coordinamento delle Politiche Comunitarie (1990a) 'Objectives and agenda for the meeting of EEC ministers, on new problems of territorial planning and balanced regional development connected with the implementation of the single market', Turin, 22–24 November.

Presidenza del consiglio dei Ministri, Dipartimento per il Coordinamento delle Politiche Comunitarie (1990b) 'Territorial planning and new regional policies, technical reports synthesis', Turin, 22–24 November.

Presidenza del consiglio dei Ministri, Dipartimento per il Coordinamento delle Politiche Comunitarie (1996) 'European spatial planning', ministerial meeting on regional policy and spatial planning, Venice, 3–4 May.

Priemus, H. (1999) 'Four ministries, four spatial planning perspectives? Dutch evidence on the persistent problem of horizontal coordination', *European Planning Studies* 5 (5): 563–85.

Putnam, R.D. (1993) *Making Democracy Work: Civic Traditions in Modern Italy*, Princeton: Princeton University Press.

Richardson, T. (1997) 'The trans-European transport network: environmental policy integration in the European Union', *European Urban and Regional Studies* 4: 333–46.

Richardson, T. and Jensen, O.B. (2000) 'Discourses of mobility and polycentric development: a contested view of European spatial planning', *European Planning Studies* 8 (4): 503–20.

Ritaine, E. (1998) 'The political capacity of southern European regions', in P. Le Galès and C. Lequesne (eds) *Regions in Europe*, London: Routledge: 67–88.

Robert, J. (1995) 'Action areas in the formulation of the European Spatial Development Perspective', prepared on the request of the Federal Ministry for Regional Planning, Bonn, November.

Rosamond, B. (2000) *Theories of European Integration*, Houndmills/Basingstoke/London: Macmillan Press Ltd.

Ross, G. (1995) *Jacques Delors and European Integration*, Cambridge, UK: Polity Press.

Ross, G. (1998) 'The Euro, the "French Model of Society", and French politics', *French Politics and Society* 16 (4): 1–16.

Rusca, R. (1998) 'The development of a European spatial planning policy: a learning-by-doing experience in the framework of intergovernmental co-operation', in C. Bengs and K. Böhme (eds) *The Progress of European Spatial Planning* (Nordregio Report 1), Stockholm: Nordregio: 35–47.

Sbragia, A.M. (2000) 'Environmental policy: economic constraints and external pressures', in H. Wallace and W. Wallace (eds) *Policy-making in the European Union*, Oxford: Oxford University Press: 293–316.

Scharpf, F. (1999) *Governing in Europe: Effective and Democratic?*, Oxford: Oxford University Press.

Schön, K.P. (2000) 'Einführung – das Europäische Raumentwicklungskonzept und die Raumordnung in Deutschland', *Informationen zur Raumentwicklung* 3–4: I–VII.

Schrumpf, H. (1997) 'The effects of European regional pollicy on the Federal Republic of Germany', in J. Bachtler and I. Turok (eds) *The Coherence of EU Regional Policy: Contrasting Perspectives on the Structural Funds* (Regional Policy and Development Series 17) London/Philadelphia: Jessica Kingsley Publishers: 246–59.

Selke, A. (1991) 'Raumordnungspolitische Aufbaustrategie für den Osten Deutschlands', *Informationen zur Raumentwicklung* 11–12: 747–53.

Selke, W. (1999) 'Einbindung in die Bundesraumordnung und in die europäische Raumordnungspolitik', in Akademie für Raumforschung und Landesplanung (ed.) *Grundriß der Landes und Regionalplanung*, Hanover: Akademie für Raumforschung und Landesplanung: 115–30.

Shaw, D.P. (2000) 'The Europeanisation of strategic spatial planning activities in the UK', paper for the annual conference of the Association of Collegiate Schools of Planning, Atlanta, Georgia, 2–5 November.

Sinz, M. (1994) 'Comprehensive regional development planning at the federal level in Germany', Conference on 'Comprehensive Physical Development in the Matured Society', Taipei (Taiwan), Republic of China, 17 January.

Sinz, M. (2000) 'Gibt es Auswirkungen der europäischen Raumentwicklungspolitik auf nationaler, regionaler oder kommunaler Ebene?', *Informationen zur Raumentwicklung* 3–4: 109–15.

Sinz, M. and Steinle, W.J. (1989) 'Regionale Wettbewerbsfähigkeit und europäischer Binnenmarkt', *Raumforschung und Raumordnung* 47 (1): 10–21.

Spatial Vision Group (2000) *A Spatial Vision for North-West Europe: Building Cooperation*, The Hague: National Spatial Planning Agency, Ministry of Housing, Spatial Planning and the Environment.

Steiner, J. (2001) 'Der Marathon zur EU-Erweiterung: Die Stunde der Endorphine', *Raum* 42: 20–25.

Strassoldo, R. (1997) 'Perspectives on frontiers: the case of Alpe Adria', in: M. Anderson and E. Bort (eds) *The Frontiers of Europe*, London/Washington: Pinter: 75–90.

Swyngedouw, E.A. (1994) 'De produktie van de Europese maatschappelijke ruimte', in W. Zonneveld and F. D'hondt (eds) *Europese ruimtelijke ordening: Impressies en visies vanuit Vlaanderen en Nederland*, Ghent/The Hague: Vlaamse Federatie voor Planologie, Nederlands Instituut voor Ruimtelijke Ordening en Volkshuisvesting: 47–58.

Tampere Ministerial (1999) *Informal Meeting of EU Ministers responsible for Spatial Planning and Urban/Regional Policy of the European Union*, Tampere, Saarijärvi: Gummerus Printing.

Taulelle, F. (2000) 'Le SDEC: instrument de l'aménagement du territoire européenne?', *Territoires 2020: Revue d'études et de prospective* 1: 58–66.

Teitsch, F. (1999) 'Aktuelle Entwicklungen der deutschen und europäischen Regionalpolitik', in Akademie für Raumforschung und Landesplanung, *Europäische Einflüsse auf die Raum- und Regionalentwicklung am Beispiel des Naturschutzes, der Agenda 2000 und des regionalen Milieus* (Arbeitsmaterial 257), Hanover: Akademie für Raumforschung und Landesplanung: 105–18.

Tewdwr-Jones, M., Bishop, K. and Wilkinson, D. (2000) '"Euroscepticism", political agendas and spatial planning: British national and regional planning policy in uncertain times', *European Planning Studies* 8 (5): 651–68.

Wallace, W. (2000) 'Collective governance: the EU political process', in H. Wallace and W. Wallace (eds) *Policy-making in the European Union*, Oxford: Oxford University Press: 523–43.

Walloon Presidency (1993) 'For a significant step towards a co-ordinated spatial organisation of Europe. Note of the Presidency concerning the spatial planning discussion of 13 November', informal meeting of ministers responsible for regional policy and spatial planning, Liège, 12–13 November.

Waterhout, B. and Faludi, A. (2000) *The Application of the European Spatial Development Perspective (ESDP) – A Case Study of the North-West Metropolitan Area (NWMA), Polycentric Urban Regions in the North-Western Metropolitan Area*, a report produced within the framework of Action 3 of Eurbanet (proj.no 0002/B), co-financed by the European Union under the INTERREG IIC Programme, Delft: OTB.

Waterhout, B. and Zonneveld, W. (2000a) 'Vakdepartementen vrezen het EROP. Ongewild in Den Haag', *Stedenbouw en Ruimtelijke Ordening* 81 (1): 7–12.

Waterhout, B. and Zonneveld, W. (2000b) *Onbekend en ongewild. Het Europees Ruimtelijk Ontwikkelingsperspectief in Nederland*, Amsterdam: Amsterdam Study Centre for the Metropolitan Environment (AME).

Weigall, D. and Stirk, P. (eds) (1992) *The Development of the European Community*, Leicester/London: Leicester University Press.

Williams, R.H. (1996) *European Union Spatial Policy and Planning*, London: Chapman Publishing.

Williams, R.H. (1999) 'Research networking and expert participation in EU policy-making', paper to the XIII AESOP Congress, Bergen, Norway, 7–11 July.

Williams, R.H. (2000) 'Constructing the European Spatial Development Perspective: for whom?', *European Planning Studies* 8 (3): 357–65.

Wong, C., Ravetz, J. and Turner, J. (2000) *The United Kingdom Spatial Planning Framework: A Discussion*, London: The Royal Town Planning Institute.

Wulf-Mathies, M. (1995) 'The European Dimension of Spatial Planning', paper presented at the informal ministerial meeting of ministers responsible for spatial planning, Madrid, 1 December.

Zonneveld, W. (2000) 'Discursive aspects of strategic planning: a deconstruction of the "Balanced Competitiveness" concept in European spatial planning', in W. Salet and A. Faludi (eds) *The Revival of Strategic Planning*, Amsterdam: Royal Netherlands Academy of Arts and Sciences: 267–80.

Zonneveld, W. and Faludi, A. (1997) 'Introduction', *Built Environment* 23 (1): 5–13.

INDEX

accession states 3, 6, 8, 128, 131, 134, 141, 150, 156, 165, 173
administration, administrative élite 9, 29, 31, 32, 47, 67, 166, 179
Africa 39, 133
Agenda 2000 143, 163
Aguilar, S. 87, 181
Alden, J. 120, 181
Allen, D. 4, 6, 181
Alps 41, 130, 133, 155
Alvergne, C. 81, 164, 181
Amsterdam 2
Andersen, J.J. 45, 181
Arbter, R. xvii
Arc Atlantique 36
Article 10 ERDF xviii, 32, 34, 43, 50, 56, 60, 65, 79, 84, 88, 89, 134, 161, 167
Article 235 (now Article 308) of the EC Treaty 6, 19, 166, 168, 171
Ash, T.G. 19, 20, 26, 181
Asia 39
Aspinwall, M. 7, 181
Assembly of European Regions 128
Association of European Border Regions (AEBR) 128
Association of European Schools of Planning (AESOP) 128
Austria
  and enlargement 8, 73, 86, 119
  and European spatial planning 86, 130, 139, 140, 141, 150, 155, 178
  Presidency (1998) 119, 126, 139, 141, 165, 168, 181

Bach, M. 9, 181
Baden-Würtemberg 44
Bagnasco, A. 10, 40, 181
Balme, R. 30, 31, 181
Baltic States 79
Banister, D. 8, 182
Barcelona 156
Barnier, M. 159, 163
Barthelemy, Pierre-Antoine xvii
Basque 65
Bastrup-Birk, H. 32, 63, 67, 166, 182
Bavaria (Free State of), Bavarians 1, 2, 44, 140
Belgium (*see also* Flanders, Wallonia)
  and European integration 17, 63–4
  and European spatial planning 35, 63–4, 104, 105, 124, 128, 129, 130, 161

Presidency (2001) 160, 175
Benelux 17
Benz, A. 9, 44, 152, 182
Ben-Zadok, E. 186
Berlin xiii, 133, 142
Beyers, J. 182
Biehl, D. 165
Birdlife International 128
Birds Directive 7
Bishop, K. 193
Black Sea Area 141
Blair, T. 126
Blomberg, U. xviii
Blue Banana 10–12, 30, 68
Boardman, P. 2, 182
Boer, M. de 114
Bonn xiii, 7, 70, 72, 73
Brandenburg 1, 2
Breuilly, J. 45, 182
Brunet, R. 10, 11, 182
Brussels (as seat of the European Commission) vii, 1, 24, 25, 36, 42, 44, 48, 50, 65, 70, 79, 133, 175, 178
Bulgaria 141
Bunch of Grapes 11–13, 51
Bursen, P. 6, 182

Caborn, R. 115, 120
Cádiz, J.C. 87, 182
Calussi, F.B. 4, 182
Cambridge, MA xiii
CEMAT, Conférence Européenne des Ministres de l'Aménagement du Territoire 2, 3, 35, 78, 79, 141, 151, 156, 186
CEMAT meetings
  Hanover (2000) 3, 156
  Lausanne (1988) 2, 34
  Nicosia (1997) 141
  Slovenia (2003) 156
  Torremolinos (1984) 2
Central and Eastern European Countries (CEEC) 18, 39, 41, 42, 48, 74, 79, 100, 116, 128, 165
Centre Borschette 50, 57
Channel Tunnel 2, 11
Chérèque, J. xvii, 11, 31, 34, 35, 36, 38, 65, 81
Chicoye, C. 30, 184
Churchill, W. 18
CIAM 2
Cini, M. 10, 23, 184